AUGUST WILSON
THREE PLAYS

AUGUST WILSON

THREE PLAYS

UNIVERSITY OF PITTSBURGH PRESS

Published by the University of Pittsburgh Press, Pittsburgh, Pa. 15261
Manufactured in the United States of America
Printed on acid-free paper

10   9   8   7   6   5   4   3

Ma Rainey's Black Bottom, copyright © 1984 August Wilson
Reprinted by arrangement with New American Library, a division of Penguin Books
USA Inc.

Fences, copyright ©1985, August Wilson
Reprinted by arrangement with New American Library, a division of Penguin Books
USA Inc.

Joe Turner's Come and Gone, copyright © 1988, August Wilson
Reprinted by arrangement with New American Library, a division of Penguin Books
USA Inc.

Library of Congress Cataloging-in-Publication Data

Wilson, August.
    [Plays. Selections]
    Three plays / August Wilson.
        p.   cm.
    Contents: Ma Rainey's black bottom—Fences—Joe Turner's come and gone.
    ISBN 0-8229-3666-6
    1. Afro-Americans—Drama   I. Title
PS3573.145677A6   1991   90-44105
812'.54—dc20

A catalogue record for this book is available from the British Library.
Eurospan, London

CONTENTS

Preface   vii

Ma Rainey's Black Bottom   1

Fences   95

Joe Turner's Come and Gone   197

August Wilson's Blues Poetics   291

PREFACE

"Where to begin?" is among the first questions an artist asks himself. I have always told anyone who asks for my advice to begin anywhere, and that beginning will lead them, whether backward or forward, to the place they want to go. That the place where they arrive may be a place they have wanted to go to unknowingly or perhaps even unwillingly is the crucible in which many a work of art is fired. Romare Bearden has said art is born out of, among other things, necessity. One always knows his wants better than his needs. Each of these plays was a journey. At the end of each, out of necessity, emerged an artifact that is representative, the way a travel photo is representative, of the journey itself. It is the only record.

I have said elsewhere and will repeat here that writing a play is for me like walking down the landscape of the self, unattended, unadorned, exploring what D. H. Lawrence called "the dark forest of the soul." It is a place rife with shadows, a place of suspect quality and occasional dazzling brightness. What you encounter there are your demons which you have occasionally fed, trying, as Hansel, to make your way back home. You find false trails, roads closed for repairs, impregnable fortresses, scouts, armies of memory, and impossible cartography. It is a place where the cartographers labor night and day remaking the maps. The road is sometimes welcoming and its wide passages offer endearment with each step only to narrow to a footpath that has led you, boatless, to the edge of a vast and encompassing ocean. Occasionally, if you are willing to negotiate the perils, you arrive strong, brighter of spirit, to a place that sprouts yams and bolls of cotton at your footfall.

So I will begin this preface where these plays began, in 1965, with a twenty-year-old poet wrestling with the world and his place in it, having discovered the joy and terror of remaking the world in his own image through the act of writing.

To write is to fix language, to get it down and fix it to a spot and have it have meaning and be fat with substance. It is in many ways a remaking of the self in which all of the parts have been realigned, redistributed, and reassembled into a new being of sense and harmony. You have wrought something into being, and what you have wrought is what you have learned about life, and what you have learned is always pointed toward moving the harborless parts of your being closer to home. To write is to forever circle the maps, marking it all down, the latitude and longitude of each specific bearing, giving new meaning to something very old and very sacred—life itself.

As a twenty-year-old poet faced with how little you know about life, you profess to know everything. What you know most assuredly is that you are going to live until you die. What you have, almost without knowing you have it, is a sense of immortality that allows you to approach the mine fields with the blind faith of innocence and the assurance of an indefatigable spirit that rivals St. George in his willingness to slay the dragon. *If only you could get those damn words down on paper!*

I lived in a rooming house in Pittsburgh in those early days, and as I bedded down each night with my immortal self the guns of social history and responsibility that went boom in the night and called the warriors to their stations were largely ignored. If I heard them at all they had no relation to my bearing as a poet determined to answer the question of how many angels could sit on the head of a pin, despite the fact that I was having trouble identifying the angels and the size of the pin.

Most of the truly important moments in our lives go by unnoticed. We recognize them only in retrospect after we have chosen one road or another and have seen where it has taken us. Only after we have kissed the woman for the last time unknowingly, or have left her final nakedness and been marked by the unsurety and the bruise, do these moments have any resonance.

Sometimes you are privileged to recognize these moments when they occur, and from one day to the next, life, in a single stroke of gluttony, has knocked over the lamps and rearranged the maps. One night in the fall of 1965 I put a typewritten yellow-labeled record titled "Nobody in Town Can Bake a Sweet Jellyroll Like Mine," by someone named Bessie Smith, on the turntable of my 78 rpm phonograph, and the universe stuttered and everything fell to a new place.

Although the business of poetry is to enlarge the sayable, I cannot describe or even relate what I felt. Suffice it to say it was a birth, a baptism, a resurrection, and a redemption all rolled up in one. It was the beginning of my consciousness that I was a representative of a culture and the carrier of some very valuable antecedents. With my discovery of Bessie Smith and the blues I had been given a world that contained my image, a world at once rich and varied, marked and marking, brutal and beautiful, and at crucial odds with the larger world that contained it and preyed and pressed it from every conceivable angle.

"Youth is sweet before flight, and a mighty furnace is its kiln," I have written my daughter as she approaches her twenty-first birthday and wrestles, in her becoming womanhood, with the social welter of America in the nineties. My own youth is fired in the kiln of black cultural nationalism as exemplified by Amiri Baraka in the sixties. It posited black Americans as coming from a long line of honorable people with a cultural and political history, a people of manners with a strong moral personality that had to be reclaimed by strengthening the elements of the culture that made it unique and by developing institutions for preserving and promoting it. The ideas of self-determination, self-respect, and self-defense which it espoused are still very much a part of my life as I sit down to write. I have stood them up in the world of Bessie Smith on the ground captured by the blues. Having started my beginning consciousness there it is no surprise that I would mature and my efforts at writing would come to fruition on the same ground. I saw the blues as a cultural response of a nonliterate people whose history and culture were rooted in the oral tradition. The response was to a world that was not of their making, in which the idea of themselves as a people of imminent worth that belied their recent history was continually assaulted. It was a world that did not recognize their gods, their manners, their mores. It despised their ethos and refused to even recognize humanity. In such an environment the blues was a flag bearer of self-definition, and within the scope of the larger world which lay beyond its doorstep, it carved out a life, set down rules, and urged a manner of being that corresponded to the temperament and sensibilities of its creators. It was a spiritual conduit that gave spontaneous expression to the spirit that was locked in combat and devising new strategies for engaging life and enlarging itself. It was a true and articulate literature that was in the forefront of the development of both character and consciousness.

I turned my ear, my heart, and whatever analytical tools I possessed to embrace this world. I elevated it, rightly or wrongly, to biblical status. I rooted out the ideas and attitudes expressed in the music, charted them and bent and twisted and stretched them. I tested them on the common ground of experience and evidence and gave my whole being, muscle and bone and sinew and flesh and spirit, over to the emotional reference provided by the music. I learned to read between the lines and tried to fill in the blank spaces. This was life being lived in all its timbre and horrifics, with zest and purpose and the affirmation of the self as worthy of the highest possibilities and the highest celebration. What more fertile ground could any artist want?

Though my discovery of Bessie Smith and the blues provided me with an aesthetic with which to frame my growing ideas of myself as part of something larger, it was not until I discovered the art of Romare Bearden that I was able to turn it into a narrative that would encompass all of the elements of culture and tradition, what Baldwin had so eloquently called "the field of manners and ritual of intercourse" that sustains black American life. Bearden had accomplished in painting an expression as full and varied as the blues. My discovery of his work was akin to my discovery of Bessie Smith, a moment of privilege and exaltation that comes from recognizing yourself as a vital part of a much larger world than you had imagined. "I try to explore, in terms of the life I know best, those things which are common to all cultures," Bearden had said. I took it as my credo and sought to answer Baldwin's call for a profound articulation of the black tradition that could sustain a man once he left his father's house. Armed with Bearden and the blues I began to look at myself in ways I hadn't thought of before and in which I have never ceased to think of since. I began to work with the idea that I would try to put in my work all the things I saw in his, the spirit and texture and substance and grace and elegance. But how?

Many writers anxious to see results often ignore the very thing that can produce them—craft with all its tentacles, its many facets and applications. As I was a poet and writer of short fiction, the crafting of a play was new to me. I didn't know the rules, the elements, or the tools. But, since I had been writing for fifteen years, I was not without discipline. I knew that to write and to write well one must be uncompromising and make choices based on one's heart and mind and execute them with craft. But what craft? The craft I knew was the craft of poetry and fiction. To my mind, they had to connect and intercept with the craft of playwrighting at some point and all I had to do was find that point. Fiction was a story told through character and dialogue, and a poem was a distillation of language and images designed to reveal an emotive response to phenomena that brought it into harmony with one's knowledge and experience. Why couldn't a play be both?

I thought that in order to accomplish that I had to look at black life with an anthropological eye, use language, character, and image to reveal its cultural flashpoints and in the process tell a story that further illuminated them. This is what the blues did. Why couldn't I? I was, after all, a bluesman. Never mind I couldn't play a guitar or carry a tune in a bucket. I was cut out of the same cloth and I was on the same field of manners and endeavor—to articulate the cultural response of black Americans to the world in which they found themselves. And so I began, not tentatively, but straight ahead, unswerving, unmitigating. I had, after all, nothing to lose.

An artist who stands before a blank canvas is Picasso (or Matisse, since Picasso himself said "There is no one but Matisse"), until proven otherwise. Artists have the same tools: color, line, mass, form, and their own hearts beating, their own demons, and their own necessity. When I sat down to write I realized I was sitting in the same chair as Eugene O'Neill, Tennessee Williams, Arthur

Miller, Henrik Ibsen, Amiri Baraka, and Ed Bullins. I felt empowered by the chair. I was confronted by the same blank piece of paper, the same problems of art and craft—how to invest the characters with a life and history, how to invent situations that challenged the characters' beliefs, forced them into action, and prompted them to stand beside the consequences ready to reengage life on the new field of memory and observable phenomena. Feeling that sense of power, there were no rules. I was on a new adventure, with the blues and what I call the blood's memory as my only guide and companion. These plays are the result.

I could not have accomplished any of this if the black playwrights working in the sixties had not laid the groundwork. Amiri Baraka, Ed Bullins, Philip Hayes Dean, Richard Wesley, and Ron Milner are but a few of those who were particularly vocal. I have an enormous respect for their talents and work and I place myself in that long line of the tradition of African-American letters that has nurtured us all. Also none of these plays would exist in the form they are in if it were not for Lloyd Richards and the Eugene O'Neill Theater Center. Started by George White with characteristic vision, the Eugene O'Neill Theatre Center is the home of the National Playwrights' Conference where each summer fifteen playwrights are invited, from among the approximate fifteen hundred who submit their work, to participate. My relationship with the O'Neill began in 1980 when my good friend Rob Penny sent me the O'Neill brochure inviting submissions, on which he wrote, in his increasingly cryptic style, "Do This!" I did, and they promptly rejected five of my scripts until the summer of 1982 when I submitted *Ma Rainey's Black Bottom* and was invited by Lloyd Richards and his staff to participate in the conference. That was the first of many enjoyable summers I spent at the O'Neill working on my plays. The O'Neill's contribution to the development of my plays and my work as a playwright should not be overlooked. In each instance the O'Neill conference has been the catalyst for major rewriting and rethinking. As I am not the kind of writer who sets everything in concrete with a chisel from beginning to end, from the O'Neill to Broadway each play has enjoyed the unselfish energies of many talented theater professionals who, by their insights and provocations, have contributed to important changes in the texts. I worked with Bill Partlan as the director on both Ma Rainey and Fences and benefited from his stagings. Edith Oliver provided wise and insightful comments as my dramaturge on Fences and Joe Turner. Michael Feingold, as usual witty and brilliant, was my dramaturge on Ma Rainey. Amy Saltz was the director on Joe Turner and her staging proved to be illuminating and resulted in more rewriting. Among the many happy events in my career was my meeting of Charles Dutton at the O'Neill in 1982. He is a rare actor of enormous talent whose intuitive sensibilities closely match my own. His inventive portrayal of Levee in Ma Rainey inspired me to write the roles of Harold Loomis in Joe Turner and Boy Willie in The Piano Lesson for him. I am still challenged to write a role to match his talent.

I met Lloyd Richards in the Exxon Building in New York City in 1982. The occasion was the annual luncheon given for the O'Neill playwrights. I don't think either one of us placed any undue importance on the meeting. I don't think either one of us knew what lay in store for us. When the house lights went down on the opening night performance of Ma Rainey's Black Bottom at the Yale Repertory Theatre on April 6, 1984, I marked it more as an accomplishment than as a point of departure for a journey through the landscape of the American theater. As it turns out it was both, and I count myself fortunate to have had Lloyd Richards as my guide, my mentor, and my provocateur. More than anyone, he can stand in loud witness to the birth and growth of these plays. From the O'Neill to Yale to Broadway, each step, in each guise, his hand has been firmly on the tiller as we charted the waters from draft to draft and brought the plays safely to shore without compromise. We were guided by the text, our own visions, and occasionally by the seat of our pants, to a port that has been worthy of the cruise. I count him as a true friend and invaluable colleague.

There is a moment in Joe Turner's Come and Gone at the end of the first act when the residents of the household, in an act of tribal solidarity and recognition of communal history, dance a Juba. Herald Loomis interrupts it to relate a terrifying vision of bones walking on the water. From the outset he has been a man who has suffered a spiritual dislocation and is searching for a world that contains his image. The years of bondage to Joe Turner have disrupted his life and severed his connection with his past. His vision is of bones walking on water that sink and wash up on the shore as fully fleshed humans. It is not the bones walking on the water that is the terrifying part of the vision—it is when they take on flesh and reveal themselves to be like him. "They black. Just like you and me. Ain't no difference." It is the shock of recognition that his birth has origins in the manifest act of the creator, that he is in fact akin to the gods. Somewhere in the Atlantic Ocean lie the bones of millions of Africans who died before reaching the New World. The flesh of their flesh populates the Americas from Mississippi to Montevideo. Loomis is made witness to the resurrection and restoration of these bones. He has only to reconcile this vision with his learned experiences and recognize he is one of the "bones people." At the end of the play he repudiates the idea that salvation comes from outside of himself and claims his moral personality by slashing his chest in a bloodletting rite that severs his bonds and demonstrates his willingness to bleed as an act of redemption.

I am reminded of a twenty-year-old poet in a rooming house in Pittsburgh in 1965 who came face to face with himself and did not find it wanting.

AUGUST WILSON
Seattle, Washington

MA RAINEY'S BLACK BOTTOM

They tore the railroad down
so the Sunshine Special can't run
I'm going away baby
build me a railroad of my own
　　　　　—Blind Lemon Jefferson

For my mother

CHARACTERS

STURDYVANT

IRVIN

CUTLER

TOLEDO

SLOW DRAG

LEVEE

MA RAINEY

POLICEMAN

DUSSIE MAE

SYLVESTER

Ma Rainey's Black Bottom opened on April 6, 1984, at the Yale Repertory Theater in New Haven, Connecticut, with the following cast:

STURDYVANT	Richard M. Davidson
IRVIN	Lou Criscuolo
CUTLER	Joe Seneca
TOLEDO	Robert Judd
SLOW DRAG	Leonard Jackson
LEVEE	Charles S. Dutton
MA RAINEY	Theresa Merritt
POLICEMAN	David Wayne Nelson
DUSSIE MAE	Sharon Mitchell
SYLVESTER	Steven R. Blye

Director	Lloyd Richards
Settings	Charles Henry McClennahan
Costumes	Daphne Pascucci
Lighting	Peter Maradudin
Music Director	Dwight Andrews

Ma Rainey's Black Bottom opened on October 11, 1984, at the Cort Theater on Broadway in New York City, with the following cast:

STURDYVANT	John Carpenter
IRVIN	Lou Criscuolo
CUTLER	Joe Seneca
TOLEDO	Robert Judd
SLOW DRAG	Leonard Jackson
LEVEE	Charles S. Dutton
MA RAINEY	Theresa Merritt
POLICEMAN	Christopher Loomis
DUSSIE MAE	Aleta Mitchell
SYLVESTER	Scott Davenport-Richards

Director	Lloyd Richards
Settings	Charles Henry McClennahan
Costumes	Daphne Pascucci
Lighting	Peter Maradudin
Music Director	Dwight Andrews
Producers	Ivan Bloch, Robert Cole, and Frederick M. Zollo

SETTING

There are two playing areas: what is called the "band room," and the recording studio. The band room is at stage left and is in the basement of the building. It is entered through a door up left. There are benches and chairs scattered about, a piano, a row of lockers, and miscellaneous paraphernalia stacked in a corner and long since forgotten. A mirror hangs on a wall with various posters.

The studio is upstairs at stage right, and resembles a recording studio of the late 1920s. The entrance is from a hall on the right wall. A small control booth is at the rear and its access is gained by means of a spiral staircase. Against one wall there is a line of chairs and a horn through which the control room communicates with the performers. A door in the rear wall allows access to the band room.

THE PLAY

It is early March in Chicago, 1927. There is a bit of a chill in the air. Winter has broken but the wind coming off the lake does not carry the promise of spring. The people of the city are bundled and brisk in their defense against such misfortunes as the weather, and the business of the city proceeds largely undisturbed.

Chicago in 1927 is a rough city, a bruising city, a city of millionaires and derelicts, gangsters and roughhouse dandies, whores and Irish grandmothers who move through its streets fingering long black rosaries. Somewhere a man is wrestling with the taste of a woman in his cheek. Somewhere a dog is barking. Somewhere the moon has fallen through a window and broken into thirty pieces of silver.

It is one o'clock in the afternoon. Secretaries are returning from their lunch, the noon Mass at St. Anthony's is over, and the priest is mumbling over his vestments while the altar boys practice their Latin. The procession of cattle cars through the stockyards continues unabated. The busboys in Mac's Place are cleaning away the last of the corned beef and cabbage, and on the city's South Side, sleepy-eyed negroes move lazily toward their small cold-water flats and rented rooms to await the onslaught of night, which will find them crowded in the bars and juke joints both dazed and dazzling in their rapport with life. It is with these negroes that our concern lies most heavily: their values, their attitudes, and particularly their music.

It is hard to define this music. Suffice it to say that it is music that breathes and touches. That connects. That is in itself a way of being separate and distinct from any other. This music is called blues. Whether this music came from Alabama or Mississippi or other parts of the South doesn't matter anymore. The men and women who make this music have learned it from the narrow crooked streets of East St. Louis, or the streets of the city's South Side, and the Alabama or Mississippi roots have been strangled by the northern manners and customs of free men of definite and sincere worth, men for whom this music often lies at the forefront of their conscience and concerns. Thus they are laid open to be consumed by it; its warmth and redress, its braggadocio and roughly poignant comments, its vision and prayer, which would instruct and allow them to reconnect, to reassemble and gird up for the next battle in which they would be both victim and the ten thousand slain.

ACT ONE

The lights come up in the studio. IRVIN *enters, carrying a microphone. He is a tall, fleshy man who prides himself on his knowledge of blacks and his ability to deal with them. He hooks up the microphone, blows into it, taps it, etc. He crosses over to the piano, opens it, and fingers a few keys.* STURDYVANT *is visible in the control booth. Preoccupied with money, he is insensitive to black performers and prefers to deal with them at arm's length. He puts on a pair of earphones.*

STURDYVANT: (*Over speaker.*) Irv . . . let's crack that mike, huh? Let's do a check on it.

IRVIN: (*Crosses to mike, speaks into it.*) Testing . . . one . . . two . . . three . . .
(*There is a loud feedback.* STURDYVANT *fiddles with the dials.*)
Testing . . . one . . . two . . . three . . . testing. How's that, Mel?
(STURDYVANT *doesn't respond.*)
Testing . . . one . . . two . . .

STURDYVANT: (*Taking off earphones.*) Okay . . . that checks. We got a good reading.
(*Pause.*)
You got that list, Irv?

IRVIN: Yeah . . . yeah, I got it. Don't worry about nothing.

STURDYVANT: Listen, Irv . . . you keep her in line, okay? I'm holding you responsible for her . . . If she starts any of her . . .

11

IRVIN: Mel, what's with the goddamn horn? You wanna talk to me . . . okay! I can't talk to you over the goddamn horn . . . Christ!

STURDYVANT: I'm not putting up with any shenanigans. You hear, Irv?
(IRVIN *crosses over to the piano and mindlessly runs his fingers over the keys.*)
I'm just not gonna stand for it. I want you to keep her in line. Irv?
(STURDYVANT *enters from the control booth.*)
Listen, Irv . . . you're her manager . . . she's your responsibility . . .

IRVIN: Okay, okay, Mel . . . let me handle it.

STURDYVANT: She's your responsibility. I'm not putting up with any Royal Highness . . . Queen of the Blues bullshit!

IRVIN: Mother of the Blues, Mel. Mother of the Blues.

STURDYVANT: I don't care what she calls herself. I'm not putting up with it. I just want to get her in here . . . record those songs on that list . . . and get her out. Just like clockwork, huh?

IRVIN: Like clockwork, Mel. You just stay out of the way and let me handle it.

STURDYVANT: Yeah . . . yeah . . . you handled it last time. Remember? She marches in here like she owns the damn place . . . doesn't like the songs we picked out . . . says her throat is sore . . . doesn't want to do more than one take . . .

IRVIN: Okay . . . okay . . . I was here! I know all about it.

STURDYVANT: Complains about the building being cold . . . and then . . . trips over the mike wire and threatens to sue me. That's taking care of it?

IRVIN: I've got it all worked out this time. I talked with her last night. Her throat is fine . . . We went over the songs together . . . I got everything straight, Mel.

STURDYVANT: Irv, that horn player . . . the one who gave me those songs . . . is he gonna be here today? Good. I want to hear more of that sound. Times are changing. This is a tricky business now. We've got to jazz it up . . . put in something different. You know, something wild . . . with a lot of rhythm.
(*Pause.*)
You know what we put out last time, Irv? We put out garbage last time. It was garbage. I don't even know why I bother with this anymore.

IRVIN: You did alright last time, Mel. Not as good as you did before, but you did alright.

STURDYVANT: You know how many records we sold in New York? You wanna see the sheet? And you know what's in New York, Irv? Harlem. Harlem's in New York, Irv.

IRVIN: Okay, so they didn't sell in New York. But look at Memphis . . . Birmingham . . . Atlanta. Christ, you made a bundle.

STURDYVANT: It's not the money, Irv. You know I couldn't sleep last night? This business is bad for my nerves. My wife is after me to slow down and take a vacation. Two more years and I'm gonna get out . . . get into something respectable. Textiles. That's a respectable business. You know what you could do with a ship-load of textiles from Ireland?
(*A buzzer is heard offstage.*)

IRVIN: Why don't you go upstairs and let me handle it, Mel?

STURDYVANT: Remember . . . you're responsible for her.
(STURDYVANT *exits to the control booth.* IRVIN *crosses to get the door.* CUTLER, SLOW DRAG, *and* TOLEDO *enter.* CUTLER *is in his mid-fifties, as are most of the others. He plays guitar and trombone and is the leader of the group, possibly because he is the most sensible. His playing is solid and almost totally unembellished. His understanding of his music is limited to the chord he is playing at the time he is playing it. He has all the qualities of a loner except the introspection.* SLOW DRAG, *the bass player, is perhaps the one most bored by life. He resembles* CUTLER, *but lacks* CUTLER's *energy. He is deceptively*

intelligent, though, as his name implies, he appears to be slow. He is a rather large man with a wicked smile. Innate African rhythms underlie everything he plays, and he plays with an ease that is at times startling. TOLEDO is the piano player. In control of his instrument, he understands and recognizes that its limitations are an extension of himself. He is the only one in the group who can read. He is self-taught but misunderstands and misapplies his knowledge, though he is quick to penetrate to the core of a situation and his insights are thought-provoking. All of the men are dressed in a style of clothing befitting the members of a successful band of the era.)

IRVIN: How you boys doing, Cutler? Come on in.
(Pause.)
Where's Ma? Is she with you?

CUTLER: I don't know, Mr. Irvin. She told us to be here at one o'clock. That's all I know.

IRVIN: Where's . . . huh . . . the horn player? Is he coming with Ma?

CUTLER: Levee's supposed to be here same as we is. I reckon he'll be here in a minute. I can't rightly say.

IRVIN: Well, come on . . . I'll show you to the band room, let you get set up and rehearsed. You boys hungry? I'll call over to the deli and get some sandwiches. Get you fed and ready to make some music. Cutler . . . here's the list of songs we're gonna record.

STURDYVANT: *(Over speaker.)* Irvin, what's happening? Where's Ma?

IRVIN: Everything under control, Mel. I got it under control.

STURDYVANT: Where's Ma? How come she isn't with the band?

IRVIN: She'll be here in a minute, Mel. Let me get these fellows down to the band room, huh?
(They exit the studio. The lights go down in the studio and up in the band room. IRVIN opens the door and allows them to pass as they enter.)

You boys go ahead and rehearse. I'll let you know when Ma comes.

(IRVIN *exits.* CUTLER *hands* TOLEDO *the list of songs.*)

CUTLER: What we got here, Toledo?

TOLEDO: (*Reading.*) We got . . . "Prove It on Me" . . . "Hear Me Talking to You" . . . "Ma Rainey's Black Bottom" . . . and "Moonshine Blues."

CUTLER: Where Mr. Irvin go? Them ain't the songs Ma told me.

SLOW DRAG: I wouldn't worry about it if I were you, Cutler. They'll get it straightened out. Ma will get it straightened out.

CUTLER: I just don't want no trouble about these songs, that's all. Ma ain't told me them songs. She told me something else.

SLOW DRAG: What she tell you?

CUTLER: This "Moonshine Blues" wasn't in it. That's one of Bessie's songs.

TOLEDO: Slow Drag's right . . . I wouldn't worry about it. Let them straighten it up.

CUTLER: Levee know what time he supposed to be here?

SLOW DRAG: Levee gone out to spend your four dollars. He left the hotel this morning talking about he was gonna go buy some shoes. Say it's the first time he ever beat you shooting craps.

CUTLER: Do he know what time he supposed to be here? That's what I wanna know. I ain't thinking about no four dollars.

SLOW DRAG: Levee sure was thinking about it. That four dollars liked to burn a hole in his pocket.

CUTLER: Well, he's supposed to be here at one o'clock. That's what time Ma said. That nigger get out in the streets with that four dollars and ain't no telling when he's liable to show. You ought to have seen him at the club last night, Toledo. Trying to talk to some gal Ma had with her.

15

TOLEDO: You ain't got to tell me. I know how Levee do.
(*Buzzer is heard offstage.*)

SLOW DRAG: Levee tried to talk to that gal and got his feelings hurt. She didn't want no part of him. She told Levee he'd have to turn his money green before he could talk with her.

CUTLER: She out for what she can get. Anybody could see that.

SLOW DRAG: That's why Levee run out to buy some shoes. He's looking to make an impression on that gal.

CUTLER: What the hell she gonna do with his shoes? She can't do nothing with the nigger's shoes.
(SLOW DRAG *takes out a pint bottle and drinks.*)

TOLEDO: Let me hit that, Slow Drag.

SLOW DRAG: (*Handing him the bottle.*) This some of that good Chicago bourbon!
(*The door opens and* LEVEE *enters, carrying a shoe box. In his early thirties,* LEVEE *is younger than the other men. His flamboyance is sometimes subtle and sneaks up on you. His temper is rakish and bright. He lacks fuel for himself and is somewhat of a buffoon. But it is an intelligent buffoonery, clearly calculated to shift control of the situation to where he can grasp it. He plays trumpet. His voice is strident and totally dependent on his manipulation of breath. He plays wrong notes frequently. He often gets his skill and talent confused with each other.*)

CUTLER: Levee . . . where Mr. Irvin go?

LEVEE: Hell, I don't know. I ain't none of his keeper.

SLOW DRAG: What you got there, Levee?

LEVEE: Look here, Cutler . . . I got me some shoes!

CUTLER: Nigger, I ain't studying you.
(LEVEE *takes the shoes out of the box and starts to put them on.*)

TOLEDO: How much you pay for something like that, Levee?

LEVEE: Eleven dollars. Four dollars of it belong to Cutler.

SLOW DRAG: Levee say if it wasn't for Cutler . . . he wouldn't have no new shoes.

CUTLER: I ain't thinking about Levee or his shoes. Come on . . . let's get ready to rehearse.

SLOW DRAG: I'm with you on that score, Cutler. I wanna get out of here. I don't want to be around here all night. When it comes time to go up there and record them songs . . . I just wanna go up there and do it. Last time it took us all day and half the night.

TOLEDO: Ain't but four songs on the list. Last time we recorded six songs.

SLOW DRAG: It felt like it was sixteen!

LEVEE: (*Finishes with his shoes.*) Yeah! Now I'm ready! I can play some good music now!
(*He goes to put up his old shoes and looks around the room.*)
Damn! They done changed things around. Don't never leave well enough alone.

TOLEDO: Everything changing all the time. Even the air you breathing change. You got, monoxide, hydrogen . . . changing all the time. Skin changing . . . different molecules and everything.

LEVEE: Nigger, what is you talking about? I'm talking about the room. I ain't talking about no skin and air. I'm talking about something I can see! Last time the band room was upstairs. This time it's downstairs. Next time it be over there. I'm talking about what I can see. I ain't talking about no molecules or nothing.

TOLEDO: Hell, I know what you talking about. I just said everything changing. I know what you talking about, but you don't know what I'm talking about.

LEVEE: That door! Nigger, you see that door? That's what I'm talking about. That door wasn't there before.

17

CUTLER: Levee, you wouldn't know your right from your left. This is where they used to keep the recording horns and things . . . and damn if that door wasn't there. How in hell else you gonna get in here? Now, if you talking about they done switched rooms, you right. But don't go telling me that damn door wasn't there!

SLOW DRAG: Damn the door and let's get set up. I wanna get out of here.

LEVEE: Toledo started all that about the door. I'm just saying that things change.

TOLEDO: What the hell you think I was saying? Things change. The air and everything. Now you gonna say you was saying it. You gonna fit two propositions on the same track . . . run them into each other, and because they crash, you gonna say it's the same train.

LEVEE: Now this nigger talking about trains! We done went from the air to the skin to the door . . . and now trains. Toledo, I'd just like to be inside your head for five minutes. Just to see how you think. You done got more shit piled up and mixed up in there than the devil got sinners. You been reading too many goddamn books.

TOLEDO: What you care about how much I read? I'm gonna ignore you cause you ignorant.
(LEVEE *takes off his coat and hangs it in the locker.*)

SLOW DRAG: Come on, let's rehearse the music.

LEVEE: You ain't gotta rehearse that . . . ain't nothing but old jug band music. They need one of them jug bands for this.

SLOW DRAG: Don't make me no difference. Long as we get paid.

LEVEE: That ain't what I'm talking about, nigger. I'm talking about art!

SLOW DRAG: What's drawing got to do with it?

18

LEVEE: Where you get this nigger from, Cutler? He sound like one of them Alabama niggers.

CUTLER: Slow Drag's alright. It's you talking all that weird shit about art. Just play the piece, nigger. You wanna be one of them . . . what you call . . . virtuoso or something, you in the wrong place. You ain't no Buddy Bolden or King Oliver . . . you just an old trumpet player come a dime a dozen. Talking about art.

LEVEE: What is you? I don't see your name in lights.

CUTLER: I just play the piece. Whatever they want. I don't go talking about art and criticizing other people's music.

LEVEE: I ain't like you, Cutler. I got talent! Me and this horn . . . we's tight. If my daddy knowed I was gonna turn out like this, he would've named me Gabriel. I'm gonna get me a band and make me some records. I done give Mr. Sturdyvant some of my songs I wrote and he say he's gonna let me record them when I get my band together.
(*Takes some papers out of his pocket.*)
I just gotta finish the last part of this song. And Mr. Sturdyvant want me to write another part to this song.

SLOW DRAG: How you learn to write music, Levee?

LEVEE: I just picked it up . . . like you pick up anything. Miss Eula used to play the piano . . . she learned me a lot. I knows how to play *real* music . . . not this old jug band shit. I got style!

TOLEDO: Everybody got style. Style ain't nothing but keeping the same idea from beginning to end. Everybody got it.

LEVEE: But everybody can't play like I do. Everybody can't have their own band.

CUTLER: Well, until you get your own band where you can play what you want, you just play the piece and stop complaining. I told you when you came on here, this ain't none of them hot bands. This is an accompaniment band. You play Ma's music when you here.

LEVEE: I got sense enough to know that. Hell, I can look at you all and see what kind of band it is. I can look at Toledo and see what kind of band it is.

TOLEDO: Toledo ain't said nothing to you now. Don't let Toledo get started. You can't even spell music, much less play it.

LEVEE: What you talking about? I can spell music. I got a dollar say I can spell it! Put your dollar up. Where your dollar?
(TOLEDO *waves him away.*)
Now come on. Put your dollar up. Talking about I can't spell music.
(LEVEE *peels a dollar off his roll and slams it down on the bench beside* TOLEDO.)

TOLEDO: Alright, I'm gonna show you. Cutler. Slow Drag. You hear this? The nigger betting me a dollar he can spell music. I don't want no shit now!
(TOLEDO *lays a dollar down beside* LEVEE's.)
Alright. Go ahead. Spell it.

LEVEE: It's a bet then. Talking about I can't spell music.

TOLEDO: Go ahead, then. Spell it. Music. Spell it.

LEVEE: I can spell it, nigger! M-U-S-I-K. There!
(*He reaches for the money.*)

TOLEDO: Naw! Naw! Leave that money alone! You ain't spelled it.

LEVEE: What you mean I ain't spelled it? I said M-U-S-I-K!

TOLEDO: That ain't how you spell it! That ain't how you spell it! It's M-U-S-I-C! C, nigger. Not K! C! M-U-S-I-C!

LEVEE: What you mean, C? Who say it's C?

TOLEDO: Cutler. Slow Drag. Tell this fool.
(*They look at each other and then away.*)
Well, I'll be a monkey's uncle!

(TOLEDO *picks up the money and hands* LEVEE *his dollar back.*)
Here's your dollar back, Levee. I done won it, you understand. I
done won the dollar. But if don't nobody know but me, how am I
gonna prove it to you?

LEVEE: You just mad cause I spelled it.

TOLEDO: Spelled what! M-U-S-I-K don't spell nothing. I just wish
there was some way I could show you the right and wrong of it.
How you gonna know something if the other fellow don't know if
you're right or not? Now I can't even be sure that I'm spelling it
right.

LEVEE: That's what I'm talking about. You don't know it. Talking
about C. You ought to give me that dollar I won from you.

TOLEDO: Alright. Alright. I'm gonna show you how ridiculous you
sound. You know the Lord's Prayer?

LEVEE: Why? You wanna bet a dollar on that?

TOLEDO: Just answer the question. Do you know the Lord's Prayer
or don't you?

LEVEE: Yeah, I know it. What of it?

TOLEDO: Cutler?

CUTLER: What you Cutlering me for? I ain't got nothing to do
with it.

TOLEDO: I just want to show the man how ridiculous he is.

CUTLER: Both of you all sound like damn fools. Arguing about
something silly. Yeah, I know the Lord's Prayer. My daddy was a
deacon in the church. Come asking me if I know the Lord's
Prayer. Yeah, I know it.

TOLEDO: Slow Drag?

SLOW DRAG: Yeah.

TOLEDO: Alright. Now I'm gonna tell you a story to show just how
ridiculous he sound. There was these two fellows, see. So, the

21

one of them go up to this church and commence to taking up the church learning. The other fellow see him out on the road and he say, "I done heard you taking up the church learning," say, "Is you learning anything up there?" The other one say, "Yeah, I done take up the church learning and I's learning all kinds of things about the Bible and what it say and all. Why you be asking?" The other one say, "Well, do you know the Lord's Prayer?" And he say, "Why, sure I know the Lord's Prayer, I'm taking up learning at the church ain't I? I know the Lord's Prayer backwards and forwards." And the other fellow says, "I bet you five dollars you don't know the Lord's Prayer, cause I don't think you knows it. I think you be going up to the church cause the Widow Jenkins be going up there and you just wanna be sitting in the same room with her when she cross them big, fine, pretty legs she got." And the other one say, "Well, I'm gonna prove you wrong and I'm gonna bet you that five dollars." So he say, "Well, go on and say it then." So he commenced to saying the Lord's Prayer. He say, "Now I lay me down to sleep, I pray the Lord my soul to keep." The other one say, "Here's your five dollars. I didn't think you knew it."
(*They all laugh.*)
Now, that's just how ridiculous Levee sound. Only cause I knowed how to spell music, I still got my dollar.

LEVEE: That don't prove nothing. What's that supposed to prove?
(TOLEDO *takes a newspaper out of his back pocket and begins to read.*)

TOLEDO: I'm through with it.

SLOW DRAG: Is you all gonna rehearse this music or ain't you?
(CUTLER *takes out some papers and starts to roll a reefer.*)

LEVEE: How many times you done played them songs? What you gotta rehearse for?

SLOW DRAG: This a recording session. I wanna get it right the first time and get on out of here.

22

CUTLER: Slow Drag's right. Let's go on and rehearse and get it over with.

LEVEE: You all go and rehearse, then. I got to finish this song for Mr. Sturdyvant.

CUTLER: Come on, Levee . . . I don't want no shit now. You rehearse like everybody else. You in the band like everybody else. Mr. Sturdyvant just gonna have to wait. You got to do that on your own time. This is the band's time.

LEVEE: Well, what is you doing? You sitting there rolling a reefer talking about let's rehearse. Toledo reading a newspaper. Hell, I'm ready if you wanna rehearse. I just say there ain't no point in it. Ma ain't here. What's the point in it?

CUTLER: Nigger, why you gotta complain all the time?

TOLEDO: Levee would complain if a gal ain't laid across his bed just right.

CUTLER: That's what I know. That's why I try to tell him just play the music and forget about it. It ain't no big thing.

TOLEDO: Levee ain't got an eye for that. He wants to tie on to some abstract component and sit down on the elemental.

LEVEE: This is get-on-Levee time, huh? Levee ain't said nothing except this some old jug band music.

TOLEDO: Under the right circumstances you'd play anything. If you know music, then you play it. Straight on or off to the side. Ain't nothing abstract about it.

LEVEE: Toledo, you sound like you got a mouth full of marbles. You the only cracker-talking nigger I know.

TOLEDO: You ought to have learned yourself to read . . . then you'd understand the basic understanding of everything.

SLOW DRAG: Both of you all gonna drive me crazy with that philosophy bullshit. Cutler, give me a reefer.

CUTLER: Ain't you got some reefer? Where's your reefer? Why you all the time asking me?

SLOW DRAG: Cutler, how long I done known you? How long we been together? Twenty-two years. We been doing this together for twenty-two years. All up and down the back roads, the side roads, the front roads . . . We done played the juke joints, the whorehouses, the barn dances, and city sit-downs . . . I done lied for you and lied with you . . . We done laughed together, fought together, slept in the same bed together, done sucked on the same titty . . . and now you don't wanna give me no reefer.

CUTLER: You see this nigger trying to talk me out of my reefer, Toledo? Running all that about how long he done knowed me and how we done sucked on the same titty. Nigger, you *still* ain't getting none of my reefer!

TOLEDO: That's African.

SLOW DRAG: What? What you talking about? What's African?

LEVEE: I know he ain't talking about me. You don't see me running around in no jungle with no bone between my nose.

TOLEDO: Levee, you worse than ignorant. You ignorant without a premise.
(*Pauses.*)
Now, what I was saying is what Slow Drag was doing is African. That's what you call an African conceptualization. That's when you name the gods or call on the ancestors to achieve whatever your desires are.

SLOW DRAG: Nigger, I ain't no African! I ain't doing no African nothing!

TOLEDO: Naming all those things you and Cutler done together is like trying to solicit some reefer based on a bond of kinship. That's African. An ancestral retention. Only you forgot the name of the gods.

24

SLOW DRAG: I ain't forgot nothing. I was telling the nigger how cheap he is. Don't come talking that African nonsense to me.

TOLEDO: You just like Levee. No eye for taking an abstract and fixing it to a specific. There's so much that goes on around you and you can't even see it.

CUTLER: Wait a minute . . . wait a minute. Toledo, now when this nigger . . . when an African do all them things you say and name all the gods and whatnot . . . then what happens?

TOLEDO: Depends on if the gods is sympathetic with his cause for which he is calling them with the right names. Then his success comes with the right proportion of his naming. That's the way that go.

CUTLER: (*Taking out a reefer.*) Here, Slow Drag. Here's a reefer. You done talked yourself up on that one.

SLOW DRAG: Thank you. You ought to have done that in the first place and saved me all the aggravation.

CUTLER: What I wants to know is . . . what's the same titty we done sucked on. That's what I want to know.

SLOW DRAG: Oh, I just threw that in there to make it sound good. (*They all laugh.*)

CUTLER: Nigger, you ain't right.

SLOW DRAG: I knows it.

CUTLER: Well, come on . . . let's get it rehearsed. Time's wasting. (*The musicians pick up their instruments.*)
Let's do it. "Ma Rainey's Black Bottom." One . . . two . . . You know what to do.
(*They begin to play.* LEVEE *is playing something different. He stops.*)

LEVEE: Naw! Naw! We ain't doing it that way.
(TOLEDO *stops playing, then* SLOW DRAG.)
We doing my version. It say so right there on that piece of paper

you got. Ask Toledo. That's what Mr. Irvin told me . . . say it's on the list he gave you.

CUTLER: Let me worry about what's on the list and what ain't on the list. How you gonna tell me what's on the list?

LEVEE: Cause I know what Mr. Irvin told me! Ask Toledo!

CUTLER: Let me worry about what's on the list. You just play the song I say.

LEVEE: What kind of sense it make to rehearse the wrong version of the song? That's what I wanna know. Why you wanna rehearse that version?

SLOW DRAG: You supposed to rehearse what you gonna play. That's the way they taught me. Now, *whatever* version we gonna play . . . let's go on and rehearse it.

LEVEE: That's what I'm trying to tell the man.

CUTLER: You trying to tell me what we is and ain't gonna play. And that ain't none of your business. Your business is to play what I say.

LEVEE: Oh, I see now. You done got jealous cause Mr. Irvin using my version. You done got jealous cause I proved I know something about music.

CUTLER: What the hell . . . nigger, you talk like a fool! What the hell I got to be jealous of you about? The day I get jealous of you I may as well lay down and die.

TOLEDO: Levee started all that cause he too lazy to rehearse.
(*To* LEVEE.)
You ought to just go on and play the song . . . What difference does it make?

LEVEE: Where's the paper? Look at the paper! Get the paper and look at it! See what it say. Gonna tell me I'm too lazy to rehearse.

CUTLER: We ain't talking about the paper. We talking about you

26

understanding where you fit in when you around here. You just play what I say.

LEVEE: Look . . . I don't care what you play! Alright? It don't matter to me. Mr. Irvin gonna straighten it up! I don't care what you play.

CUTLER: Thank you.
(*Pauses.*)
Let's play this "Hear Me Talking to You" till we find out what's happening with the "Black Bottom." Slow Drag, you sing Ma's part.
(*Pauses.*)
"Hear Me Talking to You." Let's do it. One . . . Two . . . You know what to do.
(*They play.*)

SLOW DRAG: (*Singing*)
Rambling man makes no change in me
I'm gonna ramble back to my used-to-be
Ah, you hear me talking to you
I don't bite my tongue
You wants to be my man
You got to fetch it with you when you come.

Eve and Adam in the garden taking a chance
Adam didn't take time to get his pants
Ah, you hear me talking to you
I don't bite my tongue
You wants to be my man
You got to fetch it with you when you come.

Our old cat swallowed a ball of yarn
When the kittens were born they had sweaters on
Ah, you hear me talking to you
I don't bite my tongue
You wants to be my man
You got to fetch it with you when you come.
(IRVIN *enters. The musicians stop playing.*)

27

IRVIN: Any of you boys know what's keeping Ma?

CUTLER: Can't say, Mr. Irvin. She'll be along directly, I reckon. I talked to her this morning. She say she'll be here in time to rehearse.

IRVIN: Well, you boys go ahead.
(*He starts to exit.*)

CUTLER: Mr. Irvin, about these songs . . . Levee say . . .

IRVIN: Whatever's on the list, Cutler. You got that list I gave you?

CUTLER: Yessir, I got it right here.

IRVIN: Whatever's on there. Whatever that says.

CUTLER: I'm asking about this "Black Bottom" piece . . . Levee say . . .

IRVIN: Oh, it's on the list. "Ma Rainey's Black Bottom" is on the list.

CUTLER: I know it's on the list. I wanna know what version. We got two versions of that song.

IRVIN: Oh. Levee's arrangement. We're using Levee's arrangement.

CUTLER: Okay. I got that straight. Now, this "Moonshine Blues" . . .

IRVIN: We'll work it out with Ma, Cutler. Just rehearse whatever's on the list and use Levee's arrangement on that "Black Bottom" piece.
(*He exits.*)

LEVEE: See, I told you! It don't mean nothing when I say it. You got to wait for Mr. Irvin to say it. Well, I told you the way it is.

CUTLER: Levee, the sooner you understand it ain't what you say, or what Mr. Irvin say . . . it's what Ma say that counts.

SLOW DRAG: Don't nobody say when it come to Ma. She's gonna do what she wants to do. Ma says what happens with her.

28

LEVEE: Hell, the man's the one putting out the record! He's gonna put out what he wanna put out!

SLOW DRAG: He's gonna put out what Ma want him to put out.

LEVEE: You heard what the man told you . . . "Ma Rainey's Black Bottom," Levee's arrangement. There you go! That's what he told you.

SLOW DRAG: What you gonna do, Cutler?

CUTLER: Ma ain't told me what version. Let's go on and play it Levee's way.

TOLEDO: See, now . . . I'll tell you something. As long as the colored man look to white folks to put the crown on what he say . . . as long as he looks to white folks for approval . . . then he ain't never gonna find out who he is and what he's about. He's just gonna be about what white folks want him to be about. That's one sure thing.

LEVEE: I'm just trying to show Cutler where he's wrong.

CUTLER: Cutler don't need you to show him nothing.

SLOW DRAG: (Irritated.) Come on, let's get this shit rehearsed! You all can bicker afterward!

CUTLER: Levee's confused about who the boss is. He don't know Ma's the boss.

LEVEE: Ma's the boss on the road! We at a recording session. Mr. Sturdyvant and Mr. Irvin say what's gonna be here! We's in Chicago, we ain't in Memphis! I don't know why you all wanna pick with me about it, shit! I'm with Slow Drag . . . Let's go on and get it rehearsed.

CUTLER: Alright. Alright. I know how to solve this. "Ma Rainey's Black Bottom." Levee's version. Let's do it. Come on.

TOLEDO: How that first part go again, Levee?

LEVEE: It go like this.

(*He plays.*)
That's to get the people's attention to the song. That's when you and Slow Drag come in with the rhythm part. Me and Cutler play on the breaks.
(*Becoming animated.*)
Now we gonna dance it . . . but we ain't gonna countrify it. This ain't no barn dance. We gonna play it like . . .

CUTLER: The man ask you how the first part go. He don't wanna hear all that. Just tell him how the piece go.

TOLEDO: I got it. I got it. Let's go. I know how to do it.

CUTLER: "Ma Rainey's Black Bottom." One . . . Two . . . You know what to do.
(*They begin to play.* LEVEE *stops.*)

LEVEE: You all got to keep up now. You playing in the wrong time. Ma come in over the top. She got to find her own way in.

CUTLER: Nigger, will you let us play this song? When you get your own band . . . then you tell them that nonsense. We know how to play the piece. I was playing music before you was born. Gonna tell me how to play . . . Alright. Let's try it again.

SLOW DRAG: Cutler, wait till I fix this. This string started to unravel.
(*Playfully.*)
And you know I want to play Levee's music right.

LEVEE: If you was any kind of musician, you'd take care of your instrument. Keep it in tip-top order. If you was any kind of musician, I'd let you be in my band.

SLOW DRAG: Shhheeeeet!
(*He crosses to get his string and steps on* LEVEE'*s shoes.*)

LEVEE: Damn, Slow Drag! Watch them big-ass shoes you got.

SLOW DRAG: Boy, ain't nobody done nothing to you.

LEVEE: You done stepped on my shoes.°

SLOW DRAG: Move them the hell out the way, then. You was in my way . . . I wasn't in your way.

(CUTLER *lights up another reefer.* SLOW DRAG *rummages around in his belongings for a string.* LEVEE *takes out a rag and begins to shine his shoes.*)

You can shine these when you get done, Levee.

CUTLER: If I had them shoes Levee got, I could buy me a whole suit of clothes.

LEVEE: What kind of difference it make what kind of shoes I got? Ain't nothing wrong with having nice shoes. I ain't said nothing about your shoes. Why you wanna talk about me and my Florsheims?

CUTLER: Any man who takes a whole week's pay and puts it on some shoes—you understand what I mean, what you walk around on the ground with—is a fool! And I don't mind telling you.

LEVEE: (*Irritated.*) What difference it make to you, Cutler?

SLOW DRAG: The man ain't said nothing about your shoes. Ain't nothing wrong with having nice shoes. Look at Toledo.

TOLEDO: What about Toledo?

SLOW DRAG: I said ain't nothing wrong with having nice shoes.

LEVEE: Nigger got them clodhoppers! Old brogans! He ain't nothing but a sharecropper.

TOLEDO: You can make all the fun you want. It don't mean nothing. I'm satisfied with them and that's what counts.

LEVEE: Nigger, why don't you get some decent shoes? Got nerve to put on a suit and tie with them farming boots.

CUTLER: What you just tell me? It don't make no difference about the man's shoes. That's what you told me.

LEVEE: Aw, hell, I don't care what the nigger wear. I'll be honest with you. I don't care if he went barefoot.

(SLOW DRAG *has put his string on the bass and is tuning it.*)

Play something for me, Slow Drag.
(SLOW DRAG *plays.*)
A man got to have some shoes to dance like this! You can't
dance like this with them clodhoppers Toledo got.
(LEVEE *sings.*)
Hello Central give me Doctor Jazz
He's got just what I need I'll say he has
When the world goes wrong and I have got the blues
He's the man who makes me get on my dancing shoes.

TOLEDO: That's the trouble with colored folks . . . always wanna
have a good time. Good times done got more niggers killed than
God got ways to count. What the hell having a good time mean?
That's what I wanna know.

LEVEE: Hell, nigger . . . it don't need explaining. Ain't you never
had no good time before?

TOLEDO: The more niggers get killed having a good time, the more
good times niggers wanna have.
(SLOW DRAG *stops playing.*)
There's more to life than having a good time. If there ain't, then
this is a piss-poor life we're having . . . if that's all there is to be
got out of it.

SLOW DRAG: Toledo, just cause you like to read them books and
study and whatnot . . . that's your good time. People got other
things they likes to do to have a good time. Ain't no need you
picking them about it.

CUTLER: Niggers been having a good time before you was born, and
they gonna keep having a good time after you gone.

TOLEDO: Yeah, but what else they gonna do? Ain't nobody talking
about making the lot of the colored man better for him here in
America.

LEVEE: Now you gonna be Booker T. Washington.

TOLEDO: Everybody worried about having a good time. Ain't nobody thinking about what kind of world they gonna leave their

younguns. "Just give me the good time, that's all I want." It just makes me sick.

SLOW DRAG: Well, the colored man's gonna be alright. He got through slavery, and he'll get through whatever else the white man put on him. I ain't worried about that. Good times is what makes life worth living. Now, you take the white man . . . The white man don't know how to have a good time. That's why he's troubled all the time. He don't know how to have a good time. He don't know how to laugh at life.

LEVEE: That's what the problem is with Toledo . . . reading all them books and things. He done got to the point where he forgot how to laugh and have a good time. Just like the white man.

TOLEDO: I know how to have a good time as well as the next man. I said, there's got to be more to life than having a good time. I said the colored man ought to be doing more than just trying to have a good time all the time.

LEVEE: Well, what is you doing, nigger? Talking all them high-falutin ideas about making a better world for the colored man. What is you doing to make it better? You playing the music and looking for your next piece of pussy same as we is. What is you doing? That's what I wanna know. Tell him, Cutler.

CUTLER: You all leave Cutler out of this. Cutler ain't got nothing to do with it.

TOLEDO: Levee, you just about the most ignorant nigger I know. Sometimes I wonder why I ever bother to try and talk with you.

LEVEE: Well, what is you doing? Talking that shit to me about I'm ignorant! What is you doing? You just a whole lot of mouth. A great big windbag. Thinking you smarter than everybody else. What is you doing, huh?

TOLEDO: It ain't just me, fool! It's everybody! What you think . . . I'm gonna solve the colored man's problems by myself? I said, we. You understand that? We. That's every living colored man in the world got to do his share. Got to do his part. I ain't talking about

33

what I'm gonna do . . . or what you or Cutler or Slow Drag or anybody else. I'm talking about all of us together. What all of us is gonna do. That's what I'm talking about, nigger!

LEVEE: Well, why didn't you say that, then?

CUTLER: Toledo, I don't know why you waste your time on this fool.

TOLEDO: That's what I'm trying to figure out.

LEVEE: Now there go Cutler with his shit. Calling me a fool. You wasn't even in the conversation. Now you gonna take sides and call me a fool.

CUTLER: Hell, I was listening to the man. I got sense enough to know what he was saying. I could tell it straight back to you.

LEVEE: Well, you go on with it. But I'll tell you this . . . I ain't gonna be too many more of your fools. I'll tell you that. Now you put that in your pipe and smoke it.

CUTLER: Boy, ain't nobody studying you. Telling me what to put in my pipe. Who's you to tell me what to do?

LEVEE: Alright, I ain't nobody. Don't pay me no mind. I ain't nobody.

TOLEDO: Levee, you ain't nothing but the devil.

LEVEE: There you go! That's who I am. I'm the devil. I ain't nothing but the devil.

CUTLER: I can see that. That's something you know about. You know all about the devil.

LEVEE: I ain't saying what I know. I know plenty. What you know about the devil? Telling me what I know. What you know?

SLOW DRAG: I know a man sold his soul to the devil.

LEVEE: There you go! That's the only thing I ask about the devil . . . to see him coming so I can sell him this one I got. Cause if there's a God up there, he done went to sleep.

SLOW DRAG: Sold his soul to the devil himself. Name of Eliza Cottor. Lived in Tuscaloosa County, Alabama. The devil came by and he done upped and sold him his soul.

CUTLER: How you know the man done sold his soul to the devil, nigger? You talking that old-woman foolishness.

SLOW DRAG: Everybody know. It wasn't no secret. He went around working for the devil and everybody knowed it. Carried him a bag . . . one of them carpetbags. Folks say he carried the devil's papers and whatnot where he put your fingerprint on the paper with blood.

LEVEE: Where he at now? That's what I want to know. He can put my whole handprint if he want to!

CUTLER: That's the damndest thing I ever heard! Folks kill me with that talk.

TOLEDO: Oh, that's real enough, alright. Some folks go arm in arm with the devil, shoulder to shoulder, and talk to him all the time. That's real. Ain't nothing wrong in believing that.

SLOW DRAG: That's what I'm saying. Eliza Cotter is one of them. Alright. The man living up in an old shack on Ben Foster's place, shoeing mules and horses, making them charms and things in secret. He done hooked up with the devil, showed up one day all fancied out with just the finest clothes you ever seen on a colored man . . . dressed just like one of them crackers . . . and carrying this bag with them papers and things. Alright. Had a pocketful of money, just living the life of a rich man. Ain't done no more work or nothing. Just had him a string of women he run around with and throw his money away on. Bought him a big fine house . . . Well, it wasn't all that big, but it did have one of them white picket fences around it. Used to hire a man once a week just to paint that fence. Messed around there and one of the fellows of them gals he was messing with got fixed on him wrong and Eliza killed him. And he laughed about it. Sheriff come and arrest him, and then let him go. And he went around in that town laughing about killing this fellow. Trial come up, and the judge cut him loose. He must have been in converse with the devil too . . . cause he cut him loose and give him a bottle of whiskey! Folks ask what done happened to make him change, and he'd tell them straight out he done sold his soul to the devil and ask them if they wanted to sell theirs cause he could arrange it for them. Preacher see him coming, used to cross on the other side of the road. He'd just stand there and laugh at the preacher and call him a fool to his face.

CUTLER: Well, whatever happened to this fellow? What come of him? A man who, as you say, done sold his soul to the devil is bound to come to a bad end.

TOLEDO: I don't know about that. The devil's strong. The devil ain't no pushover.

SLOW DRAG: Oh, the devil had him under his wing, alright. Took good care of him. He ain't wanted for nothing.

CUTLER: What happened to him? That's what I want to know.

SLOW DRAG: Last I heard, he headed north with that bag of his, handing out hundred-dollar bills on the spot to whoever wanted to sign on with the devil. That's what I hear tell of him.

CUTLER: That's a bunch of fool talk. I don't know how you fix your mouth to tell that story. I don't believe that.

SLOW DRAG: I ain't asking you to believe it. I'm just telling you the facts of it.

LEVEE: I sure wish I knew where he went. He wouldn't have to convince me long. Hell, I'd even help him sign people up.

CUTLER: Nigger, God's gonna strike you down with that blasphemy you talking.

LEVEE: Oh, shit! God don't mean nothing to me. Let him strike me! Here I am, standing right here. What you talking about he's gonna strike me? Here I am! Let him strike me! I ain't scared of him. Talking that stuff to me.

CUTLER: Alright. You gonna be sorry. You gonna fix yourself to have bad luck. Ain't nothing gonna work for you.
(*Buzzer sounds offstage.*)

LEVEE: Bad luck? What I care about some bad luck? You talking simple. I ain't knowed nothing but bad luck all my life. Couldn't get no worse. What the hell I care about some bad luck? Hell, I eat it everyday for breakfast! You dumber than I thought you was . . . talking about bad luck.

CUTLER: Alright, nigger, you'll see! Can't tell a fool nothing. You'll see!

IRVIN: (IRVIN *enters the studio, checks his watch, and calls down the stairs.*) Cutler . . . you boys' sandwiches are up here . . . Cutler?

CUTLER: Yessir, Mr. Irvin . . . be right there.

TOLEDO: I'll walk up there and get them.
(TOLEDO *exits. The lights go down in the band room and up in the studio.* IRVIN *paces back and forth in an agitated manner.* STURDY-VANT *enters.*)

STURDYVANT: Irv, what's happening? Is she here yet? Was that her?

IRVIN: It's the sandwiches, Mel. I told you . . . I'll let you know when she comes, huh?

STURDYVANT: What's keeping her? Do you know what time it is? Have you looked at the clock? You told me she'd be here. You told me you'd take care of it.

IRVIN: Mel, for Chrissakes! What do you want from me? What do you want me to do?

STURDYVANT: Look what time it is, Irv. You told me she'd be here.

IRVIN: She'll be here, okay? I don't know what's keeping her. You know they're always late, Mel.

STURDYVANT: You should have went by the hotel and made sure

37

she was on time. You should have taken care of this. That's what you told me, huh? "I'll take care of it."

IRVIN: Okay! Okay! I didn't go by the hotel! What do you want me to do? She'll be here, okay? The band's here . . . she'll be here.

STURDYVANT: Okay, Irv. I'll take your word. But if she doesn't come . . . if she doesn't come . . .
(STURDYVANT *exits to the control booth as* TOLEDO *enters.*)

TOLEDO: Mr. Irvin . . . I come up to get the sandwiches.

IRVIN: Say . . . uh . . . look . . . one o'clock, right? She said one o'clock.

TOLEDO: That's what time she told us. Say be here at one o'clock.

IRVIN: Do you know what's keeping her? Do you know why she ain't here?

TOLEDO: I can't say, Mr. Irvin. Told us one o'clock.
(*The buzzer sounds.* IRVIN *goes to the door. There is a flurry of commotion as* MA RAINEY *enters, followed closely by the* POLICE-MAN, DUSSIE MAE *and* SYLVESTER. MA RAINEY *is a short, heavy woman. She is dressed in a full-length fur coat with matching hat, an emerald green dress, and several strands of pearls of varying lengths. Her hair is secured by a headband that matches her dress. Her manner is simple and direct, and she carries herself in a royal fashion.* DUSSIE MAE *is a young, dark-skinned woman whose greatest asset is the sensual energy which seems to flow from her. She is dressed in a fur jacket and a tight-fitting canary yellow dress.* SYLVESTER *is an Arkansas country boy, the size of a fullback. He wears a new suit and coat, in which he is obviously uncomfortable. Most of the time he stutters when he speaks.*)

MA RAINEY: Irvin . . . you better tell this man who I am! You better get him straight!

IRVIN: Ma, do you know what time it is? Do you have any idea? We've been waiting . . .

DUSSIE MAE: (*To* SYLVESTER.) If you was watching where you was going . . .

SYLVESTER: I was watching . . . What you mean?

IRVIN: (*Notices* POLICEMAN.) What's going on here? Officer, what's the matter?

MA RAINEY: Tell the man who he's messing with!

POLICEMAN: Do you know this lady?

MA RAINEY: Just tell the man who I am! That's all you gotta do.

POLICEMAN: Lady, will you let me talk, huh?

MA RAINEY: Tell the man who I am!

IRVIN: Wait a minute . . . wait a minute! Let me handle it. Ma, will you let me handle it?

MA RAINEY: Tell him who he's messing with!

IRVIN: Okay! Okay! Give me a chance! Officer, this is one of our recording artists . . . Ma Rainey.

MA RAINEY: Madame Rainey! Get it straight! Madame Rainey! Talking about taking me to jail!

IRVIN: Look, Ma . . . give me a chance, okay? Here . . . sit down. I'll take care of it. Officer, what's the problem?

DUSSIE MAE: (*To* SYLVESTER.) It's all your fault.

SYLVESTER: I ain't done nothing . . . Ask Ma.

POLICEMAN: Well . . . when I walked up on the incident . . .

DUSSIE MAE: Sylvester wrecked Ma's car.

SYLVESTER: I d-d-did not! The m-m-man ran into me!

POLICEMAN: (*To* IRVIN.) Look, buddy . . . if you want it in a nutshell, we got her charged with assault and battery.

MA RAINEY: Assault and what for what!

DUSSIE MAE: See . . . we was trying to get a cab . . . and so Ma . . .

MA RAINEY: Wait a minute! I'll tell you if you wanna know what happened. (*She points to* SYLVESTER.)
Now, that's Sylvester. That's my nephew. He was driving my car . . .

POLICEMAN: Lady, we don't know whose car he was driving.

MA RAINEY: That's my car!

DUSSIE MAE and SYLVESTER: That's Ma's car!

MA RAINEY: What you mean you don't know whose car it is? I bought and paid for that car.

POLICEMAN: That's what you say, lady . . . We still gotta check. (*To* IRVIN.)
They hit a car on Market Street. The guy said the kid ran a stoplight.

SYLVESTER: What you mean? The man c-c-come around the corner and hit m-m-me!

POLICEMAN: While I was calling a paddy wagon to haul them to the station, they try to hop into a parked cab. The cabbie said he was waiting on a fare . . .

MA RAINEY: The man was just sitting there. Wasn't waiting for nobody. I don't know why he wanna tell that lie.

POLICEMAN: Look, lady . . . will you let me tell the story?

MA RAINEY: Go ahead and tell it then. But tell it right!

POLICEMAN: Like I say . . . she tries to get in this cab. The cabbie's waiting on a fare. She starts creating a disturbance. The cabbie gets out to try and explain the situation to her . . . and she knocks him down.

DUSSIE MAE: She ain't hit him! He just fell!

SYLVESTER: He just s-s-s-slipped!

POLICEMAN: He claims she knocked him down. We got her charged with assault and battery.

MA RAINEY: If that don't beat all to hell. I ain't touched the man! The man was trying to reach around me to keep his car door closed. I opened the door and it hit him and he fell down. I ain't touched the man!

IRVIN: Okay. Okay . . . I got it straight now, Ma. You didn't touch him. Alright? Officer, can I see you for a minute?

DUSSIE MAE: Ma was just trying to open the door.

SYLVESTER: He j-j-just got in th-th-the way!

MA RAINEY: Said he wasn't gonna haul no colored folks . . . if you want to know the truth of it.

IRVIN: Okay, Ma . . . I got it straight now. Officer?
(IRVIN *pulls the* POLICEMAN *off to the side.*)

MA RAINEY: (*Noticing* TOLEDO.) Toledo, Cutler and everybody here?

TOLEDO: Yeah, they down in the band room. What happened to your car?

STURDYVANT: (*Entering.*) Irv, what's the problem? What's going on? Officer . . .

IRVIN: Mel, let me take care of it. I can handle it.

STURDYVANT: What's happening? What the hell's going on?

IRVIN: Let me handle it, Mel, huh?
(STURDYVANT *crosses over to* MA RAINEY.)

STURDYVANT: What's going on, Ma. What'd you do?

MA RAINEY: Sturdyvant, get on away from me! That's the last thing I need . . . to go through some of your shit!

IRVIN: Mel, I'll take care of it. I'll explain it all to you. Let me handle it, huh?

(STURDYVANT *reluctantly returns to the control booth.*)

POLICEMAN: Look, buddy, like I say . . . we got her charged with assault and battery . . . and the kid with threatening the cabbie.

SYLVESTER: I ain't done n-n-nothing!

MA RAINEY: You leave the boy out of it. He ain't done nothing. What's he supposed to have done?

POLICEMAN: He threatened the cabbie, lady! You just can't go around threatening people.

SYLVESTER: I ain't done nothing to him! He's the one talking about he g-g-gonna get a b-b-baseball bat on me! I just told him what I'd do with it. But I ain't done nothing cause he didn't get the b-b-bat!

IRVIN: (*Pulling the* POLICEMAN *aside.*) Officer . . . look here . . .

POLICEMAN: We was on our way down to the precinct . . . but I figured I'd do you a favor and bring her by here. I mean, if she's as important as she says she is . . .

IRVIN: (*Slides a bill from his pocket.*) Look, officer . . . I'm Madame Rainey's manager . . . It's good to meet you.
(*He shakes the* POLICEMAN'*s hand and passes him the bill.*)
As soon as we're finished with the recording session, I'll personally stop by the precinct house and straighten up this misunderstanding.

POLICEMAN: Well . . . I guess that's alright. As long as someone is responsible for them.
(*He pockets the bill and winks at* IRVIN.)
No need to come down . . . I'll take care of it myself. Of course, we wouldn't want nothing like this to happen again.

IRVIN: Don't worry, officer . . . I'll take care of everything. Thanks for your help.
(IRVIN *escorts the* POLICEMAN *to the door and returns. He crosses over to* MA RAINEY.)
Here, Ma . . . let me take your coat.

(*To* SYLVESTER.)
I don't believe I know you.

MA RAINEY: That's my nephew, Sylvester.

IRVIN: I'm very pleased to meet you. Here . . . you can give me your coat.

MA RAINEY: That there is Dussie Mae.

IRVIN: Hello . . .
(DUSSIE MAE *hands* IRVIN *her coat.*)
Listen, Ma, just sit there and relax. The boys are in the band room rehearsing. You just sit and relax a minute.

MA RAINEY: I ain't for no sitting. I ain't never heard of such. Talking about taking me to jail. Irvin, call down there and see about my car.

IRVIN: Okay, Ma . . . I'll take care of it. You just relax.
(IRVIN *exits with the coats.*)

MA RAINEY: Why you all keep it so cold in here? Sturdyvant try and pinch every penny he can. You all wanna make some records, you better put some heat on in here or give me back my coat.

IRVIN: (*Entering.*) We got the heat turned up, Ma. It's warming up. It'll be warm in a minute.

DUSSIE MAE: (*Whispering to* MA RAINEY.) Where's the bathroom?

MA RAINEY: It's in the back. Down the hall next to Sturdyvant's office. Come on, I'll show you where it is. Irvin, call down there and see about my car. I want my car fixed today.

IRVIN: I'll take care of everything, Ma.
(*He notices* TOLEDO.)
Say . . . uh . . . uh . . .

TOLEDO: Toledo.

IRVIN: Yeah . . . Toledo. I got the sandwiches, you can take them down to the rest of the boys. We'll be ready to go in a minute.

Give you boys a chance to eat and then we'll be ready to go. (IRVIN *and* TOLEDO *exit. The lights go down in the studio and come up in the band room.*)

LEVEE: Slow Drag, you ever been to New Orleans?

SLOW DRAG: What's in New Orleans that I want?

LEVEE: How you call yourself a musician and ain't never been to New Orleans?

SLOW DRAG: You ever been to Fat Back, Arkansas?
(*Pauses.*)
Alright, then. Ain't never been nothing in New Orleans that I couldn't get in Fat Back.

LEVEE: That's why you backwards. You just an old country boy talking about Fat Back, Arkansas, and New Orleans in the same breath.

CUTLER: I been to New Orleans. What about it?

LEVEE: You ever been to Lula White's?

CUTLER: Lula White's? I ain't never heard of it.

LEVEE: Man, they got some gals in there just won't wait! I seen a man get killed in there once. Got drunk and grabbed one of the gals wrong. I don't know what the matter of it was. But he grabbed her and she stuck a knife in him all the way up to the hilt. He ain't even fell. He just stood there and choked on his own blood. I was just asking Slow Drag cause I was gonna take him to Lula White's when we get down to New Orleans and show him a good time. Introduce him to one of them gals I know down there.

CUTLER: Slow Drag don't need you to find him no pussy. He can take care of his own self. Fact is . . . you better watch your gal when Slow Drag's around. They don't call him Slow Drag for nothing.
(*He laughs.*)
Tell him how you got your name, Slow Drag.

SLOW DRAG: I ain't thinking about Levee.

CUTLER: Slow Drag break a woman's back when he dance. They had this contest one time in this little town called Bolingbroke about a hundred miles outside of Macon. We was playing for this dance and they was giving twenty dollars to the best slow draggers. Slow Drag looked over the competition, got down off the bandstand, grabbed hold of one of them gals, and stuck to her like a fly to jelly. Like wood to glue. Man had that gal whooping and hollering so . . . everybody stopped to watch. This fellow come in . . . this gal's fellow . . . and pulled a knife a foot long on Slow Drag. Member that, Slow Drag?

SLOW DRAG: Boy that mama was hot! The front of her dress was wet as a dishrag!

LEVEE: So what happened? What the man do?

CUTLER: Slow Drag ain't missed a stroke. The gal, she just look at her man with that sweet dizzy look in her eye. She ain't about to stop! Folks was clearing out, ducking and hiding under tables, figuring there's gonna be a fight. Slow Drag just looked over the gal's shoulder at the man and said, "Mister, if you'd quit hollering and wait a minute . . . you'll see I'm doing you a favor. I'm helping this gal win ten dollars so she can buy you a gold watch." The man just stood there and looked at him, all the while stroking that knife. Told Slow Drag, say, "Alright, then, nigger. You just better make damn sure you win." That's when folks started calling him Slow Drag. The women got to hanging around him so bad after that, them fellows in that town ran us out of there.
(TOLEDO *enters, carrying a small cardboard box with the sandwiches.*)

LEVEE: Yeah . . . well, them gals in Lula White's will put a harness on his ass.

TOLEDO: Ma's up there. Some kind of commotion with the police.

CUTLER: Police? What the police up there for?

TOLEDO: I couldn't get it straight. Something about her car. They

gone now . . . she's alright. Mr. Irvin sent some sandwiches.
(LEVEE *springs across the room.*)

LEVEE: Yeah, alright. What we got here?
(*He takes two sandwiches out of the box.*)

TOLEDO: What you doing grabbing two? There ain't but five in
there . . . How you figure you get two?

LEVEE: Cause I grabbed them first. There's enough for everybody . . . What you talking about? It ain't like I'm taking food
out of nobody's mouth.

CUTLER: That's alright. He can have mine too. I don't want none.
(LEVEE *starts toward the box to get another sandwich.*)

TOLEDO: Nigger, you better get out of here. Slow Drag, you want
this?

SLOW DRAG: Naw, you can have it.

TOLEDO: With Levee around, you don't have to worry about no
leftovers. I can see that.

LEVEE: What's the matter with you? Ain't you eating two sandwiches? Then why you wanna talk about me? Talking about
there won't be no leftovers with Levee around. Look at your own
self before you look at me.

TOLEDO: That's what you is. That's what we all is. A leftover from
history. You see now, I'll show you.

LEVEE: Aw, shit . . . I done got the nigger started now.

TOLEDO: Now, I'm gonna show you how this goes . . . where you
just a leftover from history. Everybody come from different places
in Africa, right? Come from different tribes and things. Soon-
awhile they began to make one big stew. You had the carrots, the
peas, and potatoes and whatnot over here. And over there you
had the meat, the nuts, the okra, corn . . . and then you mix it
up and let it cook right through to get the flavors flowing
together . . . then you got one thing. You got a stew.

46

Now you take and eat the stew. You take and make your history with that stew. Alright. Now it's over. Your history's over and you done ate the stew. But you look around and you see some carrots over here, some potatoes over there. That stew's still there. You done made your history and it's still there. You can't eat it all. So what you got? You got some leftovers. That's what it is. You got leftovers and you can't do nothing with it. You already making you another history . . . cooking you another meal, and you don't need them leftovers no more. What to do?

See, we's the leftovers. The colored man is the leftovers. Now, what's the colored man gonna do with himself? That's what we waiting to find out. But first we gotta know we the leftovers. Now, who knows that? You find me a nigger that knows that and I'll turn any whichaway you want me to. I'll bend over for you. You ain't gonna find that. And that's what the problem is. The problem ain't with the white man. The white man knows you just a leftover. Cause he the one who done the eating and he know what he done ate. But we don't know that we been took and made history out of. Done went and filled the white man's belly and now he's full and tired and wants you to get out the way and let him be by himself. Now, I know what I'm talking about. And if you wanna find out, you just ask Mr. Irvin what he had for supper yesterday. And if he's an honest white man . . . which is asking for a whole heap of a lot . . . he'll tell you he done ate your black ass and if you please I'm full up with you . . . so go on and get off the plate and let me eat something else.

SLOW DRAG: What that mean? What's eating got to do with how the white man treat you? He don't treat you no different according to what he ate.

TOLEDO: I ain't said it had nothing to do with how he treat you.

CUTLER: The man's trying to tell you something, fool!

SLOW DRAG: What he trying to tell me? Ain't you here? Why you say he was trying to tell *me* something? Wasn't he trying to tell you too?

LEVEE: He was trying alright. He was trying a whole heap. I'll say that for him. But trying ain't worth a damn. I got lost right there trying to figure out who puts nuts in their stew.

SLOW DRAG: I knowed that before. My grandpappy used to put nuts in his stew. He and my grandmama both. That ain't nothing new.

TOLEDO: They put nuts in their stew all over Africa. But the stew they eat, and the stew your grandpappy made, and all the stew that you and me eat, and the stew Mr. Irvin eats . . . ain't in no way the same stew. That's the way that go. I'm through with it. That's the last you know me to ever try and explain something to you.

CUTLER: (*After a pause.*) Well, time's getting along . . . Come on, let's finish rehearsing.

LEVEE: (*Stretching out on a bench.*) I don't feel like rehearsing. I ain't nothing but a leftover. You go and rehearse with Toledo . . . He's gonna teach you how to make a stew.

SLOW DRAG: Cutler, what you gonna do? I don't want to be around here all day.

LEVEE: I know my part. You all go on and rehearse your part. You all need some rehearsal.

CUTLER: Come on, Levee, get up off your ass and rehearse the songs.

LEVEE: I already know them songs . . . What I wanna rehearse them for?

SLOW DRAG: You in the band, ain't you? You supposed to rehearse when the band rehearse.

TOLEDO: Levee think he the king of the barnyard. He thinks he's the only rooster know how to crow.

LEVEE: Alright! Alright! Come on, I'm gonna show you I know

48

them songs. Come on, let's rehearse. I bet you the first one mess be Toledo. Come on . . . I wanna see if he know how to crow.

CUTLER: "Ma Rainey's Black Bottom," Levee's version. Let's do it. (*They begin to rehearse. The lights go down in the band room and up in the studio.* MA RAINEY *sits and takes off her shoe, rubs her foot.* DUSSIE MAE *wanders about looking at the studio.* SYLVESTER *is over by the piano.*)

MA RAINEY: (*Singing to herself.*)
Oh, Lord, these dogs of mine
They sure do worry me all the time
The reason why I don't know
Lord, I beg to be excused
I can't wear me no sharp-toed shoes.
I went for a walk
I stopped to talk
Oh, how my corns did bark.

DUSSIE MAE: It feels kinda spooky in here. I ain't never been in no recording studio before. Where's the band at?

MA RAINEY: They off somewhere rehearsing. I don't know where Irvin went to. All this hurry up and he goes off back there with Sturdyvant. I know he better come on cause Ma ain't gonna be waiting. Come here . . . let me see that dress.
(DUSSIE MAE *crosses over.* MA RAINEY *tugs at the dress around the waist, appraising the fit.*)
That dress looks nice. I'm gonna take you tomorrow and get you some more things before I take you down to Memphis. They got clothes up here you can't get in Memphis. I want you to look nice for me. If you gonna travel with the show you got to look nice.

DUSSIE MAE: I need me some more shoes. These hurt my feet.

MA RAINEY: You get you some shoes that fit your feet. Don't you be messing around with no shoes that pinch your feet. Ma know something about bad feet. Hand me my slippers out my bag over yonder.

49

(DUSSIE MAE *brings the slippers.*)

DUSSIE MAE: I just want to get a pair of them yellow ones. About a half-size bigger.

MA RAINEY: We'll get you whatever you need. Sylvester, too . . . I'm gonna get him some more clothes. Sylvester, tuck your clothes in. Straighten them up and look nice. Look like a gentleman.

DUSSIE MAE: Look at Sylvester with that hat on.

MA RAINEY: Sylvester, take your hat off inside. Act like your mama taught you something. I know she taught you better than that.
(SYLVESTER *bangs on the piano.*)
Come on over here and leave that piano alone.

SYLVESTER: I ain't d-d-doing nothing to the p-p-piano. I'm just l-l-looking at it.

MA RAINEY: Well. Come on over here and sit down. As soon as Mr. Irvin comes back, I'll have him take you down and introduce you to the band.
(SYLVESTER *comes over.*)
He's gonna take you down there and introduce you in a minute . . . have Cutler show you how your part go. And when you get your money, you gonna send some of it home to your mama. Let her know you doing alright. Make her feel good to know you doing alright in the world.
(DUSSIE MAE *wanders about the studio and opens the door leading to the band room. The strains of* LEVEE'*s version of "Ma Rainey's Black Bottom" can be heard.* IRVIN *enters.*)

IRVIN: Ma, I called down to the garage and checked on your car. It's just a scratch. They'll have it ready for you this afternoon. They're gonna send it over with one of their fellows.

MA RAINEY: They better have my car fixed right too. I ain't going for that. Brand new car . . . they better fix it like new.

IRVIN: It was just a scratch on the fender, Ma . . . They'll take care of it . . . don't worry . . . they'll have it like new.

MA RAINEY: Irvin, what is that I hear? What is that the band's rehearsing? I know they ain't rehearsing Levee's "Black Bottom." I know I ain't hearing that?

IRVIN: Ma, listen . . . that's what I wanted to talk to you about. Levee's version of that song . . . it's got a nice arrangement . . . a nice horn intro . . . It really picks it up . . .

MA RAINEY: I ain't studying Levee nothing. I know what he done to that song and I don't like to sing it that way. I'm doing it the old way. That's why I brought my nephew to do the voice intro.

IRVIN: Ma, that's what the people want now. They want something they can dance to. Times are changing. Levee's arrangement gives the people what they want. It gets them excited . . . makes them forget about their troubles.

MA RAINEY: I don't care what you say, Irvin. Levee ain't messing up my song. If he got what the people want, let him take it somewhere else. I'm singing Ma Rainey's song. I ain't singing Levee's song. Now that's all there is to it. Carry my nephew on down there and introduce him to the band. I promised my sister I'd look out for him and he's gonna do the voice intro on the song my way.

IRVIN: Ma, we just figured that . . .

MA RAINEY: Who's this "we"? What you mean "we"? I ain't studying Levee nothing. Come talking this "we" stuff. Who's "we"?

IRVIN: Me and Sturdyvant. We decided that it would . . .

MA RAINEY: You decided, huh? I'm just a bump on the log. I'm gonna go which ever way the river drift. Is that it? You and Sturdyvant decided.

IRVIN: Ma, it was just that we thought it would be better.

MA RAINEY: I ain't got good sense. I don't know nothing about

51

music. I don't know what's a good song and what ain't. You know more about my fans than I do.

IRVIN: It's not that, Ma. It would just be easier to do. It's more what the people want.

MA RAINEY: I'm gonna tell you something, Irvin . . . and you go on up there and tell Sturdyvant. What you all say don't count with me. You understand? Ma listens to her heart. Ma listens to the voice inside her. That's what counts with Ma. Now, you carry my nephew on down there . . . tell Cutler he's gonna do the voice intro on that "Black Bottom" song and that Levee ain't messing up my song with none of his music shit. Now, if that don't set right with you and Sturdyvant . . . then I can carry my black bottom on back down South to my tour, cause I don't like it up here no ways.

IRVIN: Okay, Ma . . . I don't care. I just thought . . .

MA RAINEY: Damn what you thought! What you look like telling me how to sing my song? This Levee and Sturdyvant nonsense . . . I ain't going for it! Sylvester, go on down there and introduce yourself. I'm through playing with Irvin.

SYLVESTER: Which way you go? Where they at?

MA RAINEY: Here . . . I'll carry you down there myself.

DUSSIE MAE: Can I go? I wanna see the band.

MA RAINEY: You stay your behind up here. Ain't no cause in you being down there. Come on, Sylvester.

IRVIN: Okay, Ma. Have it your way. We'll be ready to go in fifteen minutes.

MA RAINEY: We'll be ready to go when Madame says we're ready. That's the way it goes around here.
(MA RAINEY *and* SYLVESTER *exit. The lights go down in the studio and up in the band room.* MA RAINEY *enters with* SYLVESTER.)
Cutler, this here is my nephew Sylvester. He's gonna do that voice intro on the "Black Bottom" song using the old version.

LEVEE: What you talking about? Mr. Irvin say he's using my version. What you talking about?

MA RAINEY: Levee, I ain't studying you or Mr. Irvin. Cutler, get him straightened out on how to do his part. I ain't thinking about Levee. These folks done messed with the wrong person this day. Sylvester, Cutler gonna teach you your part. You go ahead and get it straight. Don't worry about what nobody else say. (MA RAINEY *exits.*)

CUTLER: Well, come on in, boy. I'm Cutler. You got Slow Drag . . . Levee . . . and that's Toledo over there. Sylvester, huh?

SYLVESTER: Sylvester Brown.

LEVEE: I done wrote a version of that song what picks it up and sets it down in the people's lap! Now she come talking this! You don't need that old circus bullshit! I know what I'm talking about. You gonna mess up the song Cutler and you know it.

CUTLER: I ain't gonna mess up nothing. Ma say . . .

LEVEE: I don't care what Ma say! I'm talking about what the intro gonna do to the song. The peoples in the North ain't gonna buy all that tent-show nonsense. They wanna hear some music!

CUTLER: Nigger, I done told you time and again . . . you just in the band. You plays the piece . . . whatever they want! Ma says what to play! Not you! You ain't here to be doing no creating. Your job is to play whatever Ma says!

LEVEE: I might not play nothing! I might quit!

CUTLER: Nigger, don't nobody care if you quit. Whose heart you gonna break?

TOLEDO: Levee ain't gonna quit. He got to make some money to keep him in shoe polish.

LEVEE: I done told you all . . . you all don't know me. You don't know what I'll do.

CUTLER: I don't think nobody too much give a damn! Sylvester,

here's the way your part go. The band plays the intro . . . I'll tell you where to come in. The band plays the intro and then you say, "Alright, boys, you done seen the rest . . . Now I'm gonna show you the best. Ma Rainey's gonna show you her black bottom." You got that?
(SYLVESTER *nods.*)
Let me hear you say it one time.

SYLVESTER: "Alright, boys, you done s-s-seen the rest n-n-now I'm gonna show you the best. M-m-m-m-m-m-ma Rainey's gonna sh-sh-show you her black b-b-bottom."

LEVEE: What kind of . . . Alright, Cutler! Let me see you fix that! You straighten that out! You hear that shit, Slow Drag? How in the hell the boy gonna do the part and he can't even talk!

SYLVESTER: W-w-w-who's you to tell me what to do, nigger! This ain't your band! Ma tell me to d-d-d-do it and I'm gonna do it. You can go to hell, n-n-n-nigger!

LEVEE: B-b-b-boy, ain't nobody studying you. You go on and fix that one, Cutler. You fix that one and I'll . . . I'll shine your shoes for you. You go on and fix that one!

TOLEDO: You say you Ma's nephew, huh?

SYLVESTER: Yeah. So w-w-what that mean?

TOLEDO: Oh, I ain't meant nothing . . . I was just asking.

SLOW DRAG: Well, come on and let's rehearse so the boy can get it right.

LEVEE: I ain't rehearsing nothing! You just wait till I get my band. I'm gonna record that song and show you how it supposed to go!

CUTLER: We can do it without Levee. Let him sit on over there. Sylvester, you remember your part?

SYLVESTER: I remember it pretty g-g-g-good.

CUTLER: Well, come on, let's do it, then.

(*The band begins to play.* LEVEE *sits and pouts.* STURDYVANT *enters the band room.*)

STURDYVANT: Good . . . you boys are rehearsing, I see.

LEVEE: (*Jumping up.*) Yessir! We rehearsing. We know them songs real good.

STURDYVANT: Good! Say, Levee, did you finish that song?

LEVEE: Yessir, Mr. Sturdyvant. I got it right here. I wrote that other part just like you say. It go like:
You can shake it, you can break it
You can dance at any hall
You can slide across the floor
You'll never have to stall
My jelly, my roll,
Sweet Mama, don't you let it fall.
Then I put that part in there for the people to dance, like you say, for them to forget about their troubles.

STURDYVANT: Good! Good! I'll just take this. I wanna see you about your songs as soon as I get the chance.

LEVEE: Yessir! As soon as you get the chance, Mr. Sturdyvant. (STURDYVANT *exits.*)

CUTLER: You hear, Levee? You hear this nigger? "Yessuh, we's rehearsing, boss."

SLOW DRAG: I heard him. Seen him too. Shuffling them feet.

TOLEDO: Aw, Levee can't help it none. He's like all of us. Spooked up with the white men.

LEVEE: I'm spooked up with him, alright. You let one of them crackers fix on me wrong. I'll show you how spooked up I am with him.

TOLEDO: That's the trouble of it. You wouldn't know if he was fixed on you wrong or not. You so spooked up by him you ain't had the time to study him.

55

LEVEE: I studies the white man. I got him studied good. The first time one fixes on me wrong, I'm gonna let him know just how much I studied. Come telling me I'm spooked up with the white man. You let one of them mess with me, I'll show you how spooked up I am.

CUTLER: You talking out your hat. The man come in here, call you a boy, tell you to get up off your ass and rehearse, and you ain't had nothing to say to him, except "Yessir!"

LEVEE: I can say "yessir" to whoever I please. What you got to do with it? I know how to handle white folks. I been handling them for thirty-two years, and now you gonna tell me how to do it. Just cause I say "yessir" don't mean I'm spooked up with him. I know what I'm doing. Let me handle him my way.

CUTLER: Well, go on and handle it, then.

LEVEE: Toledo, you always messing with somebody! Always agitating somebody with that old philosophy bullshit you be talking. You stay out of my way about what I do and say. I'm my own person. Just let me alone.

TOLEDO: You right, Levee. I apologize. It ain't none of my business that you spooked up by the white man.

LEVEE: Alright! See! That's the shit I'm talking about. You all back up and leave Levee alone.

SLOW DRAG: Aw, Levee, we was all just having fun. Toledo ain't said nothing about you he ain't said about me. You just taking it all wrong.

TOLEDO: I ain't meant nothing by it Levee.
(*Pauses.*)
Cutler, you ready to rehearse?

LEVEE: Levee got to be Levee! And he don't need nobody messing with him about the white man—cause you don't know nothing about me. You don't know Levee. You don't know nothing about what kind of blood I got! What kind of heart I got beating here!

(*He pounds his chest.*)

I was eight years old when I watched a gang of white mens come into my daddy's house and have to do with my mama any way they wanted.

(*Pauses.*)

We was living in Jefferson County, about eighty miles outside of Natchez. My daddy's name was Memphis . . . Memphis Lee Green . . . had him near fifty acres of good farming land. I'm talking about good land! Grow anything you want! He done gone off of shares and bought this land from Mr. Hallie's widow woman after he done passed on. Folks called him an uppity nigger cause he done saved and borrowed to where he could buy this land and be independent.

(*Pauses.*)

It was coming on planting time and my daddy went into Natchez to get him some seed and fertilizer. Called me, say, "Levee you the man of the house now. Take care of your mama while I'm gone." I wasn't but a little boy, eight years old.

(*Pauses.*)

My mama was frying up some chicken when them mens come in that house. Must have been eight or nine of them. She standing there frying that chicken and them mens come and took hold of her just like you take hold of a mule and make him do what you want.

(*Pauses.*)

There was my mama with a gang of white mens. She tried to fight them off, but I could see where it wasn't gonna do her any good, I didn't know what they were doing to her . . . but I figured whatever it was they may as well do to me too. My daddy had a knife that he kept around there for hunting and working and whatnot. I knew where he kept it and I went and got it.

I'm gonna show you how spooked up I was by the white man. I tried my damndest to cut one of them's throat! I hit him on the shoulder with it. He reached back and grabbed hold of that knife and whacked me across the chest with it.

(LEVEE *raises his shirt to show a long ugly scar.*)

That's what made them stop. They was scared I was gonna bleed to death. My mama wrapped a sheet around me and carried me two miles down to the Furlow place and they drove me up to Doc Albans. He was waiting on a calf to be born, and say he ain't had time to see me. They carried me up to Miss Etta, the midwife, and she fixed me up.

My daddy came back and acted like he done accepted the facts of what happened. But he got the names of them mens from mama. He found out who they was and then we announced we was moving out of that county. Said good-bye to everybody . . . all the neighbors. My daddy went and smiled in the face of one of them crackers who had been with my mama. Smiled in his face and sold him our land. We moved over with relations in Caldwell. He got us settled in and then he took off one day. I ain't never seen him since. He sneaked back, hiding up in the woods, laying to get them eight or nine men.
(Pauses.)
He got four of them before they got him. They tracked him down in the woods. Caught up with him and hung him and set him afire.
(Pauses.)
My daddy wasn't spooked up by the white man. Nosir! And that taught me how to handle them. I seen my daddy go up and grin in this cracker's face . . . smile in his face and sell him his land. All the while he's planning how he's gonna get him and what he's gonna do to him. That taught me how to handle them. So you all just back up and leave Levee alone about the white man. I can smile and say yessir to whoever I please. I got time coming to me. You all just leave Levee alone about the white man.
(There is a long pause. SLOW DRAG begins playing on the bass and sings.)

SLOW DRAG: (Singing.)
    If I had my way
    If I had my way
    If I had my way
    I would tear this old building down.

ACT TWO

(*The lights come up in the studio. The musicians are setting up their instruments.* MA RAINEY *walks about shoeless, singing softly to herself.* LEVEE *stands near* DUSSIE MAE, *who hikes up her dress and crosses her legs.* CUTLER *speaks to* IRVIN *off to the side.*)

CUTLER: Mr. Irvin, I don't know what you gonna do. I ain't got nothing to do with it, but the boy can't do the part. He stutters. He can't get it right. He stutters right through it every time.

IRVIN: Christ! Okay. We'll . . . Shit! We'll just do it like we planned. We'll do Levee's version. I'll handle it, Cutler. Come on, let's go. I'll think of something.
(*He exits to the control booth.*)

MA RAINEY: (*Calling* CUTLER *over.*) Levee's got his eyes in the wrong place. You better school him, Cutler.

CUTLER: Come on, Levee . . . let's get ready to play! Get your mind on your work!

IRVIN: (*Over speaker.*) Okay, boys, we're gonna do "Moonshine Blues" first. "Moonshine Blues," Ma.

MA RAINEY: I ain't doing no "Moonshine" nothing. I'm doing the "Black Bottom" first. Come on, Sylvester.
(*To* IRVIN.)
Where's Sylvester's mike? You need a mike for Sylvester. Irvin . . . get him a mike.

IRVIN: Uh . . . Ma, the boys say he can't do it. We'll have to do Levee's version.

MA RAINEY: What you mean he can't do it? Who say he can't do it? What boys say he can't do it?

IRVIN: The band, Ma . . . the boys in the band.

MA RAINEY: What band? The band work for me! I say what goes! Cutler, what's he talking about? Levee, this some of your shit?

IRVIN: He stutters, Ma. They say he stutters.

MA RAINEY: I don't care if he do. I promised the boy he could do the part . . . and he's gonna do it! That's all there is to it. He don't stutter all the time. Get a microphone down here for him.

IRVIN: Ma, we don't have time. We can't . . .

MA RAINEY: If you wanna make a record, you gonna find time. I ain't playing with you, Irvin. I can walk out of here and go back to my tour. I got plenty fans. I don't need to go through all of this. Just go and get the boy a microphone.
(IRVIN *and* STURDYVANT *consult in the booth.* IRVIN *exits.*)

STURDYVANT: Alright, Ma . . . we'll get him a microphone. But if he messes up . . . He's only getting one chance . . . The cost . . .

MA RAINEY: Damn the cost. You always talking about the cost. I make more money for this outfit than anybody else you got put together. If he messes up he'll just do it till he gets it right. Levee, I know you had something to do with this. You better watch yourself.

LEVEE: It was Cutler!

SYLVESTER: It was you! You the only one m-m-mad about it.

LEVEE: The boy stutter. He can't do the part. Everybody see that. I don't know why you want the boy to do the part no ways.

MA RAINEY: Well, can or can't . . . he's gonna do it! You ain't got nothing to do with it!

LEVEE: I don't care what you do! He can sing the whole goddamned song for all I care!

MA RAINEY: Well, alright. Thank you.
(IRVIN *enters with a microphone and hooks it up. He exits to the control booth.*)

MA RAINEY: Come on, Sylvester. You just stand here and hold your hands like I told you. Just remember the words and say them . . . That's all there is to it. Don't worry about messing up. If you mess up, we'll do it again. Now, let me hear you say it. Play for him, Cutler.

CUTLER: One . . . two . . . you know what to do.
(*The band begins to play and* SYLVESTER *curls his fingers and clasps his hands together in front of his chest, pulling in opposite directions as he says his lines.*)

SYLVESTER: "Alright, boys, you d-d-d-done s-s-s-seen the best . . .
(LEVEE *stops playing.*)
Now I'm g-g-g-gonna show you the rest . . . Ma R-r-rainey's gonna show you her b-b-b-black b-b-b-bottom."
(*The rest of the band stops playing.*)

MA RAINEY: That's alright. That's real good. You take your time, you'll get it right.

STURDYVANT: (*Over speaker.*) Listen, Ma . . . now, when you come in, don't wait so long to come in. Don't take so long on the intro, huh?

MA RAINEY: Sturdyvant, don't you go trying to tell me how to sing. You just take care of that up there and let me take care of this down here. Where's my Coke?

IRVIN: Okay, Ma. We're all set up to go up here. "Ma Rainey's Black Bottom," boys.

61

MA RAINEY: Where's my Coke? I need a Coke. You ain't got no Coke down here? Where's my Coke?

IRVIN: What's the matter, Ma? What's . . .

MA RAINEY: Where's my Coke? I need a Coca-Cola.

IRVIN: Uh . . . Ma, look, I forgot the Coke, huh? Let's do it without it, huh? Just this one song. What say, boys?

MA RAINEY: Damn what the band say! You know I don't sing nothing without my Coca-Cola!

STURDYVANT: We don't have any, Ma. There's no Coca-Cola here. We're all set up and we'll just go ahead and . . .

MA RAINEY: You supposed to have Coca-Cola. Irvin knew that. I ain't singing nothing without my Coca-Cola!
(*She walks away from the mike, singing to herself.* STURDYVANT *enters from the control booth.*)

STURDYVANT: Now, just a minute here, Ma. You come in an hour late . . . we're way behind schedule as it is . . . the band is set up and ready to go . . . I'm burning my lights . . . I've turned up the heat . . . We're ready to make a record and what? You decide you want a Coca-Cola?

MA RAINEY: Sturdyvant, get out of my face.
(IRVIN *enters.*)
Irvin . . . I told you keep him away from me.

IRVIN: Mel, I'll handle it.

STURDYVANT: I'm tired of her nonsense, Irv. I'm not gonna put up with this!

IRVIN: Let me handle it, Mel. I know how to handle her.
(IRVIN *to* MA RAINEY.)
Look, Ma . . . I'll call down to the deli and get you a Coke. But let's get started, huh? Sylvester's standing there ready to go . . . the band's set up . . . let's do this one song, huh?

MA RAINEY: If you too cheap to buy me a Coke, I'll buy my own.

Slow Drag! Sylvester, go with Slow Drag and get me a Coca-Cola.
(SLOW DRAG *comes over.*)
Slow Drag, walk down to that store on the corner and get me three bottles of Coca-Cola. Get out my face, Irvin. You all just wait until I get my Coke. It ain't gonna kill you.

IRVIN: Okay, Ma. Get your Coke, for Chrissakes! Get your Coke!
(IRVIN *and* STURDYVANT *exit into the hallway followed by* SLOW DRAG *and* SYLVESTER. TOLEDO, CUTLER, *and* LEVEE *head for the band room.*)

MA RAINEY: Cutler, come here a minute. I want to talk to you.
(CUTLER *crosses over somewhat reluctantly.*)
What's all this about "the boys in the band say?" I tells you what to do. I says what the matter is with the band. I say who can and can't do what.

CUTLER: We just say cause the boy stutter . . .

MA RAINEY: I know he stutters. Don't you think I know he stutters? This is what's gonna help him.

CUTLER: Well, how can he do the part if he stutters? You want him to stutter through it? We just thought it be easier to go on and let Levee do it like we planned.

MA RAINEY: I don't care if he stutters or not! He's doing the part and I don't wanna hear any more of this shit about what the band says. And I want you to find somebody to replace Levee when we get to Memphis. Levee ain't nothing but trouble.

CUTLER: Levee's alright. He plays good music when he puts his mind to it. He knows how to write music too.

MA RAINEY: I don't care what he know. He ain't nothing but bad news. Find somebody else. I know it was his idea about who to say who can do what.
(DUSSIE MAE *wanders over to where they are sitting.*)
Dussie Mae, go sit your behind down somewhere and quit flaunting yourself around.

DUSSIE MAE: I ain't doing nothing.

MA RAINEY: Well, just go on somewhere and stay out of the way.

CUTLER: I been meaning to ask you, Ma . . . about these songs. This "Moonshine Blues" . . . that's one of them songs Bessie Smith sang, I believes.

MA RAINEY: Bessie what? Ain't nobody thinking about Bessie. I taught Bessie. She ain't doing nothing but imitating me. What I care about Bessie? I don't care if she sell a million records. She got her people and I got mine. I don't care what nobody else do. Ma was the *first* and don't you forget it!

CUTLER: Ain't nobody said nothing about that. I just said that's the same song she sang.

MA RAINEY: I been doing this a long time. Ever since I was a little girl. I don't care what nobody else do. That's what gets me so mad with Irvin. White folks try to be put out with you all the time. Too cheap to buy me a Coca-Cola. I lets them know it, though. Ma don't stand for no shit. Wanna take my voice and trap it in them fancy boxes with all them buttons and dials . . . and then too cheap to buy me a Coca-Cola. And it don't cost but a nickel a bottle.

CUTLER: I knows what you mean about that.

MA RAINEY: They don't care nothing about me. All they want is my voice. Well, I done learned that, and they gonna treat me like I want to be treated no matter how much it hurt them. They back there now calling me all kinds of names . . . calling me every-thing but a child of God. But they can't do nothing else. They ain't got what they wanted yet. As soon as they get my voice down on them recording machines, then it's just like if I'd be some whore and they roll over and put their pants on. Ain't got no use for me then. I know what I'm talking about. You watch. Irvin right there with the rest of them. He don't care nothing about me either. He's been my manager for six years, always talking about sticking together, and the only time he had me in his house was to sing for some of his friends.

CUTLER: I know how they do.

MA RAINEY: If you colored and can make them some money, then you alright with them. Otherwise, you just a dog in the alley. I done made this company more money from my records than all the other recording artists they got put together. And they wanna balk about how much this session is costing them.

CUTLER: I don't see where it's costing them all what they say.

MA RAINEY: It ain't! I don't pay that kind of talk no mind.
(*The lights go down on the studio and come up on the band room.* TOLEDO *sits reading a newspaper.* LEVEE *sings and hums his song.*)

LEVEE: (*Singing.*)
You can shake it, you can break it
You can dance at any hall
You can slide across the floor
You'll never have to stall
My jelly, my roll,
Sweet Mama, don't you let it fall.
Wait till Sturdyvant hear me play that! I'm talking about some real music, Toledo! I'm talking about *real* music!
(*The door opens and* DUSSIE MAE *enters.*)
Hey, mama! Come on in.

DUSSIE MAE: Oh, hi! I just wanted to see what it looks like down here.

LEVEE: Well, come on in . . . I don't bite.

DUSSIE MAE: I didn't know you could really write music. I thought you was just jiving me at the club last night.

LEVEE: Naw, baby . . . I knows how to write music. I done give Mr. Sturdyvant some of my songs and he says he's gonna let me record them. Ask Toledo. I'm gonna have my own band! Toledo, ain't I give Mr. Sturdyvant some of my songs I wrote?

TOLEDO: Don't get Toledo mixed up in nothing.
(*He exits.*)

DUSSIE MAE: You gonna get your own band sure enough?

LEVEE: That's right! Levee Green and his Footstompers.

DUSSIE MAE: That's real nice.

LEVEE: That's what I was trying to tell you last night. A man what's gonna get his own band need to have a woman like you.

DUSSIE MAE: A woman like me wants somebody to bring it and put it in my hand. I don't need nobody wanna get something for nothing and leave me standing in my door.

LEVEE: That ain't Levee's style, sugar. I got more style than that. I knows how to treat a woman. Buy her presents and things . . . treat her like she wants to be treated.

DUSSIE MAE: That's what they all say . . . till it come time to be buying the presents.

LEVEE: When we get down to Memphis, I'm gonna show you what I'm talking about. I'm gonna take you out and show you a good time. Show you Levee knows how to treat a woman.

DUSSIE MAE: When you getting your own band?

LEVEE: (*Moves closer to slip his arm around her.*) Soon as Mr. Sturdyvant say. I done got my fellows already picked out. Getting me some good fellows know how to play real sweet music.

DUSSIE MAE: (*Moves away.*) Go on now, I don't go for all that pawing and stuff. When you get your own band, maybe we can see about this stuff you talking.

LEVEE: (*Moving toward her.*) I just wanna show you I know what the women like. They don't call me Sweet Lemonade for nothing. (*LEVEE takes her in his arms and attempts to kiss her.*)

DUSSIE MAE: Stop it now. Somebody's gonna come in here.

LEVEE: Naw they ain't. Look here, sugar . . . what I wanna know is . . . can I introduce my red rooster to your brown hen?

DUSSIE MAE: You get your band, then we'll see if that rooster know how to crow.
(*He grinds up against her and feels her buttocks.*)

LEVEE: Now I know why my grandpappy sat on the back porch with his straight razor when grandma hung out the wash.

DUSSIE MAE: Nigger, you crazy!

LEVEE: I bet you sound like the midnight train from Alabama when it crosses the Mason-Dixon line.

DUSSIE MAE: How's you get so crazy?

LEVEE: It's women like you . . . drives me that way.
(*He moves to kiss her as the lights go down in the band room and up in the studio.* MA RAINEY *sits with* CUTLER *and* TOLEDO.)

MA RAINEY: It sure done got quiet in here. I never could stand no silence. I always got to have some music going on in my head somewhere. It keeps things balanced. Music will do that. It fills things up. The more music you got in the world, the fuller it is.

CUTLER: I can agree with that. I got to have my music too.

MA RAINEY: White folks don't understand about the blues. They hear it come out, but they don't know how it got there. They don't understand that's life's way of talking. You don't sing to feel better. You sing cause that's a way of understanding life.

CUTLER: That's right. You get that understanding and you done got a grip on life to where you can hold your head up and go on to see what else life got to offer.

MA RAINEY: The blues help you get out of bed in the morning. You get up knowing you ain't alone. There's something else in the world. Something's been added by that song. This be an empty world without the blues. I take that emptiness and try to fill it up with something.

67

TOLEDO: You fill it up with something the people can't be without, Ma. That's why they call you the Mother of the Blues. You fill up that emptiness in a way ain't nobody ever thought of doing before. And now they can't be without it.

MA RAINEY: I ain't started the blues way of singing. The blues always been here.

CUTLER: In the church sometimes you find that way of singing. They got blues in the church.

MA RAINEY: They say I started it . . . but I didn't. I just helped it out. Filled up that empty space a little bit. That's all. But if they wanna call me the Mother of the Blues, that's alright with me. It don't hurt none.
(SLOW DRAG and SYLVESTER enter with the Cokes.)
It sure took you long enough. That store ain't but on the corner.

SLOW DRAG: That one was closed. We had to find another one.

MA RAINEY: Sylvester, go and find Mr. Irvin and tell him we ready to go.
(SYLVESTER exits. The lights in the band room come up while the lights in the studio stay on. LEVEE and DUSSIE MAE are kissing. SLOW DRAG enters. They break their embrace. DUSSIE MAE straightens up her clothes.)

SLOW DRAG: Cold out. I just wanted to warm up with a little sip.
(He goes to his locker, takes out his bottle and drinks.)
Ma got her Coke, Levee. We about ready to start.
(SLOW DRAG exits. LEVEE attempts to kiss DUSSIE MAE again.)

DUSSIE MAE: No . . . Come on! I got to go. You gonna get me in trouble.
(She pulls away and exits up the stairs. LEVEE watches after her.)

LEVEE: Good God! Happy birthday to the lady with the cakes!
(The lights go down in the band room and come up in the studio. MA RAINEY drinks her Coke. LEVEE enters from the band room. The musicians take their places. SYLVESTER stands by his mike. IRVIN and STURDYVANT look on from the control booth.)

IRVIN: We're all set up here, Ma. We're all set to go. You ready down there?

MA RAINEY: Sylvester you just remember your part and say it. That's all there is to it.
(*To* IRVIN.)
Yeah, we ready.

IRVIN: Okay, boys. "Ma Rainey's Black Bottom." Take one.

CUTLER: One . . . two . . . You know what to do.
(*The band plays.*)

SYLVESTER: Alright boys, you d-d-d-done s-s-seen the rest . . .

IRVIN: Hold it!
(*The band stops.* STURDYVANT *changes the recording disk and nods to* IRVIN.)
Okay. Take two.

CUTLER: One . . . Two . . . You know what to do.
(*The band plays.*)

SYLVESTER: Alright, boys, you done seen the rest . . . now I'm gonna show you the best. Ma Rainey's g-g-g-gonna sh-sh-show you her b-b-black bottom.

IRVIN: Hold it! Hold it!
(*The band stops.* STURDYVANT *changes the recording disk.*)
Okay. Take three. Ma, let's do it without the intro, huh? No voice intro . . . you just come in singing.

MA RAINEY: Irvin, I done told you . . . the boy's gonna do the part. He don't stutter all the time. Just give him a chance. Sylvester, hold your hands like I told you and just relax. Just relax and concentrate.

IRVIN: Alright. Take three.

CUTLER: One . . . Two . . . You know what to do.
(*The band plays.*)

SYLVESTER: Alright, boys, you done seen the rest . . . now, I'm

69

gonna show you the best. Ma Rainey's gonna show you her black bottom.

MA RAINEY: (*Singing.*)
Way down south in Alabamy
I got a friend they call dancing Sammy
Who's crazy about all the latest dances
Black Bottom stomping, two babies prancing

The other night at a swell affair
As soon as the boys found out that I was there
They said, come on, Ma, let's go to the cabaret.
When I got there, you ought to hear them say,

I want to see the dance you call the black bottom
I want to learn that dance
I want to see the dance you call your big black bottom
It'll put you in a trance.

All the boys in the neighborhood
They say your black bottom is really good
Come on and show me your black bottom
I want to learn that dance

I want to see the dance you call the black bottom
I want to learn that dance
Come on and show the dance you call your big black bottom
It puts you in a trance.

Early last morning about the break of day
Grandpa told my grandma, I heard him say,
Get up and show your old man your black bottom
I want to learn that dance

(*Instrumental break.*)

I done showed you all my black bottom
You ought to learn that dance.

IRVIN: Okay, that's good, Ma. That sounded great! Good job, boys!

MA RAINEY: (*To* SYLVESTER.) See! I told you. I knew you could do it. You just have to put your mind to it. Didn't he do good, Cutler? Sound real good. I told him he could do it.

CUTLER: He sure did. He did better than I thought he was gonna do.

IRVIN: (*Entering to remove* SYLVESTER's *mike.*) Okay, boys . . . Ma . . . let's do "Moonshine Blues" next, huh? "Moonshine Blues," boys.

STURDYVANT: (*over speaker.*) Irv! Something's wrong down there. We don't have it right.

IRVIN: What? What's the matter Mel . . .

STURDYVANT: We don't have it right. Something happened. We don't have the goddamn song recorded!

IRVIN: What's the matter? Mel, what happened? You sure you don't have nothing?

STURDYVANT: Check that mike, huh, Irv. It's the kid's mike. Something's wrong with the mike. We've got everything all screwed up here.

IRVIN: Christ almighty! Ma, we got to do it again. We don't have it. We didn't record the song.

MA RAINEY: What you mean you didn't record it? What was you and Sturdyvant doing up there?

IRVIN: (*Following the mike wire.*) Here . . . Levee must have kicked the plug out.

LEVEE: I ain't done nothing. I ain't kicked nothing!

SLOW DRAG: If Levee had his mind on what he's doing . . .

MA RAINEY: Levee, if it ain't one thing, it's another. You better straighten yourself up!

LEVEE: Hell . . . it ain't my fault. I ain't done nothing!

STURDYVANT: What's the matter with that mike, Irv? What's the problem?

IRVIN: It's the cord, Mel. The cord's all chewed up. We need another cord.

MA RAINEY: This is the most disorganized . . . Irvin, I'm going home! Come on. Come on, Dussie.
(MA RAINEY *walks past* STURDYVANT *as he enters from the control booth. She exits offstage to get her coat.*)

STURDYVANT: (*To* IRVIN.) Where's she going?

IRVIN: She said she's going home.

STURDYVANT: Irvin, you get her! If she walks out of here . . .
(MA RAINEY *enters carrying her and* DUSSIE MAE's *coat.*)

MA RAINEY: Come on, Sylvester.

IRVIN: (*Helping her with her coat.*) Ma . . . Ma . . . listen. Fifteen minutes! All I ask is fifteen minutes!

MA RAINEY: Come on, Sylvester, get your coat.

STURDYVANT: Ma, if you walk out of this studio . . .

IRVIN: Fifteen minutes, Ma!

STURDYVANT: You'll be through . . . washed up! If you walk out on me . . .

IRVIN: Mel, for Chrissakes, shut up and let me handle it! (*He goes after* MA RAINEY, *who has started for the door.*)
Ma, listen. These records are gonna be hits! They're gonna sell like crazy! Hell, even Sylvester will be a star. Fifteen minutes. That's all I'm asking! Fifteen minutes.

MA RAINEY: (*Crosses to a chair and sits with her coat on.*) Fifteen minutes! You hear me, Irvin? Fifteen minutes . . . and then I'm gonna take my black bottom on back down to Georgia. Fifteen minutes. Then Madame Rainey is leaving!

IRVIN: (*Kisses her.*) Alright, Ma . . . fifteen minutes. I promise.

(*To the band.*)
You boys go ahead and take a break. Fifteen minutes and we'll be ready to go.

CUTLER: Slow Drag, you got any of that bourbon left?

SLOW DRAG: Yeah, there's some down there.

CUTLER: I could use a little nip.
(CUTLER *and* SLOW DRAG *exit to the band room, followed by* LEVEE *and* TOLEDO. *The lights go down in the studio and up in the band room.*)

SLOW DRAG: Don't make me no difference if she leave or not. I was kinda hoping she would leave.

CUTLER: I'm like Mr. Irvin . . . After all this time we done put in here, it's best to go ahead and get something out of it.

TOLEDO: Ma gonna do what she wanna do, that's for sure. If I was Mr. Irvin, I'd best go on and get them cords and things hooked up right. And I wouldn't take no longer than fifteen minutes doing it.

CUTLER: If Levee had his mind on his work, we wouldn't be in this fix. We'd be up there finishing up. Now we got to go back and see if that boy get that part right. Ain't no telling if he ever get that right again in his life.

LEVEE: Hey, Levee ain't done nothing!

SLOW DRAG: Levee up there got one eye on the gal and the other on his trumpet.

CUTLER: Nigger, don't you know that's Ma's gal?

LEVEE: I don't care whose gal it is. I ain't done nothing to her. I just talk to her like I talk to anybody else.

CUTLER: Well, that being Ma's gal, and that being that boy's gal, is one and two different things. The boy is liable to kill you . . . but you ass gonna be out there scraping the concrete looking for a job if you messing with Ma's gal.

LEVEE: How am I messing with her? I ain't done nothing to the gal. I just asked her her name. Now, if you telling me I can't do that, then Ma will just have to go to hell.

CUTLER: All I can do is warn you.

SLOW DRAG: Let him hang himself, Cutler. Let him string his neck out.

LEVEE: I ain't done nothing to the gal! You all talk like I done went and done something to her. Leave me go with my business.

CUTLER: I'm through with it. Try and talk to a fool . . .

TOLEDO: Some mens got it worse than others . . . this foolishness I'm talking about. Some mens is excited to be fools. That excitement is something else. I know about it. I done experienced it. It makes you feel good to be a fool. But it don't last long. It's over in a minute. Then you got to tend with the consequences. You got to tend with what comes after. That's when you wish you had learned something about it.

LEVEE: That's the best sense you made all day. Talking about being a fool. That's the only sensible thing you said today. Admitting you was a fool.

TOLEDO: I admits it, alright. Ain't nothing wrong with it. I done been a little bit of everything.

LEVEE: Now you're talking. You's as big a fool as they make.

TOLEDO: Gonna be a bit more things before I'm finished with it. Gonna be foolish again. But I ain't never been the same fool twice. I might be a different kind of fool, but I ain't gonna be the same fool twice. That's where we parts ways.

SLOW DRAG: Toledo, you done been a fool about a woman?

TOLEDO: Sure. Sure I have. Same as everybody.

SLOW DRAG: Hell, I ain't never seen you mess with no woman. I thought them books was your woman.

TOLEDO: Sure I messed with them. Done messed with a whole heap of them. And gonna mess with some more. But I ain't gonna be no fool about them. What you think? I done come in the world full-grown, with my head in a book? I done been young. Married. Got kids. I done been around and I done loved women to where you shake in your shoes just at the sight of them. Feel it all up and down your spine.

SLOW DRAG: I didn't know you was married.

TOLEDO: Sure. Legally. I been married legally. Got the papers and all. I done been through life. Made my marks. Followed some signs on the road. Ignored some others. I done been all through it. I touched and been touched by it. But I ain't never been the same fool twice. That's what I can say.

LEVEE: But you been a fool. That's what counts. Talking about I'm a fool for asking the gal her name and here you is one yourself.

TOLEDO: Now, I married a woman. A good woman. To this day I can't say she wasn't a good woman. I can't say nothing bad about her. I married that woman with all the good graces and intentions of being hooked up and bound to her for the rest of my life. I was looking for her to put me in my grave. But, you see . . . it ain't all the time what your intentions and wishes are. She went out and joined the church. Alright. There ain't nothing wrong with that. A good Christian woman going to church and wanna do right by her God. There ain't nothing wrong with that. But she got up there, got to seeing them good Christian mens and wondering why I ain't like that. Soon she figure she got a heathen on her hands. She figured she couldn't live like that. The church was more important than I was. So she left. Packed up one day and moved out. To this day I ain't never said another word to her. Come home one day and my house was empty! And I sat down and figured out that I was a fool not to see that she needed something that I wasn't giving her. Else she wouldn't have been up there at the church in the first place. I ain't blaming her. I just said it wasn't gonna happen to me again. So, yeah, Toledo been a fool about a woman. That's part of making life.

CUTLER: Well, yeah, I been a fool too. Everybody done been a fool once or twice. But, you see, Toledo, what you call a fool and what I call a fool is two different things. I can't see where you was being a fool for that. You ain't done nothing foolish. You can't help what happened, and I wouldn't call you a fool for it. A fool is responsible for what happens to him. A fool cause it to happen. Like Levee . . . if he keeps messing with Ma's gal and his feet be out there scraping the ground. That's a fool.

LEVEE: Ain't nothing gonna happen to Levee. Levee ain't gonna let nothing happen to him. Now, I'm gonna say it again. I asked the gal her name. That's all I done. And if that's being a fool, then you looking at the biggest fool in the world . . . cause I sure as hell asked her.

SLOW DRAG: You just better not let Ma see you ask her. That's what the man's trying to tell you.

LEVEE: I don't need nobody to tell me nothing.

CUTLER: Well, Toledo, all I gots to say is that from the looks of it . . . from your story . . . I don't think life did you fair.

TOLEDO: Oh, life is fair. It's just in the taking what it gives you.

LEVEE: Life ain't shit. You can put it in a paper bag and carry it around with you. It ain't got no balls. Now, death . . . death got some style! Death will kick your ass and make you wish you never been born! That's how bad death is! But you can rule over life. Life ain't nothing.

TOLEDO: Cutler, how's your brother doing?

CUTLER: Who, Nevada? Oh, he's doing alright. Staying in St. Louis. Got a bunch of kids, last I heard.

TOLEDO: Me and him was alright with each other. Done a lot of farming together down in Plattsville.

CUTLER: Yeah, I know you all was tight. He in St. Louis now. Running an elevator, last I hear about it.

SLOW DRAG: That's better than stepping in muleshit.

TOLEDO: Oh, I don't know now. I liked farming. Get out there in the sun . . . smell that dirt. Be out there by yourself . . . nice and peaceful. Yeah, farming was alright by me. Sometimes I think I'd like to get me a little old place . . . but I done got too old to be following behind one of them balky mules now.

LEVEE: Nigger talking about life is fair. And ain't got a pot to piss in.

TOLEDO: See, now, I'm gonna tell you something. A nigger gonna be dissatisfied no matter what. Give a nigger some bread and butter . . . and he'll cry cause he ain't got no jelly. Give him some jelly, and he'll cry cause he ain't got no knife to put it on with. If there's one thing I done learned in this life, it's that you can't satisfy a nigger no matter what you do. A nigger's gonna make his own dissatisfaction.

LEVEE: Niggers got a right to be dissatisfied. Is you gonna be satisfied with a bone somebody done throwed you when you see them eating the whole hog?

TOLEDO: You lucky they let you be an entertainer. They ain't got to accept your way of entertaining. You lucky and don't even know it. You's entertaining and the rest of the people is hauling wood. That's the only kind of job for the colored man.

SLOW DRAG: Ain't nothing wrong with hauling wood. I done hauled plenty wood. My daddy used to haul wood. Ain't nothing wrong with that. That's honest work.

LEVEE: That ain't what I'm talking about. I ain't talking about hauling no wood. I'm talking about being satisfied with a bone somebody done throwed you. That's what's the matter with you all. You satisfied sitting in one place. You got to move on down the road from where you sitting . . . and all the time you got to keep an eye out for that devil who's looking to buy up souls. And hope you get lucky and find him!

CUTLER: I done told you about that blasphemy. Talking about selling your soul to the devil.

TOLEDO: We done the same thing, Cutler. There ain't no difference. We done sold Africa for the price of tomatoes. We done sold ourselves to the white man in order to be like him. Look at the way you dressed . . . That ain't African. That's the white man. We trying to be just like him. We done sold who we are in order to become someone else. We's imitation white men.

CUTLER: What else we gonna be, living over here?

LEVEE: I'm Levee. Just me. I ain't no imitation nothing!

SLOW DRAG: You can't change who you are by how you dress. That's what I got to say.

TOLEDO: It ain't all how you dress. It's how you act, how you see the world. It's how you follow life.

LEVEE: It don't matter what you talking about. I ain't no imitation white man. And I don't want to be no white man. As soon as I get my band together and make them records like Mr. Sturdyvant done told me I can make, I'm gonna be like Ma and tell the white man just what he can do. Ma tell Mr. Irvin she gonna leave . . . and Mr. Irvin get down on his knees and beg her to stay! That's the way I'm gonna be! Make the white man respect me!

CUTLER: The white man don't care nothing about Ma. The colored folks made Ma a star. White folks don't care nothing about who she is . . . what kind of music she make.

SLOW DRAG: That's the truth about that. You let her go down to one of them white-folks' hotels and see how big she is.

CUTLER: Hell, she ain't got to do that. She can't even get a cab up here in the North. I'm gonna tell you something. Reverend Gates . . . you know Reverend Gates? . . . Slow Drag know who I'm talking about. Reverend Gates . . . now I'm gonna show you how this go where the white man don't care a thing about who you is. Reverend Gates was coming from Tallahassee to Atlanta, going to see his sister, who was sick at that time with the consumption. The train come up through Thomasville, then past Moultrie, and stopped in this little town called Sigsbee . . .

LEVEE: You can stop telling that right there! That train don't stop in Sigsbee. I know what train you talking about. That train got four stops before it reach Macon to go on to Atlanta. One in Thomasville, one in Moultrie, one in Cordele . . . and it stop in Centerville.

CUTLER: Nigger, I know what I'm talking about. You gonna tell me where the train stop?

LEVEE: Hell, yeah, if you talking about it stop in Sigsbee. I'm gonna tell you the truth.

CUTLER: I'm talking about *this* train! I don't know what train you been riding. I'm talking about *this* train!

LEVEE: Ain't but one train. Ain't but one train come out of Talla-hassee heading north to Atlanta, and it don't stop at Sigsbee. Tell him, Toledo . . . that train don't stop at Sigsbee. The only train that stops at Sigsbee is the Yazoo Delta, and you have to transfer at Moultrie to get it!

CUTLER: Well, hell, maybe that what he done! I don't know. I'm just telling you the man got off the train at Sigsbee . . .

LEVEE: Alright . . . you telling it. Tell it your way. Just make up anything.

SLOW DRAG: Levee, leave the man alone and let him finish.

CUTLER: I ain't paying Levee no never mind.

LEVEE: Go on and tell it your way.

CUTLER: Anyway . . . Reverend Gates got off this train in Sigsbee. The train done stopped there and he figured he'd get off and check the schedule to be sure he arrive in time for somebody to pick him up. Alright. While he's there checking the schedule, it come upon him that he had to go to the bathroom. Now, they ain't had no colored rest rooms at the station. The only colored rest room is an outhouse they got sitting way back two hundred yards or so from the station. Alright. He in the outhouse and the train go off and leave him there. He don't know nothing about this town. Ain't never been there before—in fact, ain't never even heard of it before.

LEVEE: I heard of it! I know just where it's at . . . and he ain't got off no train coming out of Tallahassee in Sigsbee!

CUTLER: The man standing there, trying to figure out what he's gonna do . . . where this train done left him in this strange town. It started getting dark. He see where the sun's getting low in the sky and he's trying to figure out what he's gonna do, when he noticed a couple of white fellows standing across the street from this station. Just standing there, watching him. And then two or three more come up and joined the other one. He look around, ain't seen no colored folks nowhere. He didn't know what was getting in these here fellows' minds, so he commence to walking. He ain't knowed where he was going. He just walking down the railroad tracks when he hear them call him. "Hey, nigger!" See, just like that. "Hey, nigger!" He kept on walking. They called him some more and he just keep walking. Just going down the tracks. And then he heard a gunshot where somebody done fired a gun in the air. He stopped then, you know.

TOLEDO: You don't even have to tell me no more. I know the facts of it. I done heard the same story a hundred times. It happened to me too. Same thing.

CUTLER: Naw, I'm gonna show you how the white folks don't care nothing about who or what you is. They crowded around him. These gang of mens made a circle around him. Now, he's standing there, you understand . . . got his cross around his neck like them preachers wear. Had his little Bible with him what he carry all the time. So they crowd on around him and one of them ask who he is. He told them he was Reverend Gates and that he was going to see his sister who was sick and the train left without him. And they said, "Yeah, nigger . . . but can you dance?" He looked at them and commenced to dancing. One of them reached up and tore his cross off his neck. Said he was committing a heresy by dancing with a cross and Bible. Took his Bible and tore it up and had him dancing till they got tired of watching him.

SLOW DRAG: White folks ain't never had no respect for the colored minister.

CUTLER: That's the only way he got out of there alive . . . was to dance. Ain't even had no respect for a man of God! Wanna make him into a clown. Reverend Gates sat right in my house and told me that story from his own mouth. So . . . the white folks don't care nothing about Ma Rainey. She's just another nigger who they can use to make some money.

LEVEE: What I wants to know is . . . if he's a man of God, then where the hell was God when all of this was going on? Why wasn't God looking out for him? Why didn't God strike down them crackers with some of this lightning you talk about to me?

CUTLER: Levee, you gonna burn in hell.

LEVEE: What I care about burning in hell? You talk like a fool . . . burning in hell. Why didn't God strike some of them crackers down? Tell me that! That's the question! Don't come telling me this burning-in-hell shit! He a man of God . . . why didn't God strike some of them crackers down? I'll tell you why! I'll tell you the truth! It's sitting out there as plain as day! Cause he a white man's God. That's why! God ain't never listened to no nigger's prayers. God take a nigger's prayers and throw them in the garbage. God don't pay niggers no mind. In fact . . . God hate niggers! Hate them with all the fury in his heart. Jesus don't love you, nigger! Jesus hate your black ass! Come talking that shit to me. Talking about burning in hell! God can kiss my ass. (CUTLER *can stand no more. He jumps up and punches* LEVEE *in the mouth. The force of the blow knocks* LEVEE *down and* CUTLER *jumps on him.*)

81

CUTLER: You worthless . . . That's my God! That's my God! That's my God! You wanna blaspheme my God!
(TOLEDO *and* SLOW DRAG *grab* CUTLER *and try to pull him off* LEVEE.)

SLOW DRAG: Come on, Cutler . . . let it go! It don't mean nothing!
(CUTLER *has* LEVEE *down on the floor and pounds on him with a fury.*)

CUTLER: Wanna blaspheme my God! You worthless . . . talking about my God!
(TOLEDO *and* SLOW DRAG *succeed in pulling* CUTLER *off* LEVEE, *who is bleeding at the nose and mouth.*)

LEVEE: Naw, let him go! Let him go!
(*He pulls out a knife.*)
That's your God, huh? That's your God, huh? Is that right? Your God, huh? Alright. I'm gonna give your God a chance. I'm gonna give your God a chance. I'm gonna give him a chance to save your black ass.
(LEVEE *circles* CUTLER *with the knife.* CUTLER *picks up a chair to protect himself.*)

TOLEDO: Come on, Levee . . . put the knife up!

LEVEE: Stay out of this, Toledo!

TOLEDO: That ain't no way to solve nothing.
(LEVEE *alternately swipes at* CUTLER *during the following.*)

LEVEE: I'm calling Cutler's God! I'm talking to Cutler's God! You hear me? Cutler's God! I'm calling Cutler's God. Come on and save this nigger! Strike me down before I cut his throat!

SLOW DRAG: Watch him, Cutler! Put that knife up, Levee!

LEVEE: (*To* CUTLER.) I'm calling your God! I'm gonna give him a chance to save you! I'm calling your God! We gonna find out whose God he is!

CUTLER: You gonna burn in hell, nigger!

LEVEE: Cutler's God! Come on and save this nigger! Come on and save him like you did my mama! Save him like you did my mama! I heard her when she called you! I heard her when she said, "Lord, have mercy! Jesus, help me! Please, God, have mercy on me, Lord Jesus, help me!" And did you turn your back? Did you turn your back, motherfucker? Did you turn your back?

(LEVEE *becomes so caught up in his dialogue with God that he forgets about* CUTLER *and begins to stab upward in the air, trying to reach God.*)

Come on! Come on and turn your back on me! Turn your back on me! Come on! Where is you? Come on and turn your back on me! Turn your back on me, motherfucker! I'll cut your heart out! Come on, turn your back on me! Come on! What's the matter? Where is you? Come on and turn your back on me! Come on, what you scared of? Turn your back on me! Come on! Coward, motherfucker!

(LEVEE *folds his knife and stands triumphantly.*)

Your God ain't shit, Cutler.

(*The lights fade to black.*)

MA RAINEY: (*Singing.*)
Ah, you hear me talking to you
I don't bite my tongue
You wants to be my man
You got to fetch it with you when you come.

(*Lights come up in the studio. The last bars of the last song of the session are dying out.*)

IRVIN: (*Over speaker.*) Good! Wonderful! We have that, boys. Good session. That's great, Ma. We've got ourselves some winners.

TOLEDO: Well, I'm glad that's over.

MA RAINEY: Slow Drag, where you learn to play the bass at? You had it singing! I heard you! Had that bass jumping all over the place.

SLOW DRAG: I was following Toledo. Nigger got them long fingers striding all over the piano. I was trying to keep up with him.

TOLEDO: That's what you supposed to do, ain't it? Play the music. Ain't nothing abstract about it.

MA RAINEY: Cutler, you hear Slow Drag on that bass? He make it do what he want it to do! Spank it just like you spank a baby.

CUTLER: Don't be telling him that. Nigger's head get so big his hat won't fit him.

SLOW DRAG: If Cutler tune that guitar up, we would really have something!

CUTLER: You wouldn't know what a tuned-up guitar sounded like if you heard one.

TOLEDO: Cutler was talking. I heard him moaning. He was all up in it.

MA RAINEY: Levee . . . what is that you doing? Why you playing all them notes? You play ten notes for every one you supposed to play. It don't call for that.

LEVEE: You supposed to improvise on the theme. That's what I was doing.

MA RAINEY: You supposed to play the song the way I sing it. The way everybody else play it. You ain't supposed to go off by yourself and play what you want.

LEVEE: I was playing the song. I was playing it the way I felt it.

MA RAINEY: I couldn't keep up with what was going on. I'm trying to sing the song and you up there messing up my ear. That's what you was doing. Call yourself playing music.

LEVEE: Hey . . . I know what I'm doing. I know what I'm doing, alright. I know how to play music. You all back up and leave me alone about my music.

CUTLER: I done told you . . . it ain't about *your* music. It's about Ma's music.

MA RAINEY: That's alright, Cutler. I done told you what to do.

LEVEE: I don't care what you do. You supposed to improvise on the theme. Not play note for note the same thing over and over again.

MA RAINEY: You just better watch yourself. You hear me?

LEVEE: What I care what you or Cutler do? Come telling me to watch myself. What's that supposed to mean?

MA RAINEY: Alright . . . you gonna find out what it means.

LEVEE: Go ahead and fire me. I don't care. I'm gonna get my own band anyway.

MA RAINEY: You keep messing with me.

LEVEE: Ain't nobody studying you. You ain't gonna do nothing to me. Ain't nobody gonna do nothing to Levee.

MA RAINEY: Alright, nigger . . . you fired!

LEVEE: You think I care about being fired? I don't care nothing about that. You doing me a favor.

MA RAINEY: Cutler, Levee's out! He don't play in my band no more.

LEVEE: I'm fired . . . Good! Best thing that ever happened to me. I don't need this shit!
(LEVEE *exits to the band room.* IRVIN *enters from the control booth.*)

MA RAINEY: Cutler, I'll see you back at the hotel.

IRVIN: Okay, boys . . . you can pack up. I'll get your money for you.

CUTLER: That's cash money, Mr. Irvin. I don't want no check.

IRVIN: I'll see what I can do. I can't promise you nothing.

CUTLER: As long as it ain't no check. I ain't got no use for a check.

IRVIN: I'll see what I can do, Cutler.
(CUTLER, TOLEDO, *and* SLOW DRAG *exit to the band room.*)
Oh, Ma, listen . . . I talked to Sturdyvant, and he said . . .

85

Now, I tried to talk him out of it . . . He said the best he can do is to take your twenty-five dollars of your money and give it to Sylvester.

MA RAINEY: Take what and do what? If I wanted the boy to have twenty-five dollars of my money, I'd give it to him. He supposed to get his own money. He supposed to get paid like everybody else.

IRVIN: Ma, I talked to him . . . He said . . .

MA RAINEY: Go talk to him again! Tell him if he don't pay that boy, he'll never make another record of mine again. Tell him that. You supposed to be my manager. All this talk about sticking together. Start sticking! Go on up there and get that boy his money!

IRVIN: Okay, Ma . . . I'll talk to him again. I'll see what I can do.

MA RAINEY: Ain't no see about it! You bring that boy's money back here!
(IRVIN *exits. The lights stay on in the studio and come up in the band room. The men have their instruments packed and sit waiting for* IRVIN *to come and pay them.* SLOW DRAG *has a pack of cards.*)

SLOW DRAG: Come on, Levee, let me show you a card trick.

LEVEE: I don't want to see no card trick. What you wanna show me for? Why you wanna bother me with that?

SLOW DRAG: I was just trying to be nice.

LEVEE: I don't need you to be nice to me. What I need you to be nice to me for? I ain't gonna be nice to you. I ain't even gonna let you be in my band no more.

SLOW DRAG: Toledo, let me show you a card trick.

CUTLER: ᵀ just hope Mr. Irvin don't bring no check down here. What the hell I'm gonna do with a check?

SLOW DRAG: Alright now . . . pick a card. Any card . . . go on . . . take any of them. I'm gonna show you something.

TOLEDO: I agrees with you, Cutler. I don't want no check either.

CUTLER: It don't make no sense to give a nigger a check.

SLOW DRAG: Okay, now. Remember your card. Remember which one you got. Now . . . put it back in the deck. Anywhere you want. I'm gonna show you something.
(TOLEDO *puts the card in the deck.*)
You remember your card? Alright. Now I'm gonna shuffle the deck. Now . . . I'm gonna show you what card you picked. Don't say nothing now. I'm gonna tell you what card you picked.

CUTLER: Slow Drag, that trick is as old as my mama.

SLOW DRAG: Naw, naw . . . wait a minute! I'm gonna show him his card . . . There it go! The six of diamonds. Ain't that your card? Ain't that it?

TOLEDO: Yeah, that's it . . . the six of diamonds.

SLOW DRAG: Told you! Told you I'd show him what it was!
(*The lights fade in the band room and come up full on the studio.* STURDYVANT *enters with* IRVIN.)

STURDYVANT: Ma, is there something wrong? Is there a problem?

MA RAINEY: Sturdyvant, I want you to pay that boy his money.

STURDYVANT: Sure, Ma. I got it right here. Two hundred for you and twenty-five for the kid, right?
(STURDYVANT *hands the money to* IRVIN, *who hands it to* MA RAINEY *and* SYLVESTER.)
Irvin misunderstood me. It was all a mistake. Irv made a mistake.

MA RAINEY: A mistake, huh?

IRVIN: Sure, Ma. I made a mistake. He's paid, right? I straightened it out.

MA RAINEY: The only mistake was when you found out I hadn't signed the release forms. That was the mistake. Come on, Sylvester.
(*She starts to exit.*)

STURDYVANT: Hey, Ma . . . come on, sign the forms, huh?

IRVIN: Ma . . . come on now.

MA RAINEY: Get your coat, Sylvester. Irvin, where's my car?

IRVIN: It's right out front, Ma. Here . . . I got the keys right here. Come on, sign the forms, huh?

MA RAINEY: Irvin, give me my car keys!

IRVIN: Sure, Ma . . . just sign the forms, huh?
(*He gives her the keys, expecting a trade-off.*)

MA RAINEY: Send them to my address and I'll get around to them.

IRVIN: Come on, Ma . . . I took care of everything, right? I straightened everything out.

MA RAINEY: Give me the pen, Irvin.
(*She signs the forms.*)
You tell Sturdyvant . . . one more mistake like that and I can make my records someplace else.
(*She turns to exit.*)
Sylvester, straighten up your clothes. Come on, Dussie Mae.
(*She exits, followed by* DUSSIE MAE *and* SYLVESTER. *The lights go down in the studio and come up on the band room.*)

CUTLER: I know what's keeping him so long. He up there writing out checks. You watch. I ain't gonna stand for it. He ain't gonna bring me no check down here. If he do, he's gonna take it right back upstairs and get some cash.

TOLEDO: Don't get yourself all worked up about it. Wait and see. Think positive.

CUTLER: I am thinking positive. He positively gonna give me some cash. Man give me a check last time . . . you remember . . . we went all over Chicago trying to get it cashed. See a nigger with a check, the first thing they think is he done stole it someplace.

LEVEE: I ain't had no trouble cashing mine.

88

CUTLER: I don't visit no whorehouses.

LEVEE: You don't know about my business. So don't start nothing. I'm tired of you as it is. I ain't but two seconds off your ass no way.

TOLEDO: Don't you all start nothing now.

CUTLER: What the hell I care what you tired of. I wasn't even talking to you. I was talking to this man right here.
(IRVIN *and* STURDYVANT *enter.*)

IRVIN: Okay boys. Mr. Sturdyvant has your pay.

CUTLER: As long as it's cash money, Mr. Sturdyvant. Cause I have too much trouble trying to cash a check.

STURDYVANT: Oh, yes . . . I'm aware of that. Mr. Irvin told me you boys prefer cash, and that's what I have for you.
(*He starts handing out the money.*)
That was a good session you boys put in . . . That's twenty-five for you. Yessir, you boys really know your business and we are going to . . . Twenty-five for you . . . We are going to get you back in here real soon . . . twenty-five . . . and have another session so you can make some more money . . . and twenty-five for you. Okay, thank you, boys. You can get your things together and Mr. Irvin will make sure you find your way out.

IRVIN: I'll be out front when you get your things together, Cutler.
(IRVIN *exits.* STURDYVANT *starts to follow.*)

LEVEE: Mr. Sturdyvant, sir. About them songs I give you? . . .

STURDYVANT: Oh, yes, . . . uh . . . Levee. About them songs you gave me. I've thought about it and I just don't think the people will buy them. They're not the type of songs we're looking for.

LEVEE: Mr. Sturdyvant, sir . . . I done got my band picked out and they's real good fellows. They knows how to play real good. I know if the peoples hear the music, they'll buy it.

STURDYVANT: Well, Levee, I'll be fair with you . . . but they're just not the right songs.

LEVEE: Mr. Sturdyvant, you got to understand about that music. That music is what the people is looking for. They's tired of jug band music. They wants something that excites them. Something with some fire to it.

STURDYVANT: Okay, Levee. I'll tell you what I'll do. I'll give you five dollars apiece for them. Now that's the best I can do.

LEVEE: I don't want no five dollars, Mr. Sturdyvant. I wants to record them songs, like you say.

STURDYVANT: Well, Levee, like I say . . . they just aren't the kind of songs we're looking for.

LEVEE: Mr. Sturdyvant, you asked me to write them songs. Now, why didn't you tell me that before when I first give them to you? You told me you was gonna let me record them. What's the difference between then and now?

STURDYVANT: Well, look . . . I'll pay you for your trouble . . .

LEVEE: What's the difference, Mr. Sturdyvant? That's what I wanna know.

STURDYVANT: I had my fellows play your songs, and when I heard them, they just didn't sound like the kind of songs I'm looking for right now.

LEVEE: You got to hear *me* play them, Mr. Sturdyvant! You ain't heard *me* play them. That's what's gonna make them sound right.

STURDYVANT: Well, Levee, I don't doubt that really. It's just that . . . well, I don't think they'd sell like Ma's records. But I'll take them off your hands for you.

LEVEE: The people's tired of jug band music, Mr. Sturdyvant. They wants something that's gonna excite them! They wants something with some fire! I don't know what fellows you had playing

90

them songs . . . but if I could play them! I'd set them down in the people's lap! Now you told me I could record them songs!

STURDYVANT: Well, there's nothing I can do about that. Like I say, it's five dollars apiece. That's what I'll give you. I'm doing you a favor. Now, if you write any more, I'll help you out and take them off your hands. The price is five dollars apiece. Just like now.
(*He attempts to hand* LEVEE *the money, finally shoves it in* LEVEE*'s coat pocket and is gone in a flash.* LEVEE *follows him to the door and it slams in his face. He takes the money from his pocket, balls it up, and throws it on the floor. The other musicians silently gather up their belongings.* TOLEDO *walks past* LEVEE *and steps on his shoe.*)

LEVEE: Hey! Watch it . . . Shit Toledo! You stepped on my shoe!

TOLEDO: Excuse me there, Levee.

LEVEE: Look at that! Look at that! Nigger, you stepped on my shoe. What you do that for?

TOLEDO: I said I'm sorry.

LEVEE: Nigger gonna step on my goddamn shoe! You done fucked up my shoe! Look at that! Look at what you done to my shoe, nigger! I ain't stepped on your shoe! What you wanna step on my shoe for?

CUTLER: The man said he's sorry.

LEVEE: Sorry! How the hell he gonna be sorry after he gone ruint my shoe? Come talking about sorry!
(*Turns his attention back to* TOLEDO.)
Nigger, you stepped on my shoe! You know that!
(LEVEE *snatches his shoe off his foot and holds it up for* TOLEDO *to see.*)
See what you done?

TOLEDO: What you want me to do about it? It's done now. I said excuse me.

LEVEE: Wanna go and fuck up my shoe like that. I ain't done nothing to your shoe. Look at this!
(TOLEDO *turns and continues to gather up his things.* LEVEE *spins him around by his shoulder.*)

LEVEE: Naw . . . naw . . . look what you done!
(*He shoves the shoe in* TOLEDO's *face.*)
Look at that! That's my shoe! Look at that! You did it! You did it! You fucked up my shoe! You stepped on my shoe with them raggedy-ass clodhoppers!

TOLEDO: Nigger, ain't nobody studying you and your shoe! I said excuse me. If you can't accept that, then the hell with it. What you want me to do?
(LEVEE *is in a near rage, breathing hard. He is trying to get a grip on himself as even he senses, or perhaps only he senses, he is about to lose control. He looks around, uncertain of what to do.* TOLEDO *has gone back to packing, as have* CUTLER *and* SLOW DRAG. *They purposefully avoid looking at* LEVEE *in hopes he'll calm down if he doesn't have an audience. All the weight in the world suddenly falls on* LEVEE *and he rushes at* TOLEDO *with his knife in his hand.*)

LEVEE: Nigger, you stepped on my shoe!
(*He plunges the knife into* TOLEDO's *back up to the hilt.* TOLEDO *lets out a sound of surprise and agony.* CUTLER *and* SLOW DRAG *freeze.* TOLEDO *falls backward with* LEVEE, *his hand still on the knife, holding him up.* LEVEE *is suddenly faced with the realization of what he has done. He shoves* TOLEDO *forward and takes a step back.* TOLEDO *slumps to the floor.*)
He . . . he stepped on my shoe. He did. Honest, Cutler, he stepped on my shoe. What he do that for? Toledo, what you do that for? Cutler, help me. He stepped on my shoe, Cutler.
(*He turns his attention to* TOLEDO.)
Toledo! Toledo, get up.
(*He crosses to* TOLEDO *and tries to pick him up.*)
It's okay, Toledo. Come on . . . I'll help you. Come on, stand up now. Levee'll help you.
(TOLEDO *is limp and heavy and awkward. He slumps back to the*

floor. LEVEE *gets mad at him.*)
Don't look at me like that! Toledo! Nigger, don't look at me like
that! I'm warning you, nigger! Close your eyes! Don't you look at
me like that! (*He turns to* CUTLER.)
Tell him to close his eyes. Cutler. Tell him don't look at me like
that.

CUTLER: Slow Drag, get Mr. Irvin down here.
(*The sound of a trumpet is heard,* LEVEE's *trumpet, a muted trumpet
struggling for the highest of possibilities and blowing pain and warning.*)
(*Black out.*)

FENCES

When the sins of our fathers visit us
We do not have to play host.
We can banish them with forgiveness
As God, in His Largeness and Laws.
                              —August Wilson

For Lloyd Richards,
who adds to whatever he touches

CHARACTERS

TROY MAXSON

JIM BONO : TROY's *friend*

ROSE : TROY's *wife*

LYONS : TROY's *oldest son by previous marriage*

GABRIEL : TROY's *brother*

CORY : TROY *and* ROSE's *son*

RAYNELL : TROY's *daughter*

Fences opened on April 30, 1985, at the Yale Repertory Theatre in New Haven, Connecticut, with the following cast:

TROY MAXSON	James Earl Jones
JIM BONO	Ray Aranha
ROSE	Mary Alice
LYONS	Charles Brown
GABRIEL	Russell Costen
CORY	Courtney B. Vance
RAYNELL	Cristal Coleman & LaJara Henderson at alternate performances

Director	Lloyd Richards
Set Design	James D. Sandefur
Costume Design	Candice Donnelly
Light Design	Danianne Mizzy
Music Director	Dwight Andrews
Production Stage Manager	Joel Grynheim
Stage Manager	Terrence J. Witter
Casting	Meg Simon/Fran Kumin

Fences was initially presented as a staged reading at the Eugene O'Neill Theater Center's 1983 National Playwrights Conference.

Fences opened on March 26, 1987, at the 46th Street Theatre, with the following cast:

TROY MAXSON	James Earl Jones
JIM BONO	Ray Aranha
ROSE	Mary Alice
LYONS	Charles Brown
GABRIEL	Frankie R. Faison
CORY	Courtney B. Vance
RAYNELL	Karima Miller

Producer	Carole Shorenstein Hays in association with The Yale Repertory Theatre
Director	Lloyd Richards
Set Design	James D. Sandefur
Costume Design	Candice Donnelly
Light Design	Danianne Mizzy
Music Director	Dwight Andrews
Production Stage Manager	Martin Gold
General Manager	Robert Kamlot
Stage Manager	Terrence J. Witter
Casting	Meg Simon/Fran Kumin

This new edition, first printed in May 1987, reflects the final definitive text of *Fences* as performed on Broadway.

99

SETTING

The setting is the yard which fronts the only entrance to the
MAXSON household, an ancient two-story brick house set back off a
small alley in a big-city neighborhood. The entrance to the house is
gained by two or three steps leading to a wooden porch badly in need
of paint.

A relatively recent addition to the house and running its full
width, the porch lacks congruence. It is a sturdy porch with a flat
roof. One or two chairs of dubious value sit at one end where the
kitchen window opens onto the porch. An old-fashioned icebox
stands silent guard at the opposite end.

The yard is a small dirt yard, partially fenced, except for the last
scene, with a wooden sawhorse, a pile of lumber, and other fence-
building equipment set off to the side. Opposite is a tree from which
hangs a ball made of rags. A baseball bat leans against the tree. Two
oil drums serve as garbage receptacles and sit near the house at right
to complete the setting.

THE PLAY

Near the turn of the century, the destitute of Europe sprang on the city with tenacious claws and an honest and solid dream. The city devoured them. They swelled its belly until it burst into a thousand furnaces and sewing machines, a thousand butcher shops and bakers' ovens, a thousand churches and hospitals and funeral parlors and moneylenders. The city grew. It nourished itself and offered each man a partnership limited only by his talent, his guile, and his willingness and capacity for hard work. For the immigrants of Europe, a dream dared and won true.

The descendants of African slaves were offered no such welcome or participation. They came from places called the Carolinas and the Virginias, Georgia, Alabama, Mississippi, and Tennessee. They came strong, eager, searching. The city rejected them, and they fled and settled along the riverbanks and under bridges in shallow, ramshackle houses made of sticks and tar-paper. They collected rags and wood. They sold the use of their muscles and their bodies. They cleaned houses and washed clothes, they shined shoes, and in quiet desperation and vengeful pride, they stole and lived in pursuit of their own dream: That they could breathe free, finally, and stand to meet life with the force of dignity and whatever eloquence the heart could call upon.

By 1957, the hard-won victories of the European immigrants had solidified the industrial might of America. War had been confronted and won with new energies that used loyalty and patriotism as its fuel. Life was rich, full, and flourishing. The Milwaukee

103

Braves won the World Series, and the hot winds of change that would make the sixties a turbulent, racing, dangerous, and provocative decade had not yet begun to blow full.

ACT ONE: Scene One

It is 1957. TROY *and* BONO *enter the yard, engaged in conversation.*
TROY *is fifty-three years old, a large man with thick, heavy hands; it is
this largeness that he strives to fill out and make an accommodation with.
Together with his blackness, his largeness informs his sensibilities and the
choices he has made in his life.*

Of the two men, BONO *is obviously the follower. His commitment to
their friendship of thirty-odd years is rooted in his admiration of* TROY'S
honesty, capacity for hard work, and his strength, which BONO *seeks to
emulate.*

*It is Friday night, payday, and the one night of the week the two men
engage in a ritual of talk and drink.* TROY *is usually the most talkative
and at times he can be crude and almost vulgar, though he is capable of
rising to profound heights of expression. The men carry lunch buckets and
wear or carry burlap aprons and are dressed in clothes suitable to their
jobs as garbage collectors.*

BONO: Troy, you ought to stop that lying!

TROY: I ain't lying! The nigger had a watermelon this big.
(*He indicates with his hands.*)
Talking about . . . "What watermelon, Mr. Rand?" I liked to
fell out! "What watermelon, Mr. Rand?" . . . And it sitting
there big as life.

BONO: What did Mr. Rand say?

TROY: Ain't said nothing. Figure if the nigger too dumb to know he carrying a watermelon, he wasn't gonna get much sense out of him. Trying to hide that great big old watermelon under his coat. Afraid to let the white man see him carry it home.

BONO: I'm like you . . . I ain't got no time for them kind of people.

TROY: Now what he look like getting mad cause he see the man from the union talking to Mr. Rand?

BONO: He come to me talking about . . . "Maxson gonna get us fired." I told him to get away from me with that. He walked away from me calling you a troublemaker. What Mr. Rand say?

TROY: Ain't said nothing. He told me to go down the Commissioner's office next Friday. They called me down there to see them.

BONO: Well, as long as you got your complaint filed, they can't fire you. That's what one of them white fellows tell me.

TROY: I ain't worried about them firing me. They gonna fire me cause I asked a question? That's all I did. I went to Mr. Rand and asked him, "Why? Why you got the white mens driving and the colored lifting?" Told him, "What's the matter, don't I count? You think only white fellows got sense enough to drive a truck? That ain't no paper job! Hell, anybody can drive a truck. How come you got all whites driving and the colored lifting?" He told me, "take it to the union." Well, hell, that's what I done! Now they wanna come up with this pack of lies.

BONO: I told Brownie if the man come and ask him any questions . . . just tell the truth! It ain't nothing but something they done trumped up on you cause you filed a complaint on them.

TROY: Brownie don't understand nothing. All I want them to do is change the job description. Give everybody a chance to drive the truck. Brownie can't see that. He ain't got that much sense.

BONO: How you figure he be making out with that gal be up at Taylors' all the time . . . that Alberta gal?

106

TROY: Same as you and me. Getting just as much as we is. Which is to say nothing.

BONO: It is, huh? I figure you doing a little better than me . . . and I ain't saying what I'm doing.

TROY: Aw, nigger, look here . . . I know you. If you had got any-where near that gal, twenty minutes later you be looking to tell somebody. And the first one you gonna tell . . . that you gonna want to brag to . . . is gonna be me.

BONO: I ain't saying that. I see where you be eyeing her.

TROY: I eye all the women. I don't miss nothing. Don't never let nobody tell you Troy Maxson don't eye the women.

BONO: You been doing more than eyeing her. You done bought her a drink or two.

TROY: Hell yeah, I bought her a drink! What that mean? I bought you one, too. What that mean cause I buy her a drink? I'm just being polite.

BONO: It's alright to buy her one drink. That's what you call being polite. But when you wanna be buying two or three . . . that's what you call eyeing her.

TROY: Look here, as long as you known me . . . you ever known me to chase after women?

BONO: Hell yeah! Long as I done known you. You forgetting I knew you when.

TROY: Naw, I'm talking about since I been married to Rose?

BONO: Oh, not since you been married to Rose. Now, that's the truth, there. I can say that.

TROY: Alright then! Case closed.

BONO: I see you be walking up around Alberta's house. You sup-posed to be at Taylors' and you be walking up around there.

107

TROY: What you watching where I'm walking for? I ain't watching after you.

BONO: I seen you walking around there more than once.

TROY: Hell, you liable to see me walking anywhere! That don't mean nothing cause you see me walking around there.

BONO: Where she come from anyway? She just kinda showed up one day.

TROY: Tallahassee. You can look at her and tell she one of them Florida gals. They got some big healthy women down there. Grow them right up out the ground. Got a little bit of Indian in her. Most of them niggers down in Florida got some Indian in them.

BONO: I don't know about that Indian part. But she damn sure big and healthy. Woman wear some big stockings. Got them great big old legs and hips as wide as the Mississippi River.

TROY: Legs don't mean nothing. You don't do nothing but push them out of the way. But them hips cushion the ride!

BONO: Troy, you ain't got no sense.

TROY: It's the truth! Like you riding on Goodyears!
(ROSE *enters from the house. She is ten years younger than* TROY, *her devotion to him stems from her recognition of the possibilities of her life without him—a succession of abusive men and their babies, a life of partying and running the streets, the church, or aloneness with its attendant pain and frustration. She recognizes* TROY's *spirit as a fine and illuminating one and she either ignores or forgives his faults, only some of which she recognizes. Though she doesn't drink, her presence is an integral part of the Friday night rituals. She alternates between the porch and the kitchen, where supper preparations are under way.*)

ROSE: What you all out here getting into?

TROY: What you worried about what we getting into for? This is men talk, woman.

ROSE: What I care what you all talking about? Bono, you gonna stay for supper?

BONO: No, I thank you, Rose. But Lucille say she cooking up a pot of pigfeet.

TROY: Pigfeet! Hell, I'm going home with you! Might even stay the night if you got some pigfeet. You got something in there to top them pigfeet, Rose?

ROSE: I'm cooking up some chicken. I got some chicken and collard greens.

TROY: Well, go on back in the house and let me and Bono finish what we was talking about. This is men talk. I got some talk for you later. You know what kind of talk I mean. You go on and powder it up.

ROSE: Troy Maxson, don't you start that now!

TROY: (*Puts his arm around her.*) Aw, woman . . . come here. Look here, Bono . . . when I met this woman . . . I got out that place, say, "Hitch up my pony, saddle up my mare . . . there's a woman out there for me somewhere." I looked here. Looked there. Saw Rose and latched on to her. I latched on to her and told her—I'm gonna tell you the truth—I told her, "Baby, I don't wanna marry, I just wanna be your man." Rose told me . . . tell him what you told me, Rose.

ROSE: I told him if he wasn't the marrying kind, then move out the way so the marrying kind could find me.

TROY: That's what she told me. "Nigger, you in my way. You blocking the view! Move out the way so I can find me a husband." I thought it over two or three days. Come back—

ROSE: Ain't no two or three days nothing. You was back the same night.

TROY: Come back, told her . . . "Okay, baby . . . but I'm gonna buy me a banty rooster and put him out there in the backyard . . . and when he see a stranger come, he'll flap his wings

109

and crow . . ." Look here, Bono, I could watch the front door by myself . . . it was that back door I was worried about.

ROSE: Troy, you ought not talk like that. Troy ain't doing nothing but telling a lie.

TROY: Only thing is . . . when we first got married . . . forget the rooster . . . we ain't had no yard!

BONO: I hear you tell it. Me and Lucille was staying down there on Logan Street. Had two rooms with the outhouse in the back. I ain't mind the outhouse none. But when that goddamn wind blow through there in the winter . . . that's what I'm talking about! To this day I wonder why in the hell I ever stayed down there for six long years. But see, I didn't know I could do no better. I thought only white folks had inside toilets and things.

ROSE: There's a lot of people don't know they can do no better than they doing now. That's just something you got to learn. A lot of folks still shop at Bella's.

TROY: Ain't nothing wrong with shopping at Bella's. She got fresh food.

ROSE: I ain't said nothing about if she got fresh food. I'm talking about what she charge. She charge ten cents more than the A&P.

TROY: The A&P ain't never done nothing for me. I spends my money where I'm treated right. I go down to Bella, say, "I need a loaf of bread, I'll pay you Friday." She give it to me. What sense that make when I got money to go and spend it somewhere else and ignore the person who done right by me? That ain't in the Bible.

ROSE: We ain't talking about what's in the Bible. What sense it make to shop there when she overcharge?

TROY: You shop where you want to. I'll do my shopping where the people been good to me.

ROSE: Well, I don't think it's right for her to overcharge. That's all I was saying.

BONO: Look here . . . I got to get on. Lucille gonna be raising all kind of hell.

TROY: Where you going, nigger? We ain't finished this pint. Come here, finish this pint.

BONO: Well, hell, I am . . . if you ever turn the bottle loose.

TROY: (*Hands him the bottle.*) The only thing I say about the A&P is I'm glad Cory got that job down there. Help him take care of his school clothes and things. Gabe done moved out and things getting tight around here. He got that job. . . . He can start to look out for himself.

ROSE: Cory done went and got recruited by a college football team.

TROY: I told that boy about that football stuff. The white man ain't gonna let him get nowhere with that football. I told him when he first come to me with it. Now you come telling me he done went and got more tied up in it. He ought to go and get recruited in how to fix cars or something where he can make a living.

ROSE: He ain't talking about making no living playing football. It's just something the boys in school do. They gonna send a recruiter by to talk to you. He'll tell you he ain't talking about making no living playing football. It's a honor to be recruited.

TROY: It ain't gonna get him nowhere. Bono'll tell you that.

BONO: If he be like you in the sports . . . he's gonna be alright. Ain't but two men ever played baseball as good as you. That's Babe Ruth and Josh Gibson. Them's the only two men ever hit more home runs than you.

TROY: What it ever get me? Ain't got a pot to piss in or a window to throw it out of.

ROSE: Times have changed since you was playing baseball, Troy. That was before the war. Times have changed a lot since then.

111

TROY: How in hell they done changed?

ROSE: They got lots of colored boys playing ball now. Baseball and football.

BONO: You right about that, Rose. Times have changed, Troy. You just come along too early.

TROY: There ought not never have been no time called too early! Now you take that fellow . . . what's that fellow they had playing right field for the Yankees back then? You know who I'm talking about, Bono. Used to play right field for the Yankees.

ROSE: Selkirk?

TROY: Selkirk! That's it! Man batting .269, understand? .269. What kind of sense that make? I was hitting .432 with thirty-seven home runs! Man batting .269 and playing right field for the Yankees! I saw Josh Gibson's daughter yesterday. She walking around with raggedy shoes on her feet. Now I bet you Selkirk's daughter ain't walking around with raggedy shoes on her feet! I bet you that!

ROSE: They got a lot of colored baseball players now. Jackie Robinson was the first. Folks had to wait for Jackie Robinson.

TROY: I done seen a hundred niggers play baseball better than Jackie Robinson. Hell, I know some teams Jackie Robinson couldn't even make! What you talking about Jackie Robinson. Jackie Robinson wasn't nobody. I'm talking about if you could play ball then they ought to have let you play. Don't care what color you were. Come telling me I come along too early. If you could play . . . then they ought to have let you play.
(TROY *takes a long drink from the bottle.*)

ROSE: You gonna drink yourself to death. You don't need to be drinking like that.

TROY: Death ain't nothing. I done seen him. Done wrassled with him. You can't tell me nothing about death. Death ain't nothing but a fastball on the outside corner. And you know what I'll do to

112

that! Lookee here, Bono . . . am I lying? You get one of them fastballs, about waist high, over the outside corner of the plate where you can get the meat of the bat on it . . . and good God! You can kiss it good-bye. Now, am I lying?

BONO: Naw, you telling the truth there. I seen you do it.

TROY: If I'm lying . . . that 450 feet worth of lying!
(*Pause.*)
That's all death is to me. A fastball on the outside corner.

ROSE: I don't know why you want to get on talking about death.

TROY: Ain't nothing wrong with talking about death. That's part of life. Everybody gonna die. You gonna die, I'm gonna die. Bono's gonna die. Hell, we all gonna die.

ROSE: But you ain't got to talk about it. I don't like to talk about it.

TROY: You the one brought it up. Me and Bono was talking about baseball . . . you tell me I'm gonna drink myself to death. Ain't that right, Bono? You know I don't drink this but one night out of the week. That's Friday night. I'm gonna drink just enough to where I can handle it. Then I cuts it loose. I leave it alone. So don't you worry about me drinking myself to death. Cause I ain't worried about Death. I done seen him. I done wrestled with him.
   Look here, Bono . . . I looked up one day and Death was marching straight at me. Like soldiers on parade! The army of death was marching straight at me. The middle of July 1941. It got real cold just like it be winter. It seem like Death himself reached out and touched me on the shoulder. He touch me just like I touch you. I got cold as ice and Death standing there grinning at me.

ROSE: Troy, why don't you hush that talk.

TROY: I say . . . What you want, Mr. Death? You be wanting me? You done brought your army to be getting me? I looked him dead in the eye. I wasn't fearing nothing. I was ready to tangle. Just like I'm ready to tangle now. The Bible say be ever vigilant. That's why I don't get but so drunk. I got to keep watch.

113

ROSE: Troy was right down there in Mercy Hospital. You remember he had pneumonia? Laying there with a fever talking plumb out of his head.

TROY: Death standing there staring at me . . . carrying that sickle in his hand. Finally he say, "You want bound over for another year?" See, just like that . . . "You want bound over for another year?" I told him, "Bound over hell! Let's settle this now!"

It seem like he kinda fell back when I said that, and all the cold went out of me. I reached down and grabbed that sickle and threw it just as far as I could throw it . . . and me and him commenced to wrestling.

We wrestled for three days and three nights. I can't say where I found the strength from. Every time it seemed like he was gonna get the best of me, I'd reach way down deep inside myself and find the strength to do him one better.

ROSE: Every time Troy tell that story he find different ways to tell it. Different things to make up about it.

TROY: I ain't making up nothing. I'm telling you the facts of what happened. I wrestled with Death for three days and three nights and I'm standing here to tell you about it.
(*Pause.*)
Alright. At the end of the third night we done weakened each other to where we can't hardly move. Death stood up, throwed on his robe . . . had him a white robe with a hood on it. He throwed on that robe and went off to look for his sickle. Say, "I'll be back." Just like that. "I'll be back." I told him, say, "Yeah, but . . . you gonna have to find me!" I wasn't no fool. I wasn't going looking for him. Death ain't nothing to play with. And I know he's gonna get me. I know I got to join his army . . . his camp followers. But as long as I keep my strength and see him coming . . . as long as I keep up my vigilance . . . he's gonna have to fight to get me. I ain't going easy.

BONO: Well, look here, since you got to keep up your vigilance . . . let me have the bottle.

TROY: Aw hell, I shouldn't have told you that part. I should have left out that part.

ROSE: Troy be talking that stuff and half the time don't even know what he be talking about.

TROY: Bono know me better than that.

BONO: That's right. I know you. I know you got some Uncle Remus in your blood. You got more stories than the devil got sinners.

TROY: Aw hell, I done seen him too! Done talked with the devil.

ROSE: Troy, don't nobody wanna be hearing all that stuff.
(LYONS *enters the yard from the street. Thirty-four years old,* TROY'S *son by a previous marriage, he sports a neatly trimmed goatee, sport coat, white shirt, tieless and buttoned at the collar. Though he fancies himself a musician, he is more caught up in the rituals and idea of being a musician than in the actual practice of the music. He has come to borrow money from* TROY, *and while he knows he will be successful, he is uncertain as to what extent his lifestyle will be held up to scrutiny and ridicule.*)

LYONS: Hey, Pop.

TROY: What you come "Hey, Popping" me for?

LYONS: How you doing, Rose?
(*He kisses her.*)
Mr. Bono. How you doing?

BONO: Hey, Lyons . . . how you been?

TROY: He must have been doing alright. I ain't seen him around here last week.

ROSE: Troy, leave your boy alone. He come by to see you and you wanna start all that nonsense.

TROY: I ain't bothering Lyons.
(*Offers him the bottle.*)
Here . . . get you a drink. We got an understanding. I know why he come by to see me and he know I know.

115

LYONS: Come on, Pop . . . I just stopped by to say hi . . . see how you was doing.

TROY: You ain't stopped by yesterday.

ROSE: You gonna stay for supper, Lyons? I got some chicken cooking in the oven.

LYONS: No, Rose . . . thanks. I was just in the neighborhood and thought I'd stop by for a minute.

TROY: You was in the neighborhood alright, nigger. You telling the truth there. You was in the neighborhood cause it's my payday.

LYONS: Well, hell, since you mentioned it . . . let me have ten dollars.

TROY: I'll be damned! I'll die and go to hell and play blackjack with the devil before I give you ten dollars.

BONO: That's what I wanna know about . . . that devil you done seen.

LYONS: What . . . Pop done seen the devil? You too much, Pops.

TROY: Yeah, I done seen him. Talked to him too!

ROSE: You ain't seen no devil. I done told you that man ain't had nothing to do with the devil. Anything you can't understand, you want to call it the devil.

TROY: Look here, Bono . . . I went down to see Hertzberger about some furniture. Got three rooms for two-ninety-eight. That what it say on the radio. "Three rooms . . . two-ninety-eight." Even made up a little song about it. Go down there . . . man tell me I can't get no credit. I'm working every day and can't get no credit. What to do? I got an empty house with some raggedy furniture in it. Cory ain't got no bed. He's sleeping on a pile of rags on the floor. Working every day and can't get no credit. Come back here—Rose'll tell you—madder than hell. Sit down . . . try to figure what I'm gonna do. Come a knock on the door. Ain't been living here but three days. Who know I'm here? Open the door . . . devil standing there bigger than life. White fellow . . . got on good clothes and everything. Standing there with a clipboard in his hand. I ain't had to say nothing. First words come out of his mouth was . . . "I understand you need some furniture and can't get no credit." I liked to fell over. He say "I'll give you all the credit you want, but you got to pay the interest on it." I told him, "Give me three rooms worth and charge whatever you want." Next day a truck pulled up here and two men unloaded them three rooms. Man what drove the truck give me a book. Say send ten dollars, first of every month, to the address in the book and everything will be alright. Say if I miss a payment the devil was coming back and it'll be hell to pay. That was fifteen years ago. To this day . . . the first of the month I send my ten dollars, Rose'll tell you.

ROSE: Troy lying.

TROY: I ain't never seen that man since. Now you tell me who else that could have been but the devil? I ain't sold my soul or nothing like that, you understand. Naw, I wouldn't have truck with the devil about nothing like that. I got my furniture and pays my ten dollars the first of the month just like clockwork.

BONO: How long you say you been paying this ten dollars a month?

TROY: Fifteen years!

BONO: Hell, ain't you finished paying for it yet? How much the man done charged you?

TROY: Aw hell, I done paid for it. I done paid for it ten times over! The fact is I'm scared to stop paying it.

ROSE: Troy lying. We got that furniture from Mr. Glickman. He ain't paying no ten dollars a month to nobody.

TROY: Aw hell, woman. Bono know I ain't that big a fool.

LYONS: I was just getting ready to say . . . I know where there's a bridge for sale.

TROY: Look here, I'll tell you this . . . it don't matter to me if he

117

was the devil. It don't matter if the devil give credit. Somebody has got to give it.

ROSE: It ought to matter. You going around talking about having truck with the devil . . . God's the one you gonna have to answer to. He's the one gonna be at the judgment.

LYONS: Yeah, well, look here, Pop . . . let me have that ten dollars. I'll give it back to you. Bonnie got a job working at the hospital.

TROY: What I tell you, Bono? The only time I see this nigger is when he wants something. That's the only time I see him.

LYONS: Come on, Pop, Mr. Bono don't want to hear all that. Let me have the ten dollars. I told you Bonnie working.

TROY: What that mean to me? "Bonnie working." I don't care if she working. Go ask her for the ten dollars if she working. Talking about "Bonnie working." Why ain't you working?

LYONS: Aw, Pop, you know I can't find no decent job. Where am I gonna get a job at? You know I can't get no job.

TROY: I told you I know some people down there. I can get you on the rubbish if you want to work. I told you that the last time you came by here asking me for something.

LYONS: Naw, Pop . . . thanks. That ain't for me. I don't wanna be carrying nobody's rubbish. I don't wanna be punching nobody's time clock.

TROY: What's the matter, you too good to carry people's rubbish? Where you think that ten dollars you talking about come from? I'm just supposed to haul people's rubbish and give my money to you cause you too lazy to work. You too lazy to work and wanna know why you ain't got what I got.

ROSE: What hospital Bonnie working at? Mercy?

LYONS: She's down at Passavant working in the laundry.

TROY: I ain't got nothing as it is. I give you that ten dollars and I got to eat beans the rest of the week. Naw . . . you ain't getting no ten dollars here.

LYONS: You ain't got to be eating no beans. I don't know why you wanna say that.

TROY: I ain't got no extra money. Gabe done moved over to Miss Pearl's paying her the rent and things done got tight around here. I can't afford to be giving you every payday.

LYONS: I ain't asked you to give me nothing. I asked you to loan me ten dollars. I know you got ten dollars.

TROY: Yeah, I got it. You know why I got it? Cause I don't throw my money away out there in the streets. You living the fast life . . . wanna be a musician . . . running around in them clubs and things . . . then, you learn to take care of yourself. You ain't gonna find me going and asking nobody for nothing. I done spent too many years without.

LYONS: You and me is two different people, Pop.

TROY: I done learned my mistake and learned to do what's right by it. You still trying to get something for nothing. Life don't owe you nothing. You owe it to yourself. Ask Bono. He'll tell you I'm right.

LYONS: You got your way of dealing with the world . . . I got mine. The only thing that matters to me is the music.

TROY: Yeah, I can see that! It don't matter how you gonna eat . . . where your next dollar is coming from. You telling the truth there.

LYONS: I know I got to eat. But I got to live too. I need something that gonna help me to get out of the bed in the morning. Make me feel like I belong in the world. I don't bother nobody. I just stay with my music cause that's the only way I can find to live in the world. Otherwise there ain't no telling what I might do. Now I don't come criticizing you and how you live. I just come by to

119

ask you for ten dollars. I don't wanna hear all that about how I live.

TROY: Boy, your mama did a hell of a job raising you.

LYONS: You can't change me, Pop. I'm thirty-four years old. If you wanted to change me, you should have been there when I was growing up. I come by to see you . . . ask for ten dollars and you want to talk about how I was raised. You don't know nothing about how I was raised.

ROSE: Let the boy have ten dollars, Troy.

TROY: (*To* LYONS.) What the hell you looking at me for? I ain't got no ten dollars. You know what I do with my money.
(*To* ROSE.)
Give him ten dollars if you want him to have it.

ROSE: I will. Just as soon as you turn it loose.

TROY: (*Handing* ROSE *the money*.) There it is. Seventy-six dollars and forty-two cents. You see this, Bono? Now, I ain't gonna get but six of that back.

ROSE: You ought to stop telling that lie. Here, Lyons.
(*She hands him the money*.)

LYONS: Thanks, Rose. Look . . . I got to run . . . I'll see you later.

TROY: Wait a minute. You gonna say, "thanks, Rose" and ain't gonna look to see where she got that ten dollars from? See how they do me, Bono?

LYONS: I know she got it from you, Pop. Thanks. I'll give it back to you.

TROY: There he go telling another lie. Time I see that ten dollars . . . he'll be owing me thirty more.

LYONS: See you, Mr. Bono.

BONO: Take care, Lyons!

LYONS: Thanks, Pop. I'll see you again.
(LYONS *exits the yard.*)

TROY: I don't know why he don't go and get him a decent job and take care of that woman he got.

BONO: He'll be alright, Troy. The boy is still young.

TROY: The *boy* is thirty-four years old.

ROSE: Let's not get off into all that.

BONO: Look here . . . I got to be going. I got to be getting on. Lucille gonna be waiting.

TROY: (*Puts his arm around* ROSE.) See this woman, Bono? I love this woman. I love this woman so much it hurts. I love her so much . . . I done run out of ways of loving her. So I got to go back to basics. Don't you come by my house Monday morning talking about time to go to work . . . cause I'm still gonna be stroking!

ROSE: Troy! Stop it now!

BONO: I ain't paying him no mind, Rose. That ain't nothing but gin talk. Go on, Troy. I'll see you Monday.

TROY: Don't you come by my house, nigger! I done told you what I'm gonna be doing.
(*The lights go down to black.*)

121

ACT ONE: Scene Two

The lights come up on ROSE *hanging up clothes. She hums and sings softly to herself. It is the following morning.*

ROSE: (*Sings.*)
Jesus, be a fence all around me every day
Jesus, I want you to protect me as I travel on my way.
Jesus, be a fence all around me every day.
(Troy *enters from the house*)

ROSE: (*Continues.*)
Jesus, I want you to protect me
As I travel on my way.
(*To* TROY)
Morning. You ready for breakfast? I can fix it soon as I finish hanging up these clothes.

TROY: I got the coffee on. That'll be alright. I'll just drink some of that this morning.

ROSE: That 651 hit yesterday. That's the second time this month. Miss Pearl hit for a dollar . . . seem like those that need the least always get lucky. Poor folks can't get nothing.

TROY: Them numbers don't know nobody. I don't know why you fool with them. You and Lyons both.

ROSE: It's something to do.

TROY: You ain't doing nothing but throwing your money away.

ROSE: Troy, you know I don't play foolishly. I just play a nickel here and a nickel there.

TROY: That's two nickels you done thrown away.

ROSE: Now I hit sometimes . . . that makes up for it. It always comes in handy when I do hit. I don't hear you complaining then.

TROY: I ain't complaining now. I just say it's foolish. Trying to guess out of six hundred ways which way the number gonna come. If I had all the money niggers, these Negroes, throw away on numbers for one week—just one week—I'd be a rich man.

ROSE: Well, you wishing and calling it foolish ain't gonna stop folks from playing numbers. That's one thing for sure. Besides . . . some good things come from playing numbers. Look where Pope done bought him that restaurant off of numbers.

TROY: I can't stand niggers like that. Man ain't had two dimes to rub together. He walking around with his shoes all run over bumming money for cigarettes. Alright. Got lucky there and hit the numbers . . .

ROSE: Troy, I know all about it.

TROY: Had good sense, I'll say that for him. He ain't throwed his money away. I seen niggers hit the numbers and go through two thousand dollars in four days. Man bought him that restaurant down there . . . fixed it up real nice . . . and then didn't want nobody to come in it! A Negro go in there and can't get no kind of service. I seen a white fellow come in there and order a bowl of stew. Pope picked all the meat out the pot for him. Man ain't had nothing but a bowl of meat! Negro come behind him and ain't got nothing but the potatoes and carrots. Talking about what numbers do for people, you picked a wrong example. Ain't done nothing but make a worser fool out of him than he was before.

ROSE: Troy, you ought to stop worrying about what happened at work yesterday.

123

TROY: I ain't worried. Just told me to be down there at the commissioner's office on Friday. Everybody think they gonna fire me. I
ain't worried about them firing me. You ain't got to worry about
that.
(*Pause.*)
Where's Cory? Cory in the house? (*Calls.*) Cory?

ROSE: He gone out.

TROY: Out, huh? He gone out cause he know I want him to help me
with this fence. I know how he is. That boy scared of work.
(GABRIEL *enters. He comes halfway down the alley and, hearing*
TROY's *voice, stops.*)

TROY: (*Continues.*) He ain't done a lick of work in his life.

ROSE: He had to go to football practice. Coach wanted them to get
in a little extra practice before the season start.

TROY: I got his practice . . . running out of here before he get his
chores done.

ROSE: Troy, what is wrong with you this morning? Don't nothing
set right with you. Go on back in there and go to bed . . . get up
on the other side.

TROY: Why something got to be wrong with me? I ain't said nothing wrong with me.

ROSE: You got something to say about everything. First it's the
numbers . . . then it's the way the man runs his restaurant . . .
then you done got on Cory. What's it gonna be next? Take a
look up there and see if the weather suits you . . . or is it gonna
be how you gonna put up the fence with the clothes hanging in
the yard.

TROY: You hit the nail on the head then.

ROSE: I know you like I know the back of my hand. Go on in there
and get you some coffee . . . see if that straighten you up. Cause
you ain't right this morning.
(TROY *starts into the house and sees* GABRIEL. GABRIEL *starts sing-*

ing. TROY's *brother, he is seven years younger than* TROY. *Injured in World War II, he has a metal plate in his head. He carries an old trumpet tied around his waist and believes with every fiber of his being that he is the Archangel Gabriel. He carries a chipped basket with an assortment of discarded fruits and vegetables he has picked up in the Strip District and which he attempts to sell.*)

GABRIEL: (*Singing.*)
Yes, ma'am, I got plums
You ask me how I sell them
Oh ten cents apiece
Three for a quarter
Come and buy now
Cause I'm here today
And tomorrow I'll be gone
(GABRIEL *enters.*)
Hey, Rose!

ROSE: How you doing, Gabe?

GABRIEL: There's Troy . . . Hey, Troy!

TROY: Hey, Gabe.
(*Exit into kitchen.*)

ROSE: (*To* GABRIEL.) What you got there?

GABRIEL: You know what I got, Rose. I got fruits and vegetables.

ROSE: (*Looking in basket.*) Where's all these plums you talking about?

GABRIEL: I ain't got no plums today, Rose. I was just singing that. Have some tomorrow. Put me in a big order for plums. Have enough plums tomorrow for St. Peter and everybody.
(TROY *reenters from kitchen, crosses to steps.*)
(*To* ROSE.) Troy's mad at me.

TROY: I ain't mad at you. What I got to be mad at you about? You ain't done nothing to me.

GABRIEL: I just moved over to Miss Pearl's to keep out from in your way. I ain't mean no harm by it.

125

TROY: Who said anything about that? I ain't said anything about that.

GABRIEL: You ain't mad at me, is you?

TROY: Naw . . . I ain't mad at you, Gabe. If I was mad at you I'd tell you about it.

GABRIEL: Got me two rooms. In the basement. Got my own door too. Wanna see my key?
(*He holds up a key.*)
That's my own key! Ain't nobody else got a key like that. That's my key! My two rooms!

TROY: Well, that's good, Gabe. You got your own key . . . that's good.

ROSE: You hungry, Gabe? I was just fixing to cook Troy his break-fast.

GABRIEL: I'll take some biscuits. You got some biscuits? Did you know when I was in heaven . . . every morning me and St. Peter would sit down by the gate and eat some big fat biscuits? Oh, yeah! We had us a good time. We'd sit there and eat us them biscuits and then St. Peter would go off to sleep and tell me to wake him up when it's time to open the gates for the judgment.

ROSE: Well, come on . . . I'll make up a batch of biscuits.
(ROSE *exits into the house.*)

GABRIEL: Troy . . . St. Peter got your name in the book. I seen it. It say . . . Troy Maxson. I say . . . I know him! He got the same name like what I got. That's my brother!

TROY: How many times you gonna tell me that, Gabe?

GABRIEL: Ain't got my name in the book. Don't have to have my name. I done died and went to heaven. He got your name though. One morning St. Peter was looking at his book . . . marking it up for the judgment . . . and he let me see your name. Got it in there under M. Got Rose's name . . . I ain't seen it like I seen yours . . . but I know it's in there. He got a great big book. Got everybody's name what was ever been born. That's what he told me. But I seen your name. Seen it with my own eyes.

TROY: Go on in the house there. Rose going to fix you something to eat.

GABRIEL: Oh, I ain't hungry. I done had breakfast with Aunt Jemimah. She come by and cooked me up a whole mess of flapjacks. Remember how we used to eat them flapjacks?

TROY: Go on in the house and get you something to eat now.

GABRIEL: I got to go sell my plums. I done sold some tomatoes. Got me two quarters. Wanna see?
(*He shows* TROY *his quarters.*)
I'm gonna save them and buy me a new horn so St. Peter can hear me when it's time to open the gates.
(GABRIEL *stops suddenly. Listens.*)
Hear that? That's the hellhounds. I got to chase them out of here. Go on get out of here! Get out!
(GABRIEL *exits singing.*)
Better get ready for the judgment
Better get ready for the judgment
My Lord is coming down
(ROSE *enters from the house.*)

TROY: He gone off somewhere.

GABRIEL: (*Offstage*)
Better get ready for the judgment
Better get ready for the judgment morning
Better get ready for the judgment
My God is coming down

ROSE: He ain't eating right. Miss Pearl say she can't get him to eat nothing.

TROY: What you want me to do about it, Rose? I done did every-thing I can for the man. I can't make him get well. Man got half his head blown away . . . what you expect?

127

ROSE: Seem like something ought to be done to help him.

TROY: Man don't bother nobody. He just mixed up from that metal plate he got in his head. Ain't no sense for him to go back into the hospital.

ROSE: Least he be eating right. They can help him take care of himself.

TROY: Don't nobody wanna be locked up, Rose. What you wanna lock him up for? Man go over there and fight the war . . . messing around with them Japs, get half his head blown off . . . and they give him a lousy three thousand dollars. And I had to swoop down on that.

ROSE: Is you fixing to go into that again?

TROY: That's the only way I got a roof over my head . . . cause of that metal plate.

ROSE: Ain't no sense you blaming yourself for nothing. Gabe wasn't in no condition to manage that money. You done what was right by him. Can't nobody say you ain't done what was right by him. Look how long you took care of him . . . till he wanted to have his own place and moved over there with Miss Pearl.

TROY: That ain't what I'm saying, woman! I'm just stating the facts. If my brother didn't have that metal plate in his head . . . I wouldn't have a pot to piss in or a window to throw it out of. And I'm fifty-three years old. Now see if you can understand that!
(TROY *gets up from the porch and starts to exit the yard.*)

ROSE: Where you going off to? You been running out of here every Saturday for weeks. I thought you was gonna work on this fence.

TROY: I'm gonna walk down to Taylors'. Listen to the ball game. I'll be back in a bit. I'll work on it when I get back.
(*He exits the yard. The lights go to black.*)

ACT ONE: Scene Three

The lights come up on the yard. It is four hours later. ROSE *is taking down the clothes from the line.* CORY *enters carrying his football equipment.*

ROSE: Your daddy like to had a fit with you running out of here this morning without doing your chores.

CORY: I told you I had to go to practice.

ROSE: He say you were supposed to help him with this fence.

CORY: He been saying that the last four or five Saturdays, and then he don't never do nothing, but go down to Taylors'. Did you tell him about the recruiter?

ROSE: Yeah, I told him.

CORY: What he say?

ROSE: He ain't said nothing too much. You get in there and get started on your chores before he gets back. Go on and scrub down them steps before he gets back here hollering and carrying on.

CORY: I'm hungry. What you got to eat, Mama?

ROSE: Go on and get started on your chores. I got some meat loaf in there. Go on and make you a sandwich . . . and don't leave no mess in there.
(CORY *exits into the house.* ROSE *continues to take down the clothes.* TROY *enters the yard and sneaks up and grabs her from behind.*)
Troy! Go on, now. You liked to scared me to death. What was

129

the score of the game? Lucille had me on the phone and I couldn't keep up with it.

TROY: What I care about the game? Come here, woman.
(*He tries to kiss her.*)

ROSE: I thought you went down to Taylors' to listen to the game. Go on, Troy! You supposed to be putting up this fence.

TROY: (*Attempting to kiss her again.*) I'll put it up when I finish with what is at hand.

ROSE: Go on, Troy. I ain't studying you.

TROY: (*Chasing after her.*) I'm studying you . . . fixing to do my homework!

ROSE: Troy, you better leave me alone.

TROY: Where's Cory? That boy brought his butt home yet?

ROSE: He's in the house doing his chores.

TROY: (*Calling.*) Cory! Get your butt out here, boy!
(ROSE *exits into the house with the laundry.* TROY *goes over to the pile of wood, picks up a board, and starts sawing.* CORY *enters from the house.*)
You just now coming in here from leaving this morning?

CORY: Yeah, I had to go to football practice.

TROY: Yeah, what?

CORY: Yessir.

TROY: I ain't but two seconds off you noway. The garbage sitting in there overflowing . . . you ain't done none of your chores . . . and you come in here talking about "Yeah."

CORY: I was just getting ready to do my chores now, Pop . . .

TROY: Your first chore is to help me with this fence on Saturday. Everything else come after that. Now get that saw and cut them boards.

(CORY *takes the saw and begins cutting the boards.* TROY *continues working. There is a long pause.*)

CORY: Hey, Pop . . . why don't you buy a TV?

TROY: What I want with a TV? What I want one of them for?

CORY: Everybody got one. Earl, Ba Bra . . . Jesse!

TROY: I ain't asked you who had one. I say what I want with one?

CORY: So you can watch it. They got lots of things on TV. Baseball games and everything. We could watch the World Series.

TROY: Yeah . . . and how much this TV cost?

CORY: I don't know. They got them on sale for around two hundred dollars.

TROY: Two hundred dollars, huh?

CORY: That ain't that much, Pop.

TROY: Naw, it's just two hundred dollars. See that roof you got over your head at night? Let me tell you something about that roof. It's been over ten years since that roof was last tarred. See now . . . the snow come this winter and sit up there on that roof like it is . . . and it's gonna seep inside. It's just gonna be a little bit . . . ain't gonna hardly notice it. Then the next thing you know, it's gonna be leaking all over the house. Then the wood rot from all that water and you gonna need a whole new roof. Now, how much you think it cost to get that roof tarred?

CORY: I don't know.

TROY: Two hundred and sixty-four dollars . . . cash money. While you thinking about a TV, I got to be thinking about the roof . . . and whatever else go wrong around here. Now if you had two hundred dollars, what would you do . . . fix the roof or buy a TV?

CORY: I'd buy a TV. Then when the roof started to leak . . . when it needed fixing . . . I'd fix it.

TROY: Where you gonna get the money from? You done spent it for a TV. You gonna sit up and watch the water run all over your brand new TV.

CORY: Aw, Pop. You got money. I know you do.

TROY: Where I got it at, huh?

CORY: You got it in the bank.

TROY: You wanna see my bankbook? You wanna see that seventy-three dollars and twenty-two cents I got sitting up in there?

CORY: You ain't got to pay for it all at one time. You can put a down payment on it and carry it on home with you.

TROY: Not me. I ain't gonna owe nobody nothing if I can help it. Miss a payment and they come and snatch it right out your house. Then what you got? Now, soon as I get two hundred dollars clear, then I'll buy a TV. Right now, as soon as I get two hundred and sixty-four dollars, I'm gonna have this roof tarred.

CORY: Aw . . . Pop!

TROY: You go on and get you two hundred dollars and buy one if ya want it. I got better things to do with my money.

CORY: I can't get no two hundred dollars. I ain't never seen two hundred dollars.

TROY: I'll tell you what . . . you get you a hundred dollars and I'll put the other hundred with it.

CORY: Alright, I'm gonna show you.

TROY: You gonna show me how you can cut them boards right now. (CORY *begins to cut the boards. There is a long pause.*)

CORY: The Pirates won today. That makes five in a row.

TROY: I ain't thinking about the Pirates. Got an all-white team.

Got that boy . . . that Puerto Rican boy . . . Clemente. Don't even half-play him. That boy could be something if they give him a chance. Play him one day and sit him on the bench the next.

CORY: He gets a lot of chances to play.

TROY: I'm talking about playing regular. Playing every day so you can get your timing. That's what I'm talking about.

CORY: They got some white guys on the team that don't play every day. You can't play everybody at the same time.

TROY: If they got a white fellow sitting on the bench . . . you can bet your last dollar he can't play! The colored guy got to be twice as good before he get on the team. That's why I don't want you to get all tied up in them sports. Man on the team and what it get him? They got colored on the team and don't use them. Same as not having them. All them teams the same.

CORY: The Braves got Hank Aaron and Wes Covington. Hank Aaron hit two home runs today. That makes forty-three.

TROY: Hank Aaron ain't nobody. That's what you supposed to do. That's how you supposed to play the game. Ain't nothing to it. It's just a matter of timing . . . getting the right follow-through. Hell, I can hit forty-three home runs right now!

CORY: Not off no major-league pitching, you couldn't.

TROY: We had better pitching in the Negro leagues. I hit seven home runs off of Satchel Paige. You can't get no better than that!

CORY: Sandy Koufax. He's leading the league in strike-outs.

TROY: I ain't thinking of no Sandy Koufax.

CORY: You got Warren Spahn and Lew Burdette. I bet you couldn't hit no home runs off of Warren Spahn.

TROY: I'm through with it now. You go on and cut them boards. (*Pause.*)

133

Your mama tell me you done got recruited by a college football team? Is that right?

CORY: Yeah. Coach Zellman say the recruiter gonna be coming by to talk to you. Get you to sign the permission papers.

TROY: I thought you supposed to be working down there at the A&P. Ain't you suppose to be working down there after school?

CORY: Mr. Stawicki say he gonna hold my job for me until after the football season. Say starting next week I can work weekends.

TROY: I thought we had an understanding about this football stuff? You suppose to keep up with your chores and hold that job down at the A&P. Ain't been around here all day on a Saturday. Ain't none of your chores done . . . and now you telling me you done quit your job.

CORY: I'm gonna be working weekends.

TROY: You damn right you are! And ain't no need for nobody coming around here to talk to me about signing nothing.

CORY: Hey, Pop . . . you can't do that. He's coming all the way from North Carolina.

TROY: I don't care where he coming from. The white man ain't gonna let you get nowhere with that football noway. You go on and get your book learning so you can work yourself up in that A&P or learn how to fix cars or build houses or something, get you a trade. That way you have something can't nobody take away from you. You go on and learn how to put your hands to some good use. Besides hauling people's garbage.

CORY: I get good grades, Pop. That's why the recruiter wants to talk with you. You got to keep up your grades to get recruited. This way I'll be going to college. I'll get a chance . . .

TROY: First you gonna get your butt down there to the A&P and get your job back.

CORY: Mr. Stawicki done already hired somebody else cause I told him I was playing football.

TROY: You a bigger fool than I thought . . . to let somebody take away your job so you can play some football. Where you gonna get your money to take out your girlfriend and whatnot? What kind of foolishness is that to let somebody take away your job?

CORY: I'm still gonna be working weekends.

TROY: Naw . . . naw. You getting your butt out of here and finding you another job.

CORY: Come on, Pop! I got to practice. I can't work after school and play football too. The team needs me. That's what Coach Zellman say . . .

TROY: I don't care what nobody else say. I'm the boss . . . you understand? I'm the boss around here. I do the only saying what counts.

CORY: Come on, Pop!

TROY: I asked you . . . did you understand?

CORY: Yeah . . .

TROY: What?!

CORY: Yessir.

TROY: You go on down there to that A&P and see if you can get your job back. If you can't do both . . . then you quit the football team. You've got to take the crookeds with the straights.

CORY: Yessir.
(*Pause.*)
Can I ask you a question?

TROY: What the hell you wanna ask me? Mr. Stawicki the one you got the questions for.

CORY: How come you ain't never liked me?

TROY: Liked you? Who the hell say I got to like you? What law is there say I got to like you? Wanna stand up in my face and ask a damn fool-ass question like that. Talking about liking somebody. Come here, boy, when I talk to you.
(CORY *comes over to where* TROY *is working. He stands slouched over and* TROY *shoves him on his shoulder.*)
Straighten up, goddamn it! I asked you a question . . . what law is there say I got to like you?

CORY: None.

TROY: Well, alright then! Don't you eat every day?
(*Pause.*)
Answer me when I talk to you! Don't you eat every day?

CORY: Yeah.

TROY: Nigger, as long as you in my house, you put that sir on the end of it when you talk to me!

CORY: Yes . . . sir.

TROY: You eat every day?

CORY: Yessir!

TROY: Got a roof over your head.

CORY: Yessir!

TROY: Got clothes on your back.

CORY: Yessir.

TROY: Why you think that is?

CORY: Cause of you.

TROY: Aw, hell I know it's cause of me . . . but why do you think that is?

CORY: (*Hesitant.*) Cause you like me.

TROY: Like you? I go out of here every morning . . . bust my butt . . . putting up with them crackers every day . . . cause I

like you? You about the biggest fool I ever saw.
(*Pause.*)
It's my job. It's my responsibility! You understand that? A man got to take care of his family. You live in my house . . . sleep you behind on my bedclothes . . . fill you belly up with my food . . . cause you my son. You my flesh and blood. Not cause I like you! Cause it's my duty to take care of you. I owe a responsibility to you!

Let's get this straight right here . . . before it go along any further . . . I ain't got to like you. Mr. Rand don't give me my money come payday cause he likes me. He gives me cause he owe me. I done give you everything I had to give you. I gave you your life! Me and your mama worked that out between us. And liking your black ass wasn't part of the bargain. Don't you try and go through life worrying about if somebody like you or not. You best be making sure they doing right by you. You understand what I'm saying, boy?

CORY: Yessir.

TROY: Then get the hell out of my face, and get on down to that A&P.
(ROSE *has been standing behind the screen door for much of the scene. She enters as* CORY *exits.*)

ROSE: Why don't you let the boy go ahead and play football, Troy? Ain't no harm in that. He's just trying to be like you with the sports.

TROY: I don't want him to be like me! I want him to move as far away from my life as he can get. You the only decent thing that ever happened to me. I wish him that. But I don't wish him a thing else from my life. I decided seventeen years ago that boy wasn't getting involved in no sports. Not after what they did to me in the sports.

ROSE: Troy, why don't you admit you was too old to play in the major leagues? For once . . . why don't you admit that?

TROY: What do you mean too old? Don't come telling me I was too

137

old. I just wasn't the right color. Hell, I'm fifty-three years old and can do better than Selkirk's .269 right now!

ROSE: How was you gonna play ball when you were over forty? Sometimes I can't get no sense out of you.

TROY: I got good sense, woman. I got sense enough not to let my boy get hurt over playing no sports. You been mothering that boy too much. Worried about if people like him.

ROSE: Everything that boy do . . . he do for you. He wants you to say "Good job, son." That's all.

TROY: Rose, I ain't got time for that. He's alive. He's healthy. He's got to make his own way. I made mine. Ain't nobody gonna hold his hand when he get out there in that world.

ROSE: Times have changed from when you was young, Troy. People change. The world's changing around you and you can't even see it.

TROY: (Slow, methodical.) Woman . . . I do the best I can do. I come in here every Friday. I carry a sack of potatoes and a bucket of lard. You all line up at the door with your hands out. I give you the lint from my pockets. I give you my sweat and my blood. I ain't got no tears. I done spent them. We go upstairs in that room at night . . . and I fall down on you and try to blast a hole into forever. I get up Monday morning . . . find my lunch on the table. I go out. Make my way. Find my strength to carry me through to the next Friday.
(Pause.)
That's all I got, Rose. That's all I got to give. I can't give nothing else.
(TROY exits into the house. The lights go down to black.)

ACT ONE: Scene Four

It is Friday. Two weeks later. CORY *starts out of the house with his football equipment. The phone rings.*

CORY: (*Calling.*) I got it!
(*He answers the phone and stands in the screen door talking.*)
Hello? Hey, Jesse. Naw . . . I was just getting ready to leave now.

ROSE: (*Calling.*) Cory!

CORY: I told you, man, them spikes is all tore up. You can use them if you want, but they ain't no good. Earl got some spikes.

ROSE: (*Calling.*) Cory!

CORY: (*Calling to* ROSE.) Mam? I'm talking to Jesse.
(*Into phone.*)
When she say that?
(*Pause.*)
Aw, you lying, man. I'm gonna tell her you said that.

ROSE: (*Calling.*) Cory, don't you go nowhere!

CORY: I got to go to the game, Ma!
(*Into the phone.*)
Yeah, hey, look, I'll talk to you later. Yeah, I'll meet you over at Earl's house. Later. Bye, Ma.
(CORY *exits the house and starts out the yard.*)

ROSE: Cory, where you going off to? You got that stuff all pulled out and thrown all over your room.

CORY: (*In the yard.*) I was looking for my spikes. Jesse wanted to borrow my spikes.

ROSE: Get up there and get that cleaned up before your daddy get back in here.

CORY: I got to go to the game! I'll clean it up *when I get back.*
(CORY *exits.*)

ROSE: That's all he need to do is see that room all messed up.
(ROSE *exits into the house.* TROY *and* BONO *enter the yard.* TROY *is dressed in clothes other than his work clothes.*)

BONO: He told him the same thing he told you. Take it to the union.

TROY: Brownie ain't got that much sense. Man wasn't thinking about nothing. He wait until I confront them on it . . . then he wanna come crying seniority.
(*Calls.*)
Hey, Rose!

BONO: I wish I could have seen Mr. Rand's face when he told you.

TROY: He couldn't get it out of his mouth! Liked to bit his tongue! When they called me down there to the commissioner's of-fice . . . he thought they was gonna fire me. Like everybody else.

BONO: I didn't think they was gonna fire you. I thought they was gonna put you on the warning paper.

TROY: Hey, Rose!
(*To* BONO.)
Yeah, Mr. Rand liked to bit his tongue.
(TROY *breaks the seal on the bottle, takes a drink, and hands it to* BONO.)

BONO: I see you run right down to Taylors' and told that Alberta gal.

TROY: (*Calling.*) Hey Rose!
(*To* BONO.)
I told everybody. Hey, Rose! I went down there to cash my check.

ROSE: (*Entering from the house.*) Hush all that hollering, man! I know you out here. What they say down there at the commissioner's office?

TROY: You supposed to come when I call you, woman. Bono'll tell you that.
(*To* BONO.)
Don't Lucille come when you call her?

ROSE: Man, hush your mouth. I ain't no dog . . . talk about "come when you call me."

TROY: (*Puts his arm around* ROSE.) You hear this, Bono? I had me an old dog used to get uppity like that. You say, "C'mere, Blue!" . . . and he just lay there and look at you. End up getting a stick and chasing him away trying to make him come.

ROSE: I ain't studying you and your dog. I remember you used to sing that old song.

TROY: (*He sings.*)
Hear it ring! Hear it ring!
I had a dog his name was Blue.

ROSE: Don't nobody wanna hear you sing that old song.

TROY: (*Sings.*) You know Blue was mighty true.

ROSE: Used to have Cory running around here singing that song.

BONO: Hell, I remember that song myself.

TROY: (*Sings.*)
You know Blue was a good old dog.
Blue treed a possum in a hollow log.
That was my daddy's song. My daddy made up that song.

141

ROSE: I don't care who made it up. Don't nobody wanna hear you sing it.

TROY: (*Makes a song like calling a dog.*) Come here, woman.

ROSE: You come in here carrying on, I reckon they ain't fired you. What they say down there at the commissioner's office?

TROY: Look here, Rose . . . Mr. Rand called me into his office today when I got back from talking to them people down there . . . it come from up top . . . he called me in and told me they was making me a driver.

ROSE: Troy, you kidding!

TROY: No I ain't. Ask Bono.

ROSE: Well, that's great, Troy. Now you don't have to hassle them people no more.
(LYONS *enters from the street.*)

TROY: Aw hell, I wasn't looking to see you today. I thought you was in jail. Got it all over the front page of the *Courier* about them raiding Sefus' place . . . where you be hanging out with all them thugs.

LYONS: Hey, Pop . . . that ain't got nothing to do with me. I don't go down there gambling. I go down there to sit in with the band. I ain't got nothing to do with the gambling part. They got some good music down there.

TROY: They got some rogues . . . is what they got.

LYONS: How you been, Mr. Bono? Hi, Rose.

BONO: I see where you playing down at the Crawford Grill tonight.

ROSE: How come you ain't brought Bonnie like I told you? You should have brought Bonnie with you, she ain't been over in a month of Sundays.

LYONS: I was just in the neighborhood . . . thought I'd stop by.

TROY: Here he come . . .

BONO: Your daddy got a promotion on the rubbish. He's gonna be the first colored driver. Ain't got to do nothing but sit up there and read the paper like them white fellows.

LYONS: Hey, Pop . . . if you knew how to read you'd be alright.

BONO: Naw . . . naw . . . you mean if the nigger knew how to *drive* he'd be alright. Been fighting with them people about driving and ain't even got a license. Mr. Rand know you ain't got no driver's license?

TROY: Driving ain't nothing. All you do is point the truck where you want it to go. Driving ain't nothing.

BONO: Do Mr. Rand know you ain't got no driver's license? That's what I'm talking about. I ain't asked if driving was easy. I asked if Mr. Rand know you ain't got no driver's license.

TROY: He ain't got to know. The man ain't got to know my business. Time he find out, I have two or three driver's licenses.

LYONS: (*Going into his pocket.*) Say, look here, Pop . . .

TROY: I knew it was coming. Didn't I tell you, Bono? I know what kind of "Look here, Pop" that was. The nigger fixing to ask me for some money. It's Friday night. It's my payday. All them rogues down there on the avenue . . . the ones that ain't in jail . . . and Lyons is hopping in his shoes to get down there with them.

LYONS: See, Pop . . . if you give somebody else a chance to talk sometime, you'd see that I was fixing to pay you back your ten dollars like I told you. Here . . . I told you I'd pay you when Bonnie got paid.

TROY: Naw . . . you go ahead and keep that ten dollars. Put it in the bank. The next time you feel like you wanna come by here and ask me for something . . . you go on down there and get that.

LYONS: Here's your ten dollars, Pop. I told you I don't want you to give me nothing. I just wanted to borrow ten dollars.

143

TROY: Naw . . . you go on and keep that for the next time you want to ask me.

LYONS: Come on, Pop . . . here go your ten dollars.

ROSE: Why don't you go on and let the boy pay you back, Troy?

LYONS: Here you go, Rose. If you don't take it I'm gonna have to hear about it for the next six months.
(*He hands her the money.*)

ROSE: You can hand yours over here too, Troy.

TROY: You see this, Bono. You see how they do me.

BONO: Yeah, Lucille do me the same way.
(*GABRIEL is heard singing offstage. He enters.*)

GABRIEL: Better get ready for the judgment! Better get ready for . . . Hey! . . . Hey! . . . There's Troy's boy!

LYONS: How you doing, Uncle Gabe?

GABRIEL: Lyons . . . The King of the Jungle! Rose . . . hey, Rose. Got a flower for you.
(*He takes a rose from his pocket.*)
Picked it myself. That's the same rose like you is!

ROSE: That's right nice of you, Gabe.

LYONS: What you been doing, Uncle Gabe?

GABRIEL: Oh, I been chasing hellhounds and waiting on the time to tell St. Peter to open the gates.

LYONS: You been chasing hellhounds, huh? Well . . . you doing the right thing, Uncle Gabe. Somebody got to chase them.

GABRIEL: Oh, yeah . . . I know it. The devil's strong. The devil ain't no pushover. Hellhounds snipping at everybody's heels. But I got my trumpet waiting on the judgment time.

LYONS: Waiting on the Battle of Armageddon, huh?

GABRIEL: Ain't gonna be too much of a battle when God get to waving that judgment sword. But the people's gonna have a hell of a time trying to get into heaven if them gates ain't open.

LYONS: (*Putting his arm around* GABRIEL.) You hear this, Pop. Uncle Gabe, you alright!

GABRIEL: (*Laughing with* LYONS.) Lyons! King of the Jungle.

ROSE: You gonna stay for supper, Gabe. Want me to fix you a plate?

GABRIEL: I'll take a sandwich, Rose. Don't want no plate. Just wanna eat with my hands. I'll take a sandwich.

ROSE: How about you, Lyons? You staying? Got some short ribs cooking.

LYONS: Naw, I won't eat nothing till after we finished playing. (*Pause.*)
You ought to come down and listen to me play, Pop.

TROY: I don't like that Chinese music. All that noise.

ROSE: Go on in the house and wash up, Gabe . . . I'll fix you a sandwich.

GABRIEL: (*To* LYONS, *as he exits.*) Troy's mad at me.

LYONS: What you mad at Uncle Gabe for, Pop?

ROSE: He thinks Troy's mad at him cause he moved over to Miss Pearl's.

TROY: I ain't mad at the man. He can live where he want to live at.

LYONS: What he move over there for? Miss Pearl don't like nobody.

ROSE: She don't mind him none. She treats him real nice. She just don't allow all that singing.

TROY: She don't mind that rent he be paying . . . that's what she don't mind.

ROSE: Troy, I ain't going through that with you no more. He's over there cause he want to have his own place. He can come and go as he please.

145

TROY: Hell, he could come and go as he please here. I wasn't stopping him. I ain't put no rules on him.

ROSE: It ain't the same thing, Troy. And you know it.
(GABRIEL *comes to the door.*)
Now, that's the last I wanna hear about that. I don't wanna hear nothing else about Gabe and Miss Pearl. And next week . . .

GABRIEL: I'm ready for my sandwich, Rose.

ROSE: And next week . . . when that recruiter come from that school . . . I want you to sign that paper and go on and let Cory play football. Then that'll be the last I have to hear about that.

TROY: (*To* ROSE *as she exits into the house.*) I ain't thinking about Cory nothing.

LYONS: What . . . Cory got recruited? What school he going to?

TROY: That boy walking around here smelling his piss . . . thinking he's grown. Thinking he's gonna do what he want, irrespective of what I say. Look here, Bono . . . I left the Commissioner's office and went down to the A&P . . . that boy ain't working down there. He lying to me. Telling me he got his job back . . . telling me he working weekends . . . telling me he working after school . . . Mr. Stawicki tell me he ain't working down there at all!

LYONS: Cory just growing up. He's just busting at the seams trying to fill out your shoes.

TROY: I don't care what he's doing. When he get to the point where he wanna disobey me . . . then it's time for him to move on. Bono'll tell you that. I bet he ain't never disobeyed his daddy without paying the consequences.

BONO: I ain't never had a chance. My daddy came on through . . . but I ain't never knew him to see him . . . or what he had on his mind or where he went. Just moving on through. Searching out the New Land. That's what the old folks used to call it. See a fellow moving around from place to place . . . woman to woman . . . called it searching out the New Land. I can't say if he ever found it. I come along, didn't want no kids. Didn't know if I was gonna be in one place long enough to fix on them right as their daddy. I figured I was going searching too. As it turned out I been hooked up with Lucille near about as long as your daddy been with Rose. Going on sixteen years.

TROY: Sometimes I wish I hadn't known my daddy. He ain't cared nothing about no kids. A kid to him wasn't nothing. All he wanted was for you to learn how to walk so he could start you to working. When it come time for eating . . . he ate first. If there was anything left over, that's what you got. Man would sit down and eat two chickens and give you the wing.

LYONS: You ought to stop that, Pop. Everybody feed their kids. No matter how hard times is . . . everybody care about their kids. Make sure they have something to eat.

TROY: The only thing my daddy cared about was getting them bales of cotton in to Mr. Lubin. That's the only thing that mattered to him. Sometimes I used to wonder why he was living. Wonder why the devil hadn't come and got him. "Get them bales of cotton in to Mr. Lubin" and find out he owe him money . . .

LYONS: He should have just went on and left when he saw he couldn't get nowhere. That's what I would have done.

TROY: How he gonna leave with eleven kids? And where he gonna go? He ain't knew how to do nothing but farm. No, he was trapped and I think he knew it. But I'll say this for him . . . he felt a responsibility toward us. Maybe he ain't treated us the way I felt he should have . . . but without that responsibility he could have walked off and left us . . . made his own way.

BONO: A lot of them did. Back in those days what you talking about . . . they walk out their front door and just take on down one road or another and keep on walking.

LYONS: There you go! That's what I'm talking about.

BONO: Just keep on walking till you come to something else. Ain't you never heard of nobody having the walking blues? Well, that's what you call it when you just take off like that.

TROY: My daddy ain't had them walking blues! What you talking about? He stayed right there with his family. But he was just as evil as he could be. My mama couldn't stand him. Couldn't stand that evilness. She run off when I was about eight. She sneaked off one night after he had gone to sleep. Told me she was coming back for me. I ain't never seen her no more. All his women run off and left him. He wasn't good for nobody.

When my turn come to head out, I was fourteen and got to sniffing around Joe Canewell's daughter. Had us an old mule we called Greyboy. My daddy sent me out to do some plowing and I tied up Greyboy and went to fooling around with Joe Canewell's daughter. We done found us a nice little spot, got real cozy with each other. She about thirteen and we done figured we was grown anyway . . . so we down there enjoying ourselves . . . ain't thinking about nothing. We didn't know Greyboy had got loose and wandered back to the house and my daddy was looking for me. We down there by the creek enjoying ourselves when my daddy come up on us. Surprised us. He had them leather straps off the mule and commenced to whupping me like there was no tomorrow. I jumped up, mad and embarrassed. I was scared of my daddy. When he commenced to whupping on me . . . quite naturally I run to get out of the way.
(Pause.)
Now I thought he was mad cause I ain't done my work. But I see where he was chasing me off so he could have the gal for himself. When I see what the matter of it was, I lost all fear of my daddy. Right there is where I become a man . . . at fourteen years of age.
(Pause.)
Now it was my turn to run him off. I picked up them same reins that he had used on me. I picked up them reins and commenced to whupping on him. The gal jumped up and run off . . . and when my daddy turned to face me, I could see why the devil had never come to get him . . . cause he was the devil himself. I

148

don't know what happened. When I woke up, I was laying right there by the creek, and Blue . . . this old dog we had . . . was licking my face. I thought I was blind. I couldn't see nothing. Both my eyes were swollen shut. I laid there and cried. I didn't know what I was gonna do. The only thing I knew was the time had come for me to leave my daddy's house. And right there the world suddenly got big. And it was a long time before I could cut it down to where I could handle it.

Part of that cutting down was when I got to the place where I could feel him kicking in my blood and knew that the only thing that separated us was the matter of a few years.

(GABRIEL *enters from the house with a sandwich.*)

LYONS: What you got there, Uncle Gabe?

GABRIEL: Got me a ham sandwich. Rose gave me a ham sandwich.

TROY: I don't know what happened to him. I done lost touch with everybody except Gabriel. But I hope he's dead. I hope he found some peace.

LYONS: That's a heavy story, Pop. I didn't know you left home when you was fourteen.

TROY: And didn't know nothing. The only part of the world I knew was the forty-two acres of Mr. Lubin's land. That's all I knew about life.

LYONS: Fourteen's kinda young to be out on your own.
(*Phone rings.*)
I don't even think I was ready to be out on my own at fourteen. I don't know what I would have done.

TROY: I got up from the creek and walked on down to Mobile. I was through with farming. Figured I could do better in the city. So I walked the two hundred miles to Mobile.

LYONS: Wait a minute . . . you ain't walked no two hundred miles, Pop. Ain't nobody gonna walk no two hundred miles. You talking about some walking there.

149

BONO: That's the only way you got anywhere back in them days.

LYONS: Shhh. Damn if I wouldn't have hitched a ride with somebody!

TROY: Who you gonna hitch it with? They ain't had no cars and
things like they got now. We talking about 1918.

ROSE: (*Entering.*) What you all out here getting into?

TROY: (*To* ROSE.) I'm telling Lyons how good he got it. He don't
know nothing about this I'm talking.

ROSE: Lyons, that was Bonnie on the phone. She say you supposed
to pick her up.

LYONS: Yeah, okay, Rose.

TROY: I walked on down to Mobile and hitched up with some of
them fellows that was heading this way. Got up here and found
out . . . not only couldn't you get a job . . . you couldn't find
no place to live. I thought I was in freedom. Shhh. Colored folks
living down there on the riverbanks in whatever kind of shelter
they could find for themselves. Right down there under the
Brady Street Bridge. Living in shacks made of sticks and tar-
paper. Messed around there and went from bad to worse. Started
stealing. First it was food. Then I figured, hell, if I steal money I
can buy me some food. Buy me some shoes too! One thing led to
another. Met your mama. I was young and anxious to be a man.
Met your mama and had you. What I do that for? Now I got to
worry about feeding you and her. Got to steal three times as
much. Went out one day looking for somebody to rob . . . that's
what I was, a robber. I'll tell you the truth. I'm ashamed of it
today. But it's the truth. Went to rob this fellow . . . pulled out
my knife . . . and he pulled out a gun. Shot me in the chest. It
felt just like somebody had taken a hot branding iron and laid it
on me. When he shot me I jumped at him with my knife. They
told me I killed him and they put me in the penitentiary and
locked me up for fifteen years. That's where I met Bono. That's
where I learned how to play baseball. Got out that place and your

mama had taken you and went on to make life without me. Fifteen years was a long time for her to wait. But that fifteen years cured me of that robbing stuff. Rose'll tell you. She asked me when I met her if I had gotten all that foolishness out of my system. And I told her, "Baby, it's you and baseball all what count with me." You hear me, Bono? I meant it too. She say, "Which one comes first?" I told her, "Baby, ain't no doubt it's baseball . . . but you stick and get old with me and we'll both outlive this baseball." Am I right, Rose? And it's true.

ROSE: Man, hush your mouth. You ain't said no such thing. Talking about, "Baby, you know you'll always be number one with me." That's what you was talking.

TROY: You hear that, Bono. That's why I love her.

BONO: Rose'll keep you straight. You get off the track, she'll straighten you up.

ROSE: Lyons, you better get on up and get Bonnie. She waiting on you.

LYONS: (Gets up to go.) Hey, Pop, why don't you come on down to the Grill and hear me play?

TROY: I ain't going down there. I'm too old to be sitting around in them clubs.

BONO: You got to be good to play down at the Grill.

LYONS: Come on, Pop . . .

TROY: I got to get up in the morning.

LYONS: You ain't got to stay long.

TROY: Naw, I'm gonna get my supper and go on to bed.

LYONS: Well, I got to go. I'll see you again.

TROY: Don't you come around my house on my payday.

ROSE: Pick up the phone and let somebody know you coming. And bring Bonnie with you. You know I'm always glad to see her.

151

LYONS: Yeah, I'll do that, Rose. You take care now. See you, Pop. See you, Mr. Bono. See you, Uncle Gabe.

GABRIEL: Lyons! King of the Jungle!
(LYONS *exits.*)

TROY: Is supper ready, woman? Me and you got some business to take care of. I'm gonna tear it up too.

ROSE: Troy, I done told you now!

TROY: (*Puts his arm around* BONO.) Aw hell, woman . . . this is Bono. Bono like family. I done known this nigger since . . . how long I done known you?

BONO: It's been a long time.

TROY: I done known this nigger since Skippy was a pup. Me and him done been through some times.

BONO: You sure right about that.

TROY: Hell, I done known him longer than I known you. And we still standing shoulder to shoulder. Hey, look here, Bono . . . a man can't ask for no more than that.
(*Drinks to him.*)
I love you, nigger.

BONO: Hell, I love you too . . . but I got to get home see my woman. You got yours in hand. I got to go get mine.
(BONO *starts to exit as* CORY *enters the yard, dressed in his football uniform. He gives* TROY *a hard, uncompromising look.*)

CORY: What you do that for, Pop?
(*He throws his helmet down in the direction of* TROY.)

ROSE: What's the matter? Cory . . . what's the matter?

CORY: Papa done went up to the school and told Coach Zellman I can't play football no more. Wouldn't even let me play the game. Told him to tell the recruiter not to come.

ROSE: Troy . . .

152

TROY: What you Troying me for? Yeah, I did it. And the boy know why I did it.

CORY: Why you wanna do that to me? That was the one chance I had.

ROSE: Ain't nothing wrong with Cory playing football, Troy.

TROY: The boy lied to me. I told the nigger if he wanna play foot-ball . . . to keep up his chores and hold down that job at the A&P. That was the conditions. Stopped down there to see Mr. Stawicki . . .

CORY: I can't work after school during the football season, Pop! I tried to tell you that Mr. Stawicki's holding my job for me. You don't never want to listen to nobody. And then you wanna go and do this to me!

TROY: I ain't done nothing to you. You done it to yourself.

CORY: Just cause you didn't have a chance! You just scared I'm gonna be better than you, that's all.

TROY: Come here.

ROSE: Troy . . .
(CORY *reluctantly crosses over to* TROY.)

TROY: Alright! See. You done made a mistake.

CORY: I didn't even do nothing!

TROY: I'm gonna tell you what your mistake was. See . . . you swung at the ball and didn't hit it. That's strike one. See, you in the batter's box now. You swung and you missed. That's strike one. Don't you strike out!
(*Lights fade to black.*)

153

ACT TWO: Scene One

The following morning. CORY *is at the tree hitting the ball with the bat. He tries to mimic* TROY, *but his swing is awkward, less sure.* ROSE *enters from the house.*

ROSE: Cory, I want you to help me with this cupboard.

CORY: I ain't quitting the team. I don't care what Poppa say.

ROSE: I'll talk to him when he gets back. He had to go see about your Uncle Gabe. The police done arrested him. Say he was disturbing the peace. He'll be back directly. Come on in here and help me clean out the top of this cupboard.
(CORY *exits into the house.* ROSE *sees* TROY *and* BONO *coming down the alley.*)
Troy . . . what they say down there?

TROY: Ain't said nothing. I give them fifty dollars and they let him go. I'll talk to you about it. Where's Cory?

ROSE: He's in there helping me clean out these cupboards.

TROY: Tell him to get his butt out here.
(TROY *and* BONO *go over to the pile of wood.* BONO *picks up the saw and begins sawing.*)

TROY: (*To* BONO.) All they want is the money. That makes six or seven times I done went down there and got him. See me coming they stick out their *hands.*

BONO: Yeah. I know what you mean. That's all they care about . . . that money. They don't care about what's right.
(*Pause.*)
Nigger, why you got to go and get some hard wood? You ain't doing nothing but building a little old fence. Get you some soft pine wood. That's all you need.

TROY: I know what I'm doing. This is outside wood. You put pine wood inside the house. Pine wood is inside wood. This here is outside wood. Now you tell me where the fence is gonna be?

BONO: You don't need this wood. You can put it up with pine wood and it'll stand as long as you gonna be here looking at it.

TROY: How you know how long I'm gonna be here, nigger? Hell, I might just live forever. Live longer than old man Horsely.

BONO: That's what Magee used to say.

TROY: Magee's a damn fool. Now you tell me who you ever heard of gonna pull their own teeth with a pair of rusty pliers.

BONO: The old folks . . . my granddaddy used to pull his teeth with pliers. They ain't had no dentists for the colored folks back then.

TROY: Get clean pliers! You understand? Clean pliers! Sterilize them! Besides we ain't living back then. All Magee had to do was walk over to Doc Goldblum's.

BONO: I see where you and that Tallahassee gal . . . that Alberta . . . I see where you all done got tight.

TROY: What you mean "got tight?"

BONO: I see where you be laughing and joking with her all the time.

TROY: I laughs and jokes with all of them, Bono. You know me.

BONO: That ain't the kind of laughing and joking I'm talking about.
(CORY *enters from the house.*)

CORY: How you doing, Mr. Bono?

TROY: Cory? Get that saw from Bono and cut some wood. He

talking about the wood's too hard to cut. Stand back there, Jim, and let that young boy show you how it's done.

BONO: He's sure welcome to it.
(GORY *takes the saw and begins to cut the wood.*)
Whew-e-e! Look at that. Big old strong boy. Look like Joe Louis. Hell, must be getting old the way I'm watching that boy whip through that wood.

CORY: I don't see why Mama want a fence around the yard noways.

TROY: Damn if I know either. What the hell she keeping out with it? She ain't got nothing nobody want.

BONO: Some people build fences to keep people out . . . and other people build fences to keep people in. Rose wants to hold on to you all. She loves you.

TROY: Hell, nigger, I don't need nobody to tell me my wife loves me. Cory . . . go on in the house and see if you can find that other saw.

CORY: Where's it at?

TROY: I said find it! Look for it till you find it!
(CORY *exits into the house.*)
What's that supposed to mean? Wanna keep us in?

BONO: Troy . . . I done known you seem like damn near my whole life. You and Rose both. I done known both of you all for a long time. I remember when you met Rose. When you was hitting them baseball out the park. A lot of them old gals was after you then. You had the pick of the litter. When you picked Rose, I was happy for you. That was the first time I knew you had any sense. I said . . . My man Troy knows what he's doing . . . I'm gonna follow this nigger . . . he might take me somewhere. I been following you too. I done learned a whole heap of things about life watching you. I done learned how to tell where the shit lies. How to tell it from the alfalfa. You done learned me a lot of things. You showed me how to not make the same mistakes . . .

157

to take life as it comes along and keep putting one foot in front of the other.
(*Pause.*)
Rose a good woman, Troy.

TROY: Hell, nigger, I know she a good woman. I been married to her for eighteen years. What you got on your mind, Bono?

BONO: I just say she a good woman. Just like I say anything. I ain't got to have nothing on my mind.

TROY: You just gonna say she a good woman and leave it hanging out there like that? Why you telling me she a good woman?

BONO: She loves you, Troy. Rose loves you.

TROY: You saying I don't measure up. That's what you trying to say. I don't measure up cause I'm seeing this other gal. I know what you trying to say.

BONO: I know what Rose means to you, Troy. I'm just trying to say I don't want to see you mess up.

TROY: Yeah, I appreciate that, Bono. If you was messing around on Lucille I'd be telling you the same thing.

BONO: Well, that's all I got to say. I just say that because I love you both.

TROY: Hell, you know me . . . I wasn't out there looking for nothing. You can't find a better woman than Rose. I know that. But seems like this woman just stuck onto me where I can't shake her loose. I done wrestled with it, tried to throw her off me . . . but she just stuck on tighter. Now she's stuck on for good.

BONO: You's in control . . . that's what you tell me all the time. You responsible for what you do.

TROY: I ain't ducking the responsibility of it. As long as it sets right in my heart . . . then I'm okay. Cause that's all I listen to. It'll tell me right from wrong every time. And I ain't talking about doing Rose no bad turn. I love Rose. She done carried me a long ways and I love and respect her for that.

BONO: I know you do. That's why I don't want to see you hurt her. But what you gonna do when she find out? What you got then? If you try and juggle both of them . . . sooner or later you gonna drop one of them. That's common sense.

TROY: Yeah, I hear what you saying, Bono. I been trying to figure a way to work it out.

BONO: Work it out right, Troy. I don't want to be getting all up between you and Rose's business . . . but work it so it come out right.

TROY: Aw hell, I get all up between you and Lucille's business. When you gonna get that woman that refrigerator she been wanting? Don't tell me you ain't got no money now. I know who your banker is. Mellon don't need that money bad as Lucille want that refrigerator. I'll tell you that.

BONO: Tell you what I'll do . . . when you finish building this fence for Rose . . . I'll buy Lucille that refrigerator.

TROY: You done stuck your foot in your mouth now!
(TROY *grabs up a board and begins to saw.* BONO *starts to walk out the yard.*)
Hey, nigger . . . where you going?

BONO: I'm going home. I know you don't expect me to help you now. I'm protecting my money. I wanna see you put that fence up by yourself. That's what I want to see. You'll be here another six months without me.

TROY: Nigger, you ain't right.

BONO: When it comes to my money . . . I'm right as fireworks on the Fourth of July.

TROY: Alright, we gonna see now. You better get out your bank-book.

(BONO *exits, and* TROY *continues to work.* ROSE *enters from the house.*)

ROSE: What they say down there? What's happening with Gabe?

TROY: I went down there and got him out. Cost me fifty dollars. Say he was disturbing the peace. Judge set up a hearing for him in three weeks. Say to show cause why he shouldn't be recommitted.

ROSE: What was he doing that cause them to arrest him?

TROY: Some kids was teasing him and he run them off home. Say he was howling and carrying on. Some folks seen him and called the police. That's all it was.

ROSE: Well, what'd you say? What'd you tell the judge?

TROY: Told him I'd look after him. It didn't make no sense to recommit the man. He stuck out his big greasy palm and told me to give him fifty dollars and take him on home.

ROSE: Where's he at now? Where'd he go off to?

TROY: He's gone on about his business. He don't need nobody to hold his hand.

ROSE: Well, I don't know. Seem like that would be the best place for him if they did put him into the hospital. I know what you're gonna say. But that's what I think would be best.

TROY: The man done had his life ruined fighting for what? And they wanna take and lock him up. Let him be free. He don't bother nobody.

ROSE: Well, everybody got their own way of looking at it, I guess. Come on and get your lunch. I got a bowl of lima beans and some cornbread in the oven. Come on get something to eat. Ain't no sense you fretting over Gabe.
(ROSE *turns to go into the house.*)

TROY: Rose . . . got something to tell you.

ROSE: Well, come on . . . wait till I get this food on the table.

TROY: Rose!
(*She stops and turns around.*)
I don't know how to say this.
(*Pause.*)
I can't explain it none. It just sort of grows on you till it gets out of hand. It starts out like a little bush . . . and the next thing you know it's a whole forest.

ROSE: Troy . . . what is you talking about?

TROY: I'm talking, woman, let me talk. I'm trying to find a way to tell you . . . I'm gonna be a daddy. I'm gonna be somebody's daddy.

ROSE: Troy . . . you're not telling me this? You're gonna be . . . what?

TROY: Rose . . . now . . . see . . .

ROSE: You telling me you gonna be somebody's daddy? You telling your *wife* this?
(GABRIEL *enters from the street. He carries a rose in his hand.*)

GABRIEL: Hey, Troy! Hey, Rose!

ROSE: I have to wait eighteen years to hear something like this.

GABRIEL: Hey, Rose . . . I got a flower for you.
(*He hands it to her.*)
That's a rose. Same rose like you is.

ROSE: Thanks, Gabe.

GABRIEL: Troy, you ain't mad at me is you? Them bad mens come and put me away. You ain't mad at me is you?

TROY: Naw, Gabe, I ain't mad at you.

ROSE: Eighteen years and you wanna come with this.

GABRIEL: (*Takes a quarter out of his pocket.*) See what I got? Got a brand new quarter.

TROY: Rose . . . it's just . . .

161

ROSE: Ain't nothing you can say, Troy. Ain't no way of explaining that.

GABRIEL: Fellow that give me this quarter had a whole mess of them. I'm gonna keep this quarter till it stop shining.

ROSE: Gabe, go on in the house there. I got some watermelon in the Frigidaire. Go on and get you a piece.

GABRIEL: Say, Rose . . . you know I was chasing hellhounds and them bad mens come and get me and take me away. Troy helped me. He come down there and told them they better let me go before he beat them up. Yeah, he did!

ROSE: You go on and get you a piece of watermelon, Gabe. Them bad mens is gone now.

GABRIEL: Okay, Rose . . . gonna get me some watermelon. The kind with the stripes on it.
(GABRIEL *exits into the house.*)

ROSE: Why, Troy? Why? After all these years to come dragging this in to me now. It don't make no sense at your age. I could have expected this ten or fifteen years ago, but not now.

TROY: Age ain't got nothing to do with it, Rose.

ROSE: I done tried to be everything a wife should be. Everything a wife could be. Been married eighteen years and I got to live to see the day you tell me you been seeing another woman and done fathered a child by her. And you know I ain't never wanted no half nothing in my family. My whole family is half. Everybody got different fathers and mothers . . . my two sisters and my brother. Can't hardly tell who's who. Can't never sit down and talk about Papa and Mama. It's your papa and your mama and my papa and my mama . . .

TROY: Rose . . . stop it now.

ROSE: I ain't never wanted that for none of my children. And now you wanna drag your behind in here and tell me something like this.

162

TROY: You ought to know. It's time for you to know.

ROSE: Well, I don't want to know, goddamn it!

TROY: I can't just make it go away. It's done now. I can't wish the circumstance of the thing away.

ROSE: And you don't want to either. Maybe you want to wish me and my boy away. Maybe that's what you want? Well, you can't wish us away. I've got eighteen years of my life invested in you. You ought to have stayed upstairs in my bed where you belong.

TROY: Rose . . . now listen to me . . . we can get a handle on this thing. We can talk this out . . . come to an understanding.

ROSE: All of a sudden it's "we." Where was "we" at when you was down there rolling around with some godforsaken woman? "We" should have come to an understanding before you started making a damn fool of yourself. You're a day late and a dollar short when it comes to an understanding with me.

TROY: It's just . . . She gives me a different idea . . . a different understanding about myself. I can step out of this house and get away from the pressures and problems . . . be a different man. I ain't got to wonder how I'm gonna pay the bills or get the roof fixed. I can just be a part of myself that I ain't never been.

ROSE: What I want to know . . . is do you plan to continue seeing her? That's all you can say to me.

TROY: I can sit up in her house and laugh. Do you understand what I'm saying? I can laugh out loud . . . and it feels good. It reaches all the way down to the bottom of my shoes.
(*Pause.*)
Rose, I can't give that up.

ROSE: Maybe you ought to go on and stay down there with her . . . if she a better woman than me.

TROY: It ain't about nobody being a better woman or nothing. Rose, you ain't the blame. A man couldn't ask for no woman to be a better wife than you've been. I'm responsible for it. I done

163

locked myself into a pattern trying to take care of you all that I forgot about myself.

ROSE: What the hell was I there for? That was my job, not somebody else's.

TROY: Rose, I done tried all my life to live decent . . . to live a clean . . . hard . . . useful life. I tried to be a good husband to you. In every way I knew how. Maybe I come into the world backwards, I don't know. But . . . you born with two strikes on you before you come to the plate. You got to guard it closely . . . always looking for the curve ball on the inside corner. You can't afford to let none get past you. You can't afford a call strike. If you going down . . . you going down swinging. Everything lined up against you. What you gonna do? I fooled them, Rose. I bunted. When I found you and Cory and a halfway decent job . . . I was safe. Couldn't nothing touch me. I wasn't gonna strike out no more. I wasn't going back to the penitentiary. I wasn't gonna lay in the streets with a bottle of wine. I was safe. I had me a family. A job. I wasn't gonna get that last strike. I was on first looking for one of them boys to knock me in. To get me home.

ROSE: You should have stayed in my bed, Troy.

TROY: Then when I saw that gal . . . she firmed up my backbone. And I got to thinking that if I tried . . . I just might be able to steal second. Do you understand after eighteen years I wanted to steal second?

ROSE: You should have held me tight. You should have grabbed me and held on.

TROY: I stood on first base for eighteen years and I thought . . . well, goddamn it . . . go on for it!

ROSE: We're not talking about baseball! We're talking about you going off to lay in bed with another woman . . . and then bring it home to me. That's what we're talking about. We ain't talking about no baseball.

TROY: Rose, you're not listening to me. I'm trying the best I can to explain it to you. It's not easy for me to admit that I been standing in the same place for eighteen years.

ROSE: I been standing with you! I been right here with you, Troy. I got a life too. I gave eighteen years of my life to stand in the same spot with you. Don't you think I ever wanted other things? Don't you think I had dreams and hopes? What about my life? What about me? Don't you think it ever crossed my mind to want to know other men? That I wanted to lay up somewhere and forget about my responsibilities? That I wanted someone to make me laugh so I could feel good? You not the only one who's got wants and needs. But I held on to you, Troy. I took all my feelings, my wants and needs, my dreams . . . and I buried them inside you. I planted a seed and watched and prayed over it. I planted myself inside you and waited to bloom. And it didn't take me no eighteen years to find out the soil was hard and rocky and it wasn't never gonna bloom.

But I held on to you, Troy. I held you tighter. You was my husband. I owed you everything I had. Every part of me I could find to give you. And upstairs in that room . . . with the darkness falling in on me . . . I gave everything I had to try and erase the doubt that you wasn't the finest man in the world. And wherever you was going . . . I wanted to be there with you. Cause you was my husband. Cause that's the only way I was gonna survive as your wife. You always talking about what you give . . . and what you don't have to give. But you take, too. You take . . . and don't even know nobody's giving!

(ROSE *turns to exit into the house;* TROY *grabs her arm.*)

TROY: You say I take and don't give!

ROSE: Troy! You're hurting me!

TROY: You say I take and don't give.

ROSE: Troy . . . you're hurting my arm! Let go!

TROY: I done give you everything I got. Don't you tell that lie on me.

165

ROSE: Troy!

TROY: Don't you tell that lie on me!
(CORY *enters from the house.*)

CORY: Mama!

ROSE: Troy. You're hurting me.

TROY: Don't you tell me about no taking and giving.
(CORY *comes up behind* TROY *and grabs him.* TROY, *surprised, is thrown off balance just as* CORY *throws a glancing blow that catches him on the chest and knocks him down.* TROY *is stunned, as is* CORY.)

ROSE: Troy. Troy. No!
(TROY *gets to his feet and starts at* CORY.)
Troy . . . no. Please! Troy!
(ROSE *pulls on* TROY *to hold him back.* TROY *stops himself.*)

TROY: (*To* CORY.) Alright. That's strike two. You stay away from around me, boy. Don't you strike out. You living with a full count. Don't you strike out.
(TROY *exits out the yard as the lights go down.*)

ACT TWO: Scene Two

It is six months later, early afternoon. TROY *enters from the house and starts to exit the yard.* ROSE *enters from the house.*

ROSE: Troy, I want to talk to you.

TROY: All of a sudden, after all this time, you want to talk to me, huh? You ain't wanted to talk to me for months. You ain't wanted to talk to me last night. You ain't wanted no part of me then. What you wanna talk to me about now?

ROSE: Tomorrow's Friday.

TROY: I know what day tomorrow is. You think I don't know tomorrow's Friday? My whole life I ain't done nothing but look to see Friday coming and you got to tell me it's Friday.

ROSE: I want to know if you're coming home.

TROY: I always come home, Rose. You know that. There ain't never been a night I ain't come home.

ROSE: That ain't what I mean . . . and you know it. I want to know if you're coming straight home after work.

TROY: I figure I'd cash my check . . . hang out at Taylors' with the boys . . . maybe play a game of checkers . . .

ROSE: Troy, I can't live like this. I won't live like this. You livin on borrowed time with me. It's been going on six months now you ain't been coming home.

167

TROY: I be here every night. Every night of the year. That's 365 days.

ROSE: I want you to come home tomorrow after work.

TROY: Rose . . . I don't mess up my pay. You know that now. I take my pay and I give it to you. I don't have no money but what you give me back. I just want to have a little time to myself . . . a little time to enjoy life.

ROSE: What about me? When's my time to enjoy life?

TROY: I don't know what to tell you, Rose. I'm doing the best I can.

ROSE: You ain't been home from work but time enough to change your clothes and run out . . . and you wanna call that the best you can do?

TROY: I'm going over to the hospital to see Alberta. She went into the hospital this afternoon. Look like she might have the baby early. I won't be gone long.

ROSE: Well, you ought to know. They went over to Miss Pearl's and got Gabe today. She said you told them to go ahead and lock him up.

TROY: I ain't said no such thing. Whoever told you that is telling a lie. Pearl ain't doing nothing but telling a big fat lie.

ROSE: She ain't had to tell me. I read it on the papers.

TROY: I ain't told them nothing of the kind.

ROSE: I saw it right there on the papers.

TROY: What it say, huh?

ROSE: It said you told them to take him.

TROY: Then they screwed that up, just the way they screw up everything. I ain't worried about what they got on the paper.

ROSE: Say the government send part of his check to the hospital and the other part to you.

TROY: I ain't got nothing to do with that if that's the way it works. I ain't made up the rules about how it work.

ROSE: You did Gabe just like you did Cory. You wouldn't sign the paper for Cory . . . but you signed for Gabe. You signed that paper.
(*The telephone is heard ringing inside the house.*)

TROY: I told you I ain't signed nothing, woman! The only thing I signed was the release form. Hell, I can't read, I don't know what they had on that paper! I ain't signed nothing about sending Gabe away.

ROSE: I said send him to the hospital . . . you said let him be free . . . now you done went down there and signed him to the hospital for half his money. You went back on yourself, Troy. You gonna have to answer for that.

TROY: See now . . . you been over there talking to Miss Pearl. She done got mad cause she ain't getting Gabe's rent money. That's all it is. She's liable to say anything.

ROSE: Troy, I seen where you signed the paper.

TROY: You ain't seen nothing I signed. What she doing got papers on my brother anyway? Miss Pearl telling a big fat lie. And I'm gonna tell her about it too! You ain't seen nothing I signed. Say . . . you ain't seen nothing I signed.
(ROSE *exits into the house to answer the telephone. Presently she returns*).

ROSE: Troy . . . that was the hospital. Alberta had the baby.

TROY: What she have? What is it?

ROSE: It's a girl.

TROY: I better get on down to the hospital to see her.

ROSE: Troy . . .

TROY: Rose . . . I got to go see her now. That's only right . . . what's the matter . . . the baby's alright, ain't it?

169

ROSE: Alberta died having the baby.

TROY: Died . . . you say she's dead? Alberta's dead?

ROSE: They said they done all they could. They couldn't do nothing for her.

TROY: The baby? How's the baby?

ROSE: They say it's healthy. I wonder who's gonna bury her.

TROY: She had family, Rose. She wasn't living in the world by herself.

ROSE: I know she wasn't living in the world by herself.

TROY: Next thing you gonna want to know if she had any insurance.

ROSE: Troy, you ain't got to talk like that.

TROY: That's the first thing that jumped out your mouth. "Who's gonna bury her?" Like I'm fixing to take on that task for myself.

ROSE: I am your wife. Don't push me away.

TROY: I ain't pushing nobody away. Just give me some space. That's all. Just give me some room to breathe.
(ROSE *exits into the house.* TROY *walks about the yard.*)

TROY: (*With a quiet rage that threatens to consume him.*) Alright . . . Mr. Death. See now . . . I'm gonna tell you what I'm gonna do. I'm gonna take and build me a fence around this yard. See? I'm gonna build me a fence around what belongs to me. And then I want you to stay on the other side. See? You stay over there until you're ready for me. Then you come on. Bring your army. Bring your sickle. Bring your wrestling clothes. I ain't gonna fall down on my vigilance this time. You ain't gonna sneak up on me no more. When you ready for me . . . when the top of your list say Troy Maxson . . . that's when you come around here. You come up and knock on the front door. Ain't nobody else got nothing to do with this. This is between you and

me. Man to man. You stay on the other side of that fence until you ready for me. Then you come up and knock on the front door. Anytime you want. I'll be ready for you.
(*The lights go down to black.*)

ACT TWO: Scene Three

The lights come up on the porch. It is late evening three days later. ROSE *sits listening to the ball game waiting for* TROY. *The final out of the game is made and* ROSE *switches off the radio.* TROY *enters the yard carrying an infant wrapped in blankets. He stands back from the house and calls.*

(ROSE *enters and stands on the porch. There is a long, awkward silence, the weight of which grows heavier with each passing second.*)

TROY: Rose . . . I'm standing here with my daughter in my arms. She ain't but a wee bitty little old thing. She don't know nothing about grownups' business. She innocent . . . and she ain't got no mama.

ROSE: What you telling me for, Troy?
(*She turns and exits into the house.*)

TROY: Well . . . I guess we'll just sit out here on the porch.
(*He sits down on the porch. There is an awkward indelicateness about the way he handles the baby. His largeness engulfs and seems to swallow it. He speaks loud enough for* ROSE *to hear.*)
A man's got to do what's right for him. I ain't sorry for nothing I done. It felt right in my heart.
(*To the baby.*)
What you smiling at? Your daddy's a big man. Got these great big old hands. But sometimes he's scared. And right now your daddy's scared cause we sitting out here and ain't got no home. Oh, I been homeless before. I ain't had no little baby with me.

172

But I been homeless. You just be out on the road by your lone-some and you see one of them trains coming and you just kinda go like this . . .
(*He sings as a lullaby.*)
Please, Mr. Engineer let a man ride the line
Please, Mr. Engineer let a man ride the line
I ain't got no ticket please let me ride the blinds
(ROSE *enters from the house.* TROY *hearing her steps behind him, stands and faces her.*)
She's my daughter, Rose. My own flesh and blood. I can't deny her no more than I can deny them boys.
(*Pause.*)
You and them boys is my family. You and them and this child is all I got in the world. So I guess what I'm saying is . . . I'd appreciate it if you'd help me take care of her.

ROSE: Okay, Troy . . . you're right. I'll take care of your baby for you . . . cause . . . like you say . . . she's innocent . . . and you can't visit the sins of the father upon the child. A motherless child has got a hard time.
(*She takes the baby from him.*)
From right now . . . this child got a mother. But you a woman-less man.
(ROSE *turns and exits into the house with the baby. Lights go down to black.*)

173

ACT TWO: Scene Four

It is two months later. LYONS *enters from the street. He knocks on the door and calls.*

LYONS: Hey, Rose!
(*Pause.*)
Rose!

ROSE: (*From inside the house.*) Stop that yelling. You gonna wake up Raynell. I just got her to sleep.

LYONS: I just stopped by to pay Papa this twenty dollars I owe him. Where's Papa at?

ROSE: He should be here in a minute. I'm getting ready to go down to the church. Sit down and wait on him.

LYONS: I got to go pick up Bonnie over her mother's house.

ROSE: Well, sit it down there on the table. He'll get it.

LYONS: (*Enters the house and sets the money on the table.*) Tell Papa I said thanks. I'll see you again.

ROSE: Alright, Lyons. We'll see you.
(LYONS *starts to exit as* CORY *enters.*)

CORY: Hey, Lyons.

LYONS: What's happening, Cory. Say man, I'm sorry I missed your graduation. You know I had a gig and couldn't get away. Otherwise, I would have been there, man. So what you doing?

CORY: I'm trying to find a job.

LYONS: Yeah, I know how that go, man. It's rough out here. Jobs are scarce.

CORY: Yeah, I know.

LYONS: Look here, I got to run. Talk to Papa . . . he know some people. He'll be able to help get you a job. Talk to him . . . see what he say.

CORY: Yeah . . . alright, Lyons.

LYONS: You take care. I'll talk to you soon. We'll find some time to talk.
(LYONS *exits the yard.* CORY *wanders over to the tree, picks up the bat and assumes a batting stance. He studies an imaginary pitcher and swings. Dissatisfied with the result, he tries again.* TROY *enters. They eye each other for a beat.* CORY *puts the bat down and exits the yard.* TROY *starts into the house as* ROSE *exits with* RAYNELL. *She is carrying a cake.*)

TROY: I'm coming in and everybody's going out.

ROSE: I'm taking this cake down to the church for the bake sale. Lyons was by to see you. He stopped by to pay you your twenty dollars. It's laying in there on the table.

TROY: (*Going into his pocket.*) Well . . . here go this money.

ROSE: Put it in there on the table, Troy. I'll get it.

TROY: What time you coming back?

ROSE: Ain't no use in you studying me. It don't matter what time I come back.

TROY: I just asked you a question, woman. What's the matter . . . can't I ask you a question?

ROSE: Troy, I don't want to go into it. Your dinner's in there on the

175

stove. All you got to do is heat it up. And don't you be eating the rest of them cakes in there. I'm coming back for them. We having a bake sale at the church tomorrow.

(ROSE *exits the yard.* TROY *sits down on the steps, takes a pint bottle from his pocket, opens it and drinks. He begins to sing.*)

TROY:
Hear it ring! Hear it ring!
Had an old dog his name was Blue
You know Blue was mighty true
You know Blue was a good old dog
Blue treed a possum in a hollow log
You know from that he was a good old dog
(BONO *enters the yard.*)

BONO: Hey, Troy.

TROY: Hey, what's happening, Bono?

BONO: I just thought I'd stop by to see you.

TROY: What you stop by and see me for? You ain't stopped by in a month of Sundays. Hell, I must owe you money or something.

BONO: Since you got your promotion I can't keep up with you. Used to see you every day. Now I don't even know what route you working.

TROY: They keep switching me around. Got me out in Greentree now . . . hauling white folks' garbage.

BONO: Greentree, huh? You lucky, at least you ain't got to be lifting them barrels. Damn if they ain't getting heavier. I'm gonna put in my two years and call it quits.

TROY: I'm thinking about retiring myself.

BONO: You got it easy. You can *drive* for another five years.

TROY: It ain't the same, Bono. It ain't like working the back of the truck. Ain't got nobody to talk to . . . feel like you working by yourself. Naw, I'm thinking about retiring. How's Lucille?

BONO: She alright. Her arthritis get to acting up on her sometime. Saw Rose on my way in. She going down to the church, huh?

TROY: Yeah, she took up going down there. All them preachers looking for somebody to fatten their pockets.
(*Pause.*)
Got some gin here.

BONO: Naw, thanks. I just stopped by to say hello.

TROY: Hell, nigger . . . you can take a drink. I ain't never known you to say no to a drink. You ain't got to work tomorrow.

BONO: I just stopped by. I'm fixing to go over to Skinner's. We got us a domino game going over his house every Friday.

TROY: Nigger, you can't play no dominoes. I used to whup you four games out of five.

BONO: Well, that learned me. I'm getting better.

TROY: Yeah? Well, that's alright.

BONO: Look here . . . I got to be getting on. Stop by sometime, huh?

TROY: Yeah, I'll do that, Bono. Lucille told Rose you bought her a new refrigerator.

BONO: Yeah, Rose told Lucille you had finally built your fence . . . so I figured we'd call it even.

TROY: I knew you would.

BONO: Yeah . . . okay. I'll be talking to you.

TROY: Yeah, take care, Bono. Good to see you. I'm gonna stop over.

BONO: Yeah. Okay, Troy.
(BONO *exits.* TROY *drinks from the bottle.*)

TROY:
Old Blue died and I dig his grave
Let him down with a golden chain

Every night when I hear old Blue bark
I know Blue treed a possum in Noah's Ark.
Hear it ring! Hear it ring!
(CORY *enters the yard. They eye each other for a beat.* TROY *is sitting in the middle of the steps.* CORY *walks over.*)

CORY: I got to get by.

TROY: Say what? What's you say?

CORY: You in my way. I got to get by.

TROY: You got to get by where? This is my house. Bought and paid for. In full. Took me fifteen years. And if you wanna go in my house and I'm sitting on the steps . . . you say excuse me. Like your mama taught you.

CORY: Come on, Pop . . . I got to get by.
(CORY *starts to maneuver his way past* TROY. TROY *grabs his leg and shoves him back.*)

TROY: You just gonna walk over top of me?

CORY: I live here too!

TROY: (*Advancing toward him.*) You just gonna walk over top of me in my own house?

CORY: I ain't scared of you.

TROY: I ain't asked if you was scared of me. I asked you if you was fixing to walk over top of me in my own house? That's the question. You ain't gonna say excuse me? You just gonna walk over top of me?

CORY: If you wanna put it like that.

TROY: How else am I gonna put it?

CORY: I was walking by you to go into the house cause you sitting on the steps drunk, singing to yourself. You can put it like that.

TROY: Without saying excuse me???

178

(CORY *doesn't respond.*)
I asked you a question. Without saying excuse me???

CORY: I ain't got to say excuse me to you. You don't count around here no more.

TROY: Oh, I see . . . I don't count around here no more. You ain't got to say excuse me to your daddy. All of a sudden you done got so grown that your daddy don't count around here no more . . . Around here in his own house and yard that he done paid for with the sweat of his brow. You done got so grown to where you gonna take over. You gonna take over my house. Is that right? You gonna wear my pants. You gonna go in there and stretch out on my bed. You ain't got to say excuse me cause I don't count around here no more. Is that right?

CORY: That's right. You always talking this dumb stuff. Now, why don't you just get out my way.

TROY: I guess you got some place to sleep and something to put in your belly. You got that, huh? You got that? That's what you need. You got that, huh?

CORY: You don't know what I got. You ain't got to worry about what I got.

TROY: You right! You one hundred percent right! I done spent the last seventeen years worrying about what you got. Now it's your turn, see? I'll tell you what to do. You grown . . . we done established that. You a man. Now, let's see you act like one. Turn your behind around and walk out this yard. And when you get out there in the alley . . . you can forget about this house. See? Cause this is my house. You go on and be a man and get your own house. You can forget about this. Cause this is mine. You go on and get yours cause I'm through with doing for you.

CORY: You talking about what you did for me . . . what'd you ever give me?

TROY: Them feet and bones! That pumping heart, nigger! I give you more than anybody else is ever gonna give you.

179

CORY: You ain't never gave me nothing! You ain't never done nothing but hold me back. Afraid I was gonna be better than you. All you ever did was try and make me scared of you. I used to tremble every time you called my name. Every time I heard your footsteps in the house. Wondering all the time . . . what's Papa gonna say if I do this? . . . What's he gonna say if I do that? . . . What's Papa gonna say if I turn on the radio? And Mama, too . . . she tries . . . but she's scared of you.

TROY: You leave your mama out of this. She ain't got nothing to do with this.

CORY: I don't know how she stand you . . . after what you did to her.

TROY: I told you to leave your mama out of this!
(*He advances toward* CORY.)

CORY: What you gonna do . . . give me a whupping? You can't whup me no more. You're too old. You just an old man.

TROY: (*Shoves him on his shoulder.*) Nigger! That's what you are. You just another nigger on the street to me!

CORY: You crazy! You know that?

TROY: Go on now! You got the devil in you. Get on away from me!

CORY: You just a crazy old man . . . talking about I got the devil in me.

TROY: Yeah, I'm crazy! If you don't get on the other side of that yard . . . I'm gonna show you how crazy I am! Go on . . . get the hell out of my yard.

CORY: It ain't your yard. You took Uncle Gabe's money he got from the army to buy this house and then you put him out.

TROY: (*Advancing on* CORY.) Get your black ass out of my yard!
(TROY's *advance backs* CORY *up against the tree.* CORY *grabs up the bat.*)

180

CORY: I ain't going nowhere! Come on . . . put me out! I ain't scared of you.

TROY: That's my bat!

CORY: Come on!

TROY: Put my bat down!

CORY: Come on, put me out.
(CORY swings at TROY, who backs across the yard.)
What's the matter? You so bad . . . put me out!
(TROY advances toward CORY.)

CORY: (Backing up.) Come on! Come on!

TROY: You're gonna have to use it! You wanna draw that bat back on me . . . you're gonna have to use it.

CORY: Come on! . . . Come on!
(CORY swings the bat at TROY a second time. He misses. TROY continues to advance toward him.)

TROY: You're gonna have to kill me! You wanna draw that bat back on me. You're gonna have to kill me.
(CORY, backed up against the tree, can go no farther. TROY taunts him. He sticks out his head and offers him a target.)
Come on! Come on!
(CORY is unable to swing the bat. TROY grabs it.)

TROY: Then I'll show you.
(CORY and TROY struggle over the bat. The struggle is fierce and fully engaged. TROY ultimately is the stronger, and takes the bat from CORY and stands over him ready to swing. He stops himself.)
Go on and get away from around my house.
(CORY, stung by his defeat, picks himself up, walks slowly out of the yard and up the alley.)

CORY: Tell Mama I'll be back for my things.

TROY: They'll be on the other side of that fence.
(CORY exits.)

TROY: I can't taste nothing. Hallelujah! I can't taste nothing no more. (TROY *assumes a batting posture and begins to taunt Death, the fastball in the outside corner.*) Come on! It's between you and me now! Come on! Anytime you want! Come on! I be ready for you . . . but I ain't gonna be easy.
(*The lights go down on the scene.*)

ACT TWO: Scene Five

The time is 1965. The lights come up in the yard. It is the morning of
TROY's *funeral. A funeral plaque with a light hangs beside the door.*
There is a small garden plot off to the side. There is noise and activity in
the house as ROSE, LYONS, *and* BONO *have gathered. The door opens*
and RAYNELL, *seven years old, enters dressed in a flannel nightgown.*
She crosses to the garden and pokes around with a stick. ROSE *calls from*
the house.

ROSE: Raynell!

RAYNELL: Mam?

ROSE: What you doing out there?

RAYNELL: Nothing.
    (ROSE *comes to the door.*)

ROSE: Girl, get in here and get dressed. What you doing?

RAYNELL: Seeing if my garden growed.

ROSE: I told you it ain't gonna grow overnight. You got to wait.

RAYNELL: It don't look like it never gonna grow. Dag!

ROSE: I told you a watched pot never boils. Get in here and get
    dressed.

RAYNELL: This ain't even no pot, Mama.

ROSE: You just have to give it a chance. It'll grow. Now you come

183

on and do what I told you. We got to be getting ready. This ain't no morning to be playing around. You hear me?

RAYNELL: Yes, mam.

(ROSE *exits into the house.* RAYNELL *continues to poke at her garden with a stick.* CORY *enters. He is dressed in a Marine corporal's uniform and carries a duffel bag. His posture is that of a military man, and his speech has a clipped sternness.*)

CORY: (*To* RAYNELL.) Hi.
(*Pause.*)
I bet your name is Raynell.

RAYNELL: Uh huh.

CORY: Is your mama home?
(RAYNELL *runs up on the porch and calls through the screen door.*)

RAYNELL: Mama . . . there's some man out here. Mama?
(ROSE *comes to the door.*)

ROSE: Cory? Lord have mercy! Look here, you all!
(ROSE *and* CORY *embrace in a tearful reunion as* BONO *and* LYONS *enter from the house dressed in funeral clothes.*)

BONO: Aw, looka here . . .

ROSE: Done got all grown up!

CORY: Don't cry, Mama. What you crying about?

ROSE: I'm just so glad you made it.

CORY: Hey Lyons. How you doing, Mr. Bono?
(LYONS *goes to embrace* CORY.)

LYONS: Look at you, man. Look at you. Don't he look good, Rose. Got them corporal stripes.

ROSE: What took you so long?

CORY: You know how the marines are, Mama. They got to get all their paperwork straight before they let you do anything.

184

ROSE: Well, I'm sure glad you made it. They let Lyons come. Your Uncle Gabe's still in the hospital. They don't know if they gonna let him out or not. I just talked to them a little while ago.

LYONS: A corporal in the United States Marines.

BONO: Your daddy knew you had it in you. He used to tell me all the time.

LYONS: Don't he look good, Mr. Bono?

BONO: Yeah, he remind me of Troy when I first met him.
(*Pause.*)
Say, Rose, Lucille's down at the church with the choir. I'm gonna go down and get the pallbearers lined up. I'll be back to get you all.

ROSE: Thanks, Jim.

CORY: See you, Mr. Bono.

LYONS: (*With his arm around* RAYNELL.) Cory . . . look at Raynell. Ain't she precious? She gonna break a whole lot of hearts.

ROSE: Raynell, come and say hello to your brother. This is your brother, Cory. You remember Cory.

RAYNELL: No, Mam.

CORY: She don't remember me, Mama.

ROSE: Well, we talk about you. She heard us talk about you.

(*To* RAYNELL.) This is your brother, Cory. Come on and say hello.

RAYNELL: Hi.

CORY: Hi. So you're Raynell. Mama told me a lot about you.

ROSE: You all come on into the house and let me fix you some breakfast. Keep up your strength.

CORY: I ain't hungry, Mama.

LYONS: You can fix me something, Rose. I'll be in there in a minute.

ROSE: Cory, you sure you don't want nothing? I know they ain't feeding you right.

CORY: No, Mama . . . thanks. I don't feel like eating. I'll get something later.

ROSE: Raynell . . . get on upstairs and get that dress on like I told you.
(ROSE *and* RAYNELL *exit into the house.*)

LYONS: So . . . I hear you thinking about getting married.

CORY: Yeah, I done found the right one, Lyons. It's about time.

LYONS: Me and Bonnie been split up about four years now. About the time Papa retired. I guess she just got tired of all them changes I was putting her through.
(*Pause.*)
I always knew you was gonna make something out yourself. Your head was always in the right direction. So . . . you gonna stay in . . . make it a career . . . put in your twenty years?

CORY: I don't know. I got six already, I think that's enough.

LYONS: Stick with Uncle Sam and retire early. Ain't nothing out here. I guess Rose told you what happened with me. They got me down the workhouse. I thought I was being slick cashing other people's checks.

CORY: How much time you doing?

LYONS: They give me three years. I got that beat now. I ain't got but nine more months. It ain't so bad. You learn to deal with it like anything else. You got to take the crookeds with the straights. That's what Papa used to say. He used to say that when he struck out. I seen him strike out three times in a row . . . and the next time up he hit the ball over the grandstand. Right out there in Homestead Field. He wasn't satisfied hitting in the seats . . . he want to hit it over everything! After the game he

186

had two hundred people standing around waiting to shake his hand. You got to take the crookeds with the straights. Yeah, Papa was something else.

CORY: You still playing?

LYONS: Cory . . . you know I'm gonna do that. There's some fellows down there we got us a band . . . we gonna try and stay together when we get out . . . but yeah, I'm still playing. It still helps me to get out of bed in the morning. As long as it do that I'm gonna be right there playing and trying to make some sense out of it.

ROSE: (Calling.) Lyons, I got these eggs in the pan.

LYONS: Let me go on and get these eggs, man. Get ready to go bury Papa.
(Pause.)
How you doing? You doing alright?
(CORY nods. LYONS touches him on the shoulder and they share a moment of silent grief. LYONS exits into the house. CORY wanders about the yard. RAYNELL enters.)

RAYNELL: Hi.

CORY: Hi.

RAYNELL: Did you used to sleep in my room?

CORY: Yeah . . . that used to be my room.

RAYNELL: That's what Papa call it. "Cory's room." It got your football in the closet.
(ROSE comes to the door.)

ROSE: Raynell, get in there and get them good shoes on.

RAYNELL: Mama, can't I wear these? Them other ones hurt my feet.

ROSE: Well, they just gonna have to hurt your feet for a while. You ain't said they hurt your feet when you went down to the store and got them.

187

RAYNELL: They didn't hurt then. My feet done got bigger.

ROSE: Don't you give me no backtalk now. You get in there and get them shoes on.
(RAYNELL *exits into the house.*)
Ain't too much changed. He still got that piece of rag tied to that tree. He was out here swinging that bat. I was just ready to go back in the house. He swung that bat and then he just fell over. Seem like he swung it and stood there with this grin on his face . . . and then he just fell over. They carried him on down to the hospital, but I knew there wasn't no need . . . why don't you come on in the house?

CORY: Mama . . . I got something to tell you. I don't know how to tell you this . . . but I've got to tell you . . . I'm not going to Papa's funeral.

ROSE: Boy, hush your mouth. That's your daddy you talking about. I don't want to hear that kind of talk this morning. I done raised you to come to this? You standing there all healthy and grown talking about you ain't going to your daddy's funeral?

CORY: Mama . . . listen . . .

ROSE: I don't want to hear it, Cory. You just get that thought out of your head.

CORY: I can't drag Papa with me everywhere I go. I've got to say no to him. One time in my life I've got to say no.

ROSE: Don't nobody have to listen to nothing like that. I know you and your daddy ain't seen eye to eye, but I ain't got to listen to that kind of talk this morning. Whatever was between you and your daddy . . . the time has come to put it aside. Just take it and set it over there on the shelf and forget about it. Disrespecting your daddy ain't gonna make you a man, Cory. You got to find a way to come to that on your own. Not going to your daddy's funeral ain't gonna make you a man.

CORY: The whole time I was growing up . . . living in his house . . . Papa was like a shadow that followed you everywhere. It weighed on you and sunk into your flesh. It would wrap around you and lay there until you couldn't tell which one was you anymore. That shadow digging in your flesh. Trying to crawl in. Trying to live through you. Everywhere I looked, Troy Maxson was staring back at me . . . hiding under the bed . . . in the closet. I'm just saying I've got to find a way to get rid of that shadow, Mama.

ROSE: You just like him. You got him in you good.

CORY: Don't tell me that, Mama.

ROSE: You Troy Maxson all over again.

CORY: I don't want to be Troy Maxson. I want to be me.

ROSE: You can't be nobody but who you are, Cory. That shadow wasn't nothing but you growing into yourself. You either got to grow into it or cut it down to fit you. But that's all you got to make life with. That's all you got to measure yourself against that world out there. Your daddy wanted you to be everything he wasn't . . . and at the same time he tried to make you into everything he was. I don't know if he was right or wrong . . . but I do know he meant to do more good than he meant to do harm. He wasn't always right. Sometimes when he touched he bruised. And sometimes when he took me in his arms he cut.

When I first met your daddy I thought . . . Here is a man I can lay down with and make a baby. That's the first thing I thought when I seen him. I was thirty years old and had done seen my share of men. But when he walked up to me and said, "I can dance a waltz that'll make you dizzy," I thought, Rose Lee, here is a man that you can open yourself up to and be filled to bursting. Here is a man that can fill all them empty spaces you been tipping around the edges of. One of them empty spaces was being somebody's mother. I married your daddy and settled down to cooking his supper and keeping clean sheets on the bed. When your daddy walked through the house he was so big he filled it up. That was my first mistake. Not to make him leave some room for me. For my part in the matter. But at that time I

189

wanted that. I wanted a house that I could sing in. And that's what your daddy gave me. I didn't know to keep up his strength I had to give up little pieces of mine. I did that. I took on his life as mine and mixed up the pieces so that you couldn't hardly tell which was which anymore. It was my choice. It was my life, and I didn't have to live it like that. But that's what life offered me in the way of being a woman and I took it. I grabbed hold of it with both hands.

By the time Raynell came into the house, me and your daddy had done lost touch with one another. I didn't want to make my blessing off of nobody's misfortune . . . but I took on to Raynell like she was all them babies I had wanted and never had. (*The phone rings.*)
Like I'd been blessed to relive a part of my life. And if the Lord see fit to keep up my strength . . . I'm gonna do her just like your daddy did you . . . I'm gonna give her the best of what's in me.

RAYNELL: (*Entering, still with her old shoes.*) Mama . . . Reverend Tollivier on the phone.
(ROSE *exits into the house.*)

RAYNELL: Hi.

CORY: Hi.

RAYNELL: You in the army or the marines?

CORY: Marines.

RAYNELL: Papa said it was the army. Did you know Blue?

CORY: Blue? Who's Blue?

RAYNELL: Papa's dog what he sing about all the time.

CORY: (*Singing.*)
Hear it ring! Hear it ring!
I had a dog his name was Blue
You know Blue was mighty true
You know Blue was a good old dog
Blue treed a possum in a hollow log

190

You know from that he was a good old dog.
Hear it ring! Hear it ring!
(RAYNELL *joins in singing.*)

CORY and RAYNELL:
Blue treed a possum out on a limb
Blue looked at me and I looked at him
Grabbed that possum and put him in a sack
Blue stayed there till I came back
Old Blue's feets was big and round
Never allowed a possum to touch the ground.
Old Blue died and I dug his grave
I dug his grave with a silver spade
Let him down with a golden chain
And every night I call his name
Go on Blue, you good dog you
Go on Blue, you good dog you

RAYNELL:
Blue laid down and died like a man
Blue laid down and died . . .
CORY and RAYNELL:
Blue laid down and died like a man
Now he's treeing possums in the Promised Land
I'm gonna tell you this to let you know
Blue's gone where the good dogs go
When I hear old Blue bark
When I hear old Blue bark
Blue treed a possum in Noah's Ark
Blue treed a possum in Noah's Ark.
(ROSE *comes to the screen door.*)

ROSE: Cory, we gonna be ready to go in a minute.

CORY: (*To* RAYNELL.) You go on in the house and change them
shoes like Mama told you so we can go to Papa's funeral.

RAYNELL: Okay, I'll be back.
(RAYNELL *exits into the house.* CORY *gets up and crosses over to the*

191

tree. ROSE *stands in the screen door watching him.* GABRIEL *enters from the alley.*)

GABRIEL: (*Calling.*) Hey, Rose!

ROSE: Gabe?

GABRIEL: I'm here, Rose. Hey Rose, I'm here!
(ROSE *enters from the house.*)

ROSE: Lord . . . Look here, Lyons!

LYONS: See, I told you, Rose . . . I told you they'd let him come.

CORY: How you doing, Uncle Gabe?

LYONS: How you doing, Uncle Gabe?

GABRIEL: Hey, Rose. It's time. It's time to tell St. Peter to open the gates. Troy, you ready? You ready, Troy. I'm gonna tell St. Peter to open the gates. You get ready now.
(GABRIEL, *with great fanfare, braces himself to blow. The trumpet is without a mouthpiece. He puts the end of it into his mouth and blows with great force, like a man who has been waiting some twenty-odd years for this single moment. No sound comes out of the trumpet. He braces himself and blows again with the same result. A third time he blows. There is a weight of impossible description that falls away and leaves him bare and exposed to a frightful realization. It is a trauma that a sane and normal mind would be unable to withstand. He begins to dance. A slow, strange dance, eerie and life-giving. A dance of atavistic signature and ritual.* LYONS *attempts to embrace him.* GABRIEL *pushes* LYONS *away. He begins to howl in what is an attempt at song, or perhaps a song turning back into itself in an attempt at speech. He finishes his dance and the gates of heaven stand open as wide as God's closet.*)
That's the way that go!
(*Blackout.*)

JOE TURNER'S
COME AND GONE

For my daughter,
Sakina Ansari,
with love and gratitude
for her understanding

CHARACTERS

SETH HOLLY : *owner of the boardinghouse*

BERTHA HOLLY : *his wife*

BYNUM WALKER : *a rootworker*

RUTHERFORD SELIG : *a peddler*

JEREMY FURLOW : *a resident*

HERALD LOOMIS : *a resident*

ZONIA LOOMIS : *his daughter*

MATTIE CAMPBELL : *a resident*

REUBEN SCOTT : *boy who lives next door*

MOLLY CUNNINGHAM : *a resident*

MARTHA LOOMIS : *Herald Loomis' wife*

Joe Turner's Come and Gone opened on April 29, 1986, at the Yale Repertory Theatre, Lloyd Richards, Artistic Director, Benjamin Mordecai, Managing Director, in New Haven, Connecticut, with the following cast:

SETH HOLLY	Mel Winkler
BERTHA HOLLY	L. Scott Caldwell
BYNUM WALKER	Ed Hall
RUTHERFORD SELIG	Raynor Scheine
JEREMY FURLOW	Bo Rucker
HERALD LOOMIS	Charles S. Dutton
ZONIA LOOMIS	Cristal Coleman and LaJara Henderson at alternate performances
MATTIE CAMPBELL	Kimberleigh Burroughs
REUBEN MERCER	Casey Lydell Badger and LaMar James Fedrick at alternate performances
MOLLY CUNNINGHAM	Kimberly Scott
MARTHA PENTECOST	Angela Bassett

Director	Lloyd Richards
Set Design	Scott Bradley
Costume Design	Pamela Peterson
Lighting Design	Michael Gianitti

Musical Direction	Dwight Andrews
Sound Design	Matthew Wiener
Production Stage Manager	Margaret Adair
Stage Manager	Ethan Ruber
Casting	Meg Simon/Fran Kumin

Joe Turner's Come and Gone was initially presented as a staged reading at the Eugene O'Neill Theater Center's 1984 National Playwrights Conference.

The Yale Repertory Theatre production of *Joe Turner's Come and Gone* opened on October 2, 1987, at the Arena Stage, Zelda Fichandler, Producing Director, William Stewart, Managing Director, Douglas C. Wager, Associate Producing Director, in Washington, D.C., with the following cast:

SETH HOLLY	Mel Winkler
BERTHA HOLLY	L. Scott Caldwell
BYNUM WALKER	Ed Hall
RUTHERFORD SELIG	Raynor Scheine
JEREMY FURLOW	Bo Rucker
HERALD LOOMIS	Delroy Lindo
ZONIA LOOMIS	Kippen Hay and Kellie S. Williams at alternate performances
MATTIE CAMPBELL	Kimberleigh Aarn
REUBEN MERCER	LaFontaine Oliver and Vincent Prevost at alternate performances
MOLLY CUNNINGHAM	Kimberly Scott
MARTHA PENTECOST	Angela Bassett
Director	Lloyd Richards
Set Design	Scott Bradley
Costume Design	Pamela Peterson

Lighting Design	Michael Gianitti
Musical Direction	Dwight Andrews
Stage Manager	Karen L. Carpenter
Casting Consultants	Meg Simon/Fran Kumin

Joe Turner's Come and Gone opened on March 26, 1988, at the Ethel Barrymore Theatre on Broadway in New York City, with the following cast:

SETH HOLLY	Mel Winkler
BERTHA HOLLY	L. Scott Caldwell
BYNUM WALKER	Ed Hall
RUTHERFORD SELIG	Raynor Scheine
JEREMY FURLOW	Bo Rucker
HERALD LOOMIS	Delroy Lindo
ZONIA LOOMIS	Jamila Perry
MATTIE CAMPBELL	Kimberleigh Aarn
REUBEN MERCER	Richard Parnell Habersham
MOLLY CUNNINGHAM	Kimberly Scott
MARTHA PENTECOST	Angela Bassett

Director	Lloyd Richards
Set Design	Scott Bradley
Costume Design	Pamela Peterson
Lighting Design	Michael Gianitti
Musical Direction	Dwight Andrews
Production Stage Manager	Karen L. Carpenter
Stage Manager	Elliott Woodruff
Casting Consultants	Meg Simon/Fran Kumin

SETTING

August, 1911. A boardinghouse in Pittsburgh. At right is a kitchen. Two doors open off the kitchen. One leads to the outhouse and SETH's workshop. The other to SETH and BERTHA's bedroom. At left is a parlor. The front door opens into the parlor, which gives access to the stairs leading to the upstairs rooms.

There is a small outside playing area.

THE PLAY

It is August in Pittsburgh, 1911. The sun falls out of heaven like a stone. The fires of the steel mill rage with a combined sense of industry and progress. Barges loaded with coal and iron ore trudge up the river to the mill towns that dot the Monongahela and return with fresh, hard, gleaming steel. The city flexes its muscles. Men throw countless bridges across the rivers, lay roads, and carve tunnels through the hills sprouting with houses.

From the deep and the near South the sons and daughters of newly freed African slaves wander into the city. Isolated, cut off from memory, having forgotten the names of the gods and only guessing at their faces, they arrive dazed and stunned, their hearts kicking in their chest with a song worth singing. They arrive carrying Bibles and guitars, their pockets lined with dust and fresh hope, marked men and women seeking to scrape from the narrow, crooked cobbles and the fiery blasts of the coke furnace a way of bludgeoning and shaping the malleable parts of themselves into a new identity as free men of definite and sincere worth.

Foreigners in a strange land, they carry as part and parcel of their baggage a long line of separation and dispersement which informs their sensibilities and marks their conduct as they search for ways to reconnect, to reassemble, to give clear and luminous meaning to the song which is both a wail and a whelp of joy.

ACT ONE: Scene One

The lights come up on the kitchen. BERTHA *busies herself with breakfast preparations.* SETH *stands looking out the window at* BYNUM *in the yard.* SETH *is in his early fifties. Born of northern free parents, a skilled craftsman, and owner of the boardinghouse, he has a stability that none of the other characters have.* BERTHA *is five years his junior. Married for over twenty-five years, she has learned how to negotiate around* SETH's *apparent orneriness.*

SETH: (*At the window, laughing.*) If that ain't the damndest thing I seen. Look here, Bertha.

BERTHA: I done seen Bynum out there with them pigeons before.

SETH: Naw . . . naw . . . look at this. That pigeon flopped out of Bynum's hand and he about to have a fit.
(BERTHA *crosses over to the window.*)
He down there on his hands and knees behind that bush looking all over for that pigeon and it on the other side of the yard. See it over there?

BERTHA: Come on and get your breakfast and leave that man alone.

SETH: Look at him . . . he still looking. He ain't seen it yet. All that old mumbo jumbo nonsense. I don't know why I put up with it.

BERTHA: You don't say nothing when he bless the house.

SETH: I just go along with that cause of you. You around here sprinkling salt all over the place . . . got pennies lined up across the threshold . . . all that heebie-jeebie stuff. I just put up with that cause of you. I don't pay that kind of stuff no mind. And you going down there to the church and wanna come home and sprinkle salt all over the place.

BERTHA: It don't hurt none. I can't say if it help . . . but it don't hurt none.

SETH: Look at him. He done found that pigeon and now he's talking to it.

BERTHA: These biscuits be ready in a minute.

SETH: He done drew a big circle with that stick and now he's dancing around. I know he'd better not . . .
(SETH *bolts from the window and rushes to the back door.*)
Hey, Bynum! Don't be hopping around stepping in my vegetables. Hey, Bynum . . . Watch where you stepping!

BERTHA: Seth, leave that man alone.

SETH: (*Coming back into the house.*) I don't care how much he be dancing around . . . just don't be stepping in my vegetables. Man got my garden all messed up now . . . planting them weeds out there . . . burying them pigeons and whatnot.

BERTHA: Bynum don't bother nobody. He ain't even thinking about your vegetables.

SETH: I know he ain't! That's why he out there stepping on them.

BERTHA: What Mr. Johnson say down there?

SETH: I told him if I had the tools I could go out here and find me four or five fellows and open up my own shop instead of working for Mr. Olowski. Get me four or five fellows and teach them how to make pots and pans. One man making ten pots is five men making fifty. He told me he'd think about it.

BERTHA: Well, maybe he'll come to see it your way.

SETH: He wanted me to sign over the house to him. You know what I thought of that idea.

BERTHA: He'll come to see you're right.

SETH: I'm going up and talk to Sam Green. There's more than one way to skin a cat. I'm going up and talk to him. See if he got more sense than Mr. Johnson. I can't get nowhere working for Mr. Olowski and selling Selig five or six pots on the side. I'm going up and see Sam Green. See if he loan me the money. (SETH *crosses back to the window.*) Now he got that cup. He done killed that pigeon and now he's putting its blood in that little cup. I believe he drink that blood.

BERTHA: Seth Holly, what is wrong with you this morning? Come on and get your breakfast so you can go to bed. You know Bynum don't be drinking no pigeon blood.

SETH: I don't know what he do.

BERTHA: Well, watch him, then. He's gonna dig a little hole and bury that pigeon. Then he's gonna pray over that blood . . . pour it on top . . . mark out his circle and come on into the house.

SETH: That's what he doing . . . he pouring that blood on top.

BERTHA: When they gonna put you back working daytime? Told me two months ago he was gonna put you back working daytime.

SETH: That's what Mr. Olowski told me. I got to wait till he say when. He tell me what to do. I don't tell him. Drive me crazy to speculate on the man's wishes when he don't know what he want to do himself.

BERTHA: Well, I wish he go ahead and put you back working daytime. This working all hours of the night don't make no sense.

SETH: It don't make no sense for that boy to run out of here and get drunk so they lock him up either.

207

BERTHA: Who? Who they got locked up for being drunk?

SETH: That boy that's staying upstairs . . . Jeremy. I stopped down there on Logan Street on my way home from work and one of the fellows told me about it. Say he seen it when they arrested him.

BERTHA: I was wondering why I ain't seen him this morning.

SETH: You know I don't put up with that. I told him when he came . . .
(BYNUM *enters from the yard carrying some plants. He is a short, round man in his early sixties. A conjure man, or rootworker, he gives the impression of always being in control of everything. Nothing ever bothers him. He seems to be lost in a world of his own making and to swallow any adversity or interference with his grand design.*)
What you doing bringing them weeds in my house? Out there stepping on my vegetables and now wanna carry them weeds in my house.

BYNUM: Morning, Seth. Morning, Sister Bertha.

SETH: Messing up my garden growing them things out there. I ought to go out there and pull up all them weeds.

BERTHA: Some gal was by here to see you this morning, Bynum. You was out there in the yard . . . I told her to come back later.

BYNUM: (*To* SETH.) You look sick. What's the matter, you ain't eating right?

SETH: What if I was sick? You ain't getting near me with none of that stuff.
(BERTHA *sets a plate of biscuits on the table.*)

BYNUM: My . . . my . . . Bertha, your biscuits getting fatter and fatter.
(BYNUM *takes a biscuit and begins to eat.*)
Where Jeremy? I don't see him around this morning. He usually be around riffing and raffing on Saturday morning.

SETH: I know where he at. I know just where he at. They got him down there in the jail. Getting drunk and acting a fool. He down there where he belong with all that foolishness.

BYNUM: Mr. Piney's boys got him, huh? They ain't gonna do nothing but hold on to him for a little while. He's gonna be back here hungrier than a mule directly.

SETH: I don't go for all that carrying on and such. This is a respectable house. I don't have no drunkards or fools around here.

BYNUM: That boy got a lot of country in him. He ain't been up here but two weeks. It's gonna take a while before he can work that country out of him.

SETH: These niggers coming up here with that old backward country style of living. It's hard enough now without all that ignorant kind of acting. Ever since slavery got over with there ain't been nothing but foolish-acting niggers. Word get out they need men to work in the mill and put in these roads . . . and niggers drop everything and head North looking for freedom. They don't know the white fellows looking too. White fellows coming from all over the world. White fellow come over and in six months got more than what I got. But these niggers keep on coming. Walking . . . riding . . . carrying their Bibles. That boy done carried a guitar all the way from North Carolina. What he gonna find out? What he gonna do with that guitar? This the city.
(*There is a knock on the door.*)
Niggers coming up here from the backwoods . . . coming up here from the country carrying Bibles and guitars looking for freedom. They got a rude awakening.
(SETH *goes to answer the door.* RUTHERFORD SELIG *enters. About* SETH's *age, he is a thin white man with greasy hair. A peddler, he supplies* SETH *with the raw materials to make pots and pans which he then peddles door to door in the mill towns along the river. He keeps a list of his customers as they move about and is known in the various communities as the People Finder. He carries squares of sheet metal under his arm.*)
Ho! Forgot you was coming today. Come on in.

BYNUM: If it ain't Rutherford Selig . . . the People Finder himself.

SELIG: What say there, Bynum?

BYNUM: I say about my shiny man. You got to tell me something. I done give you my dollar . . . I'm looking to get a report.

SELIG: I got eight here, Seth.

SETH: (*Taking the sheet metal.*) What is this? What you giving me here? What I'm gonna do with this?

SELIG: I need some dustpans. Everybody asking me about dustpans.

SETH: Gonna cost you fifteen cents apiece. And ten cents to put a handle on them.

SELIG: I'll give you twenty cents apiece with the handles.

SETH: Alright. But I ain't gonna give you but fifteen cents for the sheet metal.

SELIG: It's twenty-five cents apiece for the metal. That's what we agreed on.

SETH: This low-grade sheet metal. They ain't worth but a dime. I'm doing you a favor giving you fifteen cents. You know this metal ain't worth no twenty-five cents. Don't come talking that twenty-five-cent stuff to me over no low-grade sheet metal.

SELIG: Alright, fifteen cents apiece. Just make me some dustpans out of them.
(SETH *exits with the sheet metal out the back door.*)

BERTHA: Sit on down there, Selig. Get you a cup of coffee and a biscuit.

BYNUM: Where you coming from this time?

SELIG: I been upriver. All along the Monongahela. Past Rankin and all up around Little Washington.

BYNUM: Did you find anybody?

SELIG: I found Sadie Jackson up in Braddock. Her mother's staying down there in Scotchbottom say she hadn't heard from her and she didn't know where she was at. I found her up in Braddock on Enoch Street. She bought a frying pan from me.

BYNUM: You around here finding everybody how come you ain't found my shiny man?

SELIG: The only shiny man I saw was the Nigras working on the road gang with the sweat glistening on them.

BYNUM: Naw, you'd be able to tell this fellow. He shine like new money.

SELIG: Well, I done told you I can't find nobody without a name.

BERTHA: Here go one of these hot biscuits, Selig.

BYNUM: This fellow don't have no name. I call him John cause it was up around Johnstown where I seen him. I ain't even so sure he's one special fellow. That shine could pass on to anybody. He could be anybody shining.

SELIG: Well, what's he look like besides being shiny? There's lots of shiny Nigras.

BYNUM: He's just a man I seen out on the road. He ain't had no special look. Just a man walking toward me on the road. He come up and asked me which way the road went. I told him everything I knew about the road, where it went and all, and he asked me did I have anything to eat cause he was hungry. Say he ain't had nothing to eat in three days. Well, I never be out there on the road without a piece of dried meat. Or an orange or an apple. So I give this fellow an orange. He take and eat that orange and told me to come and go along the road a little ways with him, that he had something he wanted to show me. He had a look about him made me wanna go with him, see what he gonna show me.

We walked on a bit and it's getting kind of far from where I met him when it come up on me all of a sudden, we wasn't going the way he had come from, we was going back my way. Since he said he ain't knew nothing about the road, I asked him about

211

this. He say he had a voice inside him telling him which way to go and if I come and go along with him he was gonna show me the Secret of Life. Quite naturally I followed him. A fellow that's gonna show you the Secret of Life ain't to be taken lightly. We get near this bend in the road . . .

(SETH *enters with an assortment of pots.*)

SETH: I got six here, Selig.

SELIG: Wait a minute, Seth. Bynum's telling me about the secret of life. Go ahead, Bynum. I wanna hear this.

(SETH *sets the pots down and exits out the back.*)

BYNUM: We get near this bend in the road and he told me to hold out my hands. Then he rubbed them together with his and I looked down and see they got blood on them. Told me to take and rub it all over me . . . say that was a way of cleaning myself. Then we went around the bend in that road. Got around that bend and it seem like all of a sudden we ain't in the same place. Turn around that bend and everything look like it was twice as big as it was. The trees and everything bigger than life! Sparrows big as eagles! I turned around to look at this fellow and he had this light coming out of him. I had to cover up my eyes to keep from being blinded. He shining like new money with that light. He shined until all the light seemed like it seeped out of him and then he was gone and I was by myself in this strange place where everything was bigger than life.

I wandered around there looking for that road, trying to find my way back from this big place . . . and I looked over and seen my daddy standing there. He was the same size he always was, except for his hands and his mouth. He had a great big old mouth that look like it took up his whole face and his hands were as big as hams. Look like they was too big to carry around. My daddy called me to him. Said he had been thinking about me and it grieved him to see me in the world carrying other people's songs and not having one of my own. Told me he was gonna show me how to find my song. Then he carried me further into this big place until we come to this ocean. Then he showed me something I ain't got words to tell you. But if you stand to witness it, you done seen something there. I stayed in that place awhile and my daddy taught me the meaning of this thing that I had seen and showed me how to find my song. I asked him about the shiny man and he told me he was the One Who Goes Before and Shows the Way. Said there was lots of shiny men and if I ever saw one again before I died then I would know that my song had been accepted and worked its full power in the world and I could lay down and die a happy man. A man who done left his mark on life. On the way people cling to each other out of the truth they find in themselves. Then he showed me how to get back to the road. I came out to where everything was its own size and I had my song. I had the Binding Song. I chose that song because that's what I seen most when I was traveling . . . people walking away and leaving one another. So I takes the power of my song and binds them together.

(SETH *enters from the yard carrying cabbages and tomatoes.*)
Been binding people ever since. That's why they call me Bynum. Just like glue I sticks people together.

SETH: Maybe they ain't supposed to be stuck sometimes. You ever think of that?

BYNUM: Oh, I don't do it lightly. It cost me a piece of myself every time I do. I'm a Binder of What Clings. You got to find out if they cling first. You can't bind what don't cling.

SELIG: Well, how is that the secret of life? I thought you said he was gonna show you the secret of life. That's what I'm waiting to find out.

BYNUM: Oh, he showed me alright. But you still got to figure it out. Can't nobody figure it out for you. You got to come to it on your own. That's why I'm looking for the shiny man.

SELIG: Well, I'll keep my eye out for him. What you got there, Seth?

SETH: Here go some cabbage and tomatoes. I got some green beans coming in real nice. I'm gonna take and start me a grapevine out

213

there next year. Butera says he gonna give me a piece of his vine and I'm gonna start that out there.

SELIG: How many of them pots you got?

SETH: I got six. That's six dollars minus eight on top of fifteen for the sheet metal come to a dollar twenty out the six dollars leave me four dollars and eighty cents.

SELIG: (*Counting out the money.*) There's four dollars . . . and . . . eighty cents.

SETH: How many of them dustpans you want?

SELIG: As many as you can make out them sheets.

SETH: You can use that many? I get to cutting on them sheets figuring how to make them dustpans . . . ain't no telling how many I'm liable to come up with.

SELIG: I can use them and you can make me some more next time.

SETH: Alright, I'm gonna hold you to that, now.

SELIG: Thanks for the biscuit, Bertha.

BERTHA: You know you welcome any time, Selig.

SETH: Which way you heading?

SELIG: Going down to Wheeling. All through West Virginia there. I'll be back Saturday. They putting in new roads down that way. Makes traveling easier.

SETH: That's what I hear. All up around here too. Got a fellow staying here working on that road by the Brady Street Bridge.

SELIG: Yeah, it's gonna make traveling real nice. Thanks for the cabbage, Seth. I'll see you on Saturday.
(SELIG *exits.*)

SETH: (*To* BYNUM) Why you wanna start all that nonsense talk with that man? All that shiny man nonsense?

BYNUM: You know it ain't no nonsense. Bertha know it ain't no nonsense. I don't know if Selig know or not.

BERTHA: Seth, when you get to making them dustpans make me a coffeepot.

SETH: What's the matter with your coffee? Ain't nothing wrong with your coffee. Don't she make some good coffee, Bynum?

BYNUM: I ain't worried about the coffee. I know she makes some good biscuits.

SETH: I ain't studying no coffeepot, woman. You heard me tell the man I was gonna cut as many dustpans as them sheets will make . . . and all of a sudden you want a coffeepot.

BERTHA: Man, hush up and go on and make me that coffeepot. (JEREMY *enters the front door. About twenty-five, he gives the impression that he has the world in his hand, that he can meet life's challenges head on. He smiles a lot. He is a proficient guitar player, though his spirit has yet to be molded into song.*)

BYNUM: I hear Mr. Piney's boys had you.

JEREMY: Fined me two dollars for nothing! Ain't done nothing.

SETH: I told you when you come on here everybody know my house. Know these is respectable quarters. I don't put up with no foolishness. Everybody know Seth Holly keep a good house. Was my daddy's house. This house been a decent house for a long time.

JEREMY: I ain't done nothing, Mr. Seth. I stopped by the Workmen's Club and got me a bottle. Me and Roper Lee from Alabama. Had us a half pint. We was fixing to cut that half in two when they came up on us. Asked us if we was working. We told them we was putting in the road over yonder and that it was our payday. They snatched hold of us to get that two dollars. Me and Roper Lee ain't even had a chance to take a drink when they grabbed us.

SETH: I don't go for all that kind of carrying on.

215

BERTHA: Leave the boy alone, Seth. You know the police do that. Figure there's too many people out on the street they take some of them off. You know that.

SETH: I ain't gonna have folks talking.

BERTHA: Ain't nobody talking nothing. That's all in your head. You want some grits and biscuits, Jeremy?

JEREMY: Thank you, Miss Bertha. They didn't give us a thing to eat last night. I'll take one of them big bowls if you don't mind.
(*There is a knock at the door.* SETH *goes to answer it. Enter* HERALD LOOMIS *and his eleven-year-old daughter,* ZONIA. HERALD LOOMIS *is thirty-two years old. He is at times possessed. A man driven not by the hellhounds that seemingly bay at his heels, but by his search for a world that speaks to something about himself. He is unable to harmonize the forces that swirl around him, and seeks to recreate the world into one that contains his image. He wears a hat and a long wool coat.*)

LOOMIS: Me and my daughter looking for a place to stay, mister. You got a sign say you got rooms.
(SETH *stares at* LOOMIS, *sizing him up.*)
Mister, if you ain't got no rooms we can go somewhere else.

SETH: How long you plan on staying?

LOOMIS: Don't know. Two weeks or more maybe.

SETH: It's two dollars a week for the room. We serve meals twice a day. It's two dollars for room and board. Pay up in advance.
(LOOMIS *reaches into his pocket.*)
It's a dollar extra for the girl.

LOOMIS: The girl sleep in the same room.

SETH: Well, do she eat off the same plate? We serve meals twice a day. That's a dollar extra for food.

LOOMIS: Ain't got no extra dollar. I was planning on asking your missus if she could help out with the cooking and cleaning and whatnot.

216

SETH: Her helping out don't put no food on the table. I need that dollar to buy some food.

LOOMIS: I'll give you fifty cents extra. She don't eat much.

SETH: Okay . . . but fifty cents don't buy but half a portion.

BERTHA: Seth, she can help me out. Let her help me out. I can use some help.

SETH: Well, that's two dollars for the week. Pay up in advance. Saturday to Saturday. You wanna stay on then it's two more come Saturday.
(LOOMIS *pays* SETH *the money.*)

BERTHA: My name's Bertha. This my husband, Seth. You got Bynum and Jeremy over there.

LOOMIS: Ain't nobody else live here? ·

BERTHA: They the only ones live here now. People come and go. They the only ones here now. You want a cup of coffee and a biscuit?

LOOMIS: We done ate this morning.

BYNUM: Where you coming from, Mister . . . I didn't get your name.

LOOMIS: Name's Herald Loomis. This my daughter, Zonia.

BYNUM: Where you coming from?

LOOMIS: Come from all over. Whichever way the road take us, that's the way we go.

JEREMY: If you looking for a job, I'm working putting in that road down there by the bridge. They can't get enough mens. Always looking to take somebody on.

LOOMIS: I'm looking for a woman named Martha Loomis. That's my wife. Got married legal with the papers and all.

217

SETH: I don't know nobody named Loomis. I know some Marthas but I don't know no Loomis.

BYNUM: You got to see Rutherford Selig if you wanna find somebody. Selig's the People Finder. Rutherford Selig's a first-class People Finder.

JEREMY: What she look like? Maybe I seen her.

LOOMIS: She a brownskin woman. Got long, pretty hair. About five feet from the ground.

JEREMY: I don't know. I might have seen her.

BYNUM: You got to see Rutherford Selig. You give him one dollar to get her name on his list . . . and after she get her name on his list Rutherford Selig will go right on out there and find her. I got him looking for somebody for me.

LOOMIS: You say he find people. How you find him?

BYNUM: You just missed him. He's gone downriver now. You got to wait till Saturday. He's gone downriver with his pots and pans. He come to see Seth on Saturdays. You got to wait till then.

SETH: Come on, I'll show you to your room.
(SETH, LOOMIS, and ZONIA exit up the stairs.)

JEREMY: Miss Bertha, I'll take that biscuit you was gonna give that fellow, if you don't mind. Say, Mr. Bynum, they got somebody like that around here sure enough? Somebody that find people?

BYNUM: Rutherford Selig. He go around selling pots and pans and every house he come to he write down the name and address of whoever lives there. So if you looking for somebody, quite naturally you go and see him . . . cause he's the only one who know where everybody live at.

JEREMY: I ought to have him look for this old gal I used to know. It be nice to see her again.

BERTHA: (Giving JEREMY a biscuit.) Jeremy, today's the day for you

218

to pull them sheets off the bed and set them outside your door. I'll set you out some clean ones.

BYNUM: Mr. Piney's boys done ruined your good time last night, Jeremy . . . what you planning for tonight?

JEREMY: They got me scared to go out, Mr. Bynum. They might grab me again.

BYNUM: You ought to take your guitar and go down to Seefus. Seefus got a gambling place down there on Wylie Avenue. You ought to take your guitar and go down there. They got guitar contest down there.

JEREMY: I don't play no contest, Mr. Bynum. Had one of them white fellows cure me of that. I ain't been nowhere near a contest since.

BYNUM: White fellow beat you playing guitar?

JEREMY: Naw, he ain't beat me. I was sitting at home just fixing to sit down and eat when somebody come up to my house and got me. Told me there's a white fellow say he was gonna give a prize to the best guitar player he could find. I take up my guitar and go down there and somebody had gone up and got Bobo Smith and brought him down there. Him and another fellow called Hooter. Old Hooter couldn't play no guitar, he do more hollering than playing, but Bobo could go at it awhile.

This fellow standing there say he the one that was gonna give the prize and me and Bobo started playing for him. Bobo play something and then I'd try to play something better than what he played. Old Hooter, he just holler and bang at the guitar. Man was the worst guitar player I ever seen. So me and Bobo played and after a while I seen where he was getting the attention of this white fellow. He'd play something and while he was playing it he be slapping on the side of the guitar, and that made it sound like he was playing more than he was. So I started doing it too. White fellow ain't knew no difference. He ain't knew as much about guitar playing as Hooter did. After we play awhile, the white fellow called us to him and said he couldn't make up his

219

mind, say all three of us was the best guitar player and we'd have to split the prize between us. Then he give us twenty-five cents. That's eight cents apiece and a penny on the side. That cured me of playing contest to this day.

BYNUM: Seefus ain't like that. Seefus give a whole dollar and a drink of whiskey.

JEREMY: What night they be down there?

BYNUM: Be down there every night. Music don't know no certain night.

BERTHA: You go down to Seefus with them people and you liable to end up in a raid and go to jail sure enough. I don't know why Bynum tell you that.

BYNUM: That's where the music at. That's where the people at. The people down there making music and enjoying themselves. Some things is worth taking the chance going to jail about.

BERTHA: Jeremy ain't got no business going down there.

JEREMY: They got some women down there, Mr. Bynum?

BYNUM: Oh, they got women down there, sure. They got women everywhere. Women be where the men is so they can find each other.

JEREMY: Some of them old gals come out there where we be putting in that road. Hanging around there trying to snatch somebody.

BYNUM: How come some of them ain't snatched hold of you?

JEREMY: I don't want them kind. Them desperate kind. Ain't nothing worse than a desperate woman. Tell them you gonna leave them and they get to crying and carrying on. That just make you want to get away quicker. They get to cutting up your clothes and things trying to keep you staying. Desperate women ain't nothing but trouble for a man.
(SETH enters from the stairs.)

SETH: Something ain't setting right with that fellow.

220

BERTHA: What's wrong with him? What he say?

SETH: I take him up there and try to talk to him and he ain't for no talking. Say he been traveling . . . coming over from Ohio. Say he a deacon in the church. Say he looking for Martha Pentecost. Talking about that's his wife.

BERTHA: How you know it's the same Martha? Could be talking about anybody. Lots of people named Martha.

SETH: You see that little girl? I didn't hook it up till he said it, but that little girl look just like her. Ask Bynum. (*To* BYNUM.) Bynum. Don't that little girl look just like Martha Pentecost?

BERTHA: I still say he could be talking about anybody.

SETH: The way he described her wasn't no doubt about who he was talking about. Described her right down to her toes.

BERTHA: What did you tell him?

SETH: I ain't told him nothing. The way that fellow look I wasn't gonna tell him nothing. I don't know what he looking for her for.

BERTHA: What else he have to say?

SETH: I told you he wasn't for no talking. I told him where the outhouse was and to keep that gal off the front porch and out of my garden. He asked if you'd mind setting a hot tub for the gal and that was about the gist of it.

BERTHA: Well, I wouldn't let it worry me if I was you. Come on get your sleep.

BYNUM: He says he looking for Martha and he a deacon in the church.

SETH: That's what he say. Do he look like a deacon to you?

BERTHA: He might be, you don't know. Bynum ain't got no special say on whether he a deacon or not.

SETH: Well, if he the deacon I'd sure like to see the preacher.

221

BERTHA: Come on get your sleep. Jeremy, don't forget to set them sheets outside the door like I told you.
(BERTHA *exits into the bedroom.*)

SETH: Something ain't setting right with that fellow, Bynum. He's one of them mean-looking niggers look like he done killed somebody gambling over a quarter.

BYNUM: He ain't no gambler. Gamblers wear nice shoes. This fellow got on clodhoppers. He been out there walking up and down them roads.
(ZONIA *enters from the stairs and looks around.*)

BYNUM: You looking for the back door, sugar? There it is. You can go out there and play. It's alright.

SETH: (*Showing her the door.*) You can go out there and play. Just don't get in my garden. And don't go messing around in my work shed.
(SETH *exits into the bedroom. There is a knock on the door.*)

JEREMY: Somebody at the door.
(JEREMY *goes to answer the door.* Enter MATTIE CAMPBELL. *She is a young woman of twenty-six whose attractiveness is hidden under the weight and concerns of a dissatisfied life. She is a woman in an honest search for love and companionship. She has suffered many defeats in her search, and though not always uncompromising, still believes in the possibility of love.*)

MATTIE: I'm looking for a man named Bynum. Lady told me to come back later.

JEREMY: Sure, he here. Mr. Bynum, somebody here to see you.

BYNUM: Come to see me, huh?

MATTIE: Are you the man they call Bynum? The man folks say can fix things?

BYNUM: Depend on what need fixing. I can't make no promises. But I got a powerful song in some matters.

222

MATTIE: Can you fix it so my man come back to me?

BYNUM: Come on in . . . have a sit down.

MATTIE: You got to help me. I don't know what else to do.

BYNUM: Depend on how all the circumstances of the thing come together. How all the pieces fit.

MATTIE: I done everything I knowed how to do. You got to make him come back to me.

BYNUM: It ain't nothing to make somebody come back. I can fix it so he can't stand to be away from you. I got my roots and powders, I can fix it so wherever he's at this thing will come up on him and he won't be able to sleep for seeing your face. Won't be able to eat for thinking of you.

MATTIE: That's what I want. Make him come back.

BYNUM: The roots is a powerful thing. I can fix it so one day he'll walk out his front door . . . won't be thinking of nothing. He won't know what it is. All he knows is that a powerful dissatisfaction done set in his bones and can't nothing he do make him feel satisfied. He'll set his foot down on the road and the wind in the trees be talking to him and everywhere he step on the road, that road'll give back your name and something will pull him right up to your doorstep. Now, I can do that. I can take my roots and fix that easy. But maybe he ain't supposed to come back. And if he ain't supposed to come back . . . then he'll be in your bed one morning and it'll come up on him that he's in the wrong place. That he's lost outside of time from his place that he's supposed to be in. Then both of you be lost and trapped outside of life and ain't no way for you to get back into it. Cause you lost from yourselves and where the places come together, where you're supposed to be alive, your heart kicking in your chest with a song worth singing.

MATTIE: Make him come back to me. Make his feet say my name on the road. I don't care what happens. Make him come back.

BYNUM: What's your man's name?

MATTIE: He go by Jack Carper. He was born in Alabama then he come to West Texas and find me and we come here. Been here three years before he left. Say I had a curse prayer on me and he started walking down the road and ain't never come back. Somebody told me, say you can fix things like that.

BYNUM: He just got up one day, set his feet on the road, and walked away?

MATTIE: You got to make him come back, mister.

BYNUM: Did he say good-bye?

MATTIE: Ain't said nothing. Just started walking. I could see where he disappeared. Didn't look back. Just kept walking. Can't you fix it so he come back? I ain't got no curse prayer on me. I know I ain't.

BYNUM: What made him say you had a curse prayer on you?

MATTIE: Cause the babies died. Me and Jack had two babies. Two little babies that ain't lived two months before they died. He say it's because somebody cursed me not to have babies.

BYNUM: He ain't bound to you if the babies died. Look like somebody trying to keep you from being bound up and he's gone on back to whoever it is cause he's already bound up to her. Ain't nothing to be done. Somebody else done got a powerful hand in it and ain't nothing to be done to break it. You got to let him go find where he's supposed to be in the world.

MATTIE: Jack done gone off and you telling me to forget about him. All my life I been looking for somebody to stop and stay with me. I done already got too many things to forget about. I take Jack Carper's hand and it feel so rough and strong. Seem like he's the strongest man in the world the way he hold me. Like he's bigger than the whole world and can't nothing bad get to me. Even when he act mean sometimes he still make everything seem okay

224

with the world. Like there's part of it that belongs just to you. Now you telling me to forget about him?

BYNUM: Jack Carper gone off to where he belong. There's somebody searching for your doorstep right now. Ain't no need you fretting over Jack Carper. Right now he's a strong thought in your mind. But every time you catch yourself fretting over Jack Carper you push that thought away. You push it out your mind and that thought will get weaker and weaker till you wake up one morning and you won't even be able to call him up on your mind.

(BYNUM *gives her a small cloth packet.*)

Take this and sleep with it under your pillow and it'll bring good luck to you. Draw it to you like a magnet. It won't be long before you forget all about Jack Carper.

MATTIE: How much . . . do I owe you?

BYNUM: Whatever you got there . . . that'll be alright.

(MATTIE *hands* BYNUM *two quarters. She crosses to the door.*)

You sleep with that under your pillow and you'll be alright.

(MATTIE *opens the door to exit and* JEREMY *crosses over to her.* BYNUM *overhears the first part of their conversation, then exits out the back.*)

JEREMY: I overheard what you told Mr. Bynum. Had me an old gal did that to me. Woke up one morning and she was gone. Just took off to parts unknown. I woke up that morning and the only thing I could do was look around for my shoes. I woke up and got out of there. Found my shoes and took off. That's the only thing I could think of to do.

MATTIE: She ain't said nothing?

JEREMY: I just looked around for my shoes and got out of there.

MATTIE: Jack ain't said nothing either. He just walked off.

JEREMY: Some mens do that. Womens too. I ain't gone off looking for her. I just let her go. Figure she had a time to come to herself. Wasn't no use of me standing in the way. Where you from?

225

MATTIE: Texas. I was born in Georgia but I went to Texas with my mama. She dead now. Was picking peaches and fell dead away. I come up here with Jack Carper.

JEREMY: I'm from North Carolina. Down around Raleigh where they got all that tobacco. Been up here about two weeks. I likes it fine except I still got to find me a woman. You got a nice look to you. Look like you have mens standing in your door. Is you got mens standing in your door to get a look at you?

MATTIE: I ain't got nobody since Jack left.

JEREMY: A woman like you need a man. Maybe you let me be your man. I got a nice way with the women. That's what they tell me.

MATTIE: I don't know. Maybe Jack's coming back.

JEREMY: I'll be your man till he come. A woman can't be by her lonesome. Let me be your man till he come.

MATTIE: I just can't go through life piecing myself out to different mens. I need a man who wants to stay with me.

JEREMY: I can't say what's gonna happen. Maybe I'll be the man. I don't know. You wanna go along the road a little ways with me?

MATTIE: I don't know. Seem like life say it's gonna be one thing and end up being another. I'm tired of going from man to man.

JEREMY: Life is like you got to take a chance. Everybody got to take a chance. Can't nobody say what's gonna be. Come on . . . take a chance with me and see what the year bring. Maybe you let me come and see you. Where you staying?

MATTIE: I got me a room up on Bedford. Me and Jack had a room together.

JEREMY: What's the address? I'll come by and get you tonight and we can go down to Seefus. I'm going down there and play my guitar.

MATTIE: You play guitar?

226

JEREMY: I play guitar like I'm born to it.

MATTIE: I live at 1727 Bedford Avenue. I'm gonna find out if you can play guitar like you say.

JEREMY: I plays it sugar, and that ain't all I do. I got a ten-pound hammer and I knows how to drive it down. Good god . . . you ought to hear my hammer ring!

MATTIE: Go on with that kind of talk, now. If you gonna come by and get me I got to get home and straighten up for you.

JEREMY: I'll be by at eight o'clock. How's eight o'clock? I'm gonna make you forget all about Jack Carper.

MATTIE: Go on, now. I got to get home and fix up for you.

JEREMY: Eight o'clock, sugar.
(*The lights go down in the parlor and come up on the yard outside.* ZONIA *is singing and playing a game.*)

ZONIA:
I went downtown
To get my grip
I came back home
Just a pullin' the skiff
I went upstairs
To make my bed
I made a mistake
And I bumped my head
Just a pullin' the skiff

I went downstairs
To milk the cow
I made a mistake
And I milked the sow
Just a pullin' the skiff

Tomorrow, tomorrow
Tomorrow never comes
The marrow the marrow

227

The marrow in the bone.
(REUBEN *enters.*)

REUBEN: Hi.

ZONIA: Hi.

REUBEN: What's your name?

ZONIA: Zonia.

REUBEN: What kind of name is that?

ZONIA: It's what my daddy named me.

REUBEN: My name's Reuben. You staying in Mr. Seth's house?

ZONIA: Yeah.

REUBEN: That your daddy I seen you with this morning?

ZONIA: I don't know. Who you see me with?

REUBEN: I saw you with some man had on a great big old coat. And you was walking up to Mr. Seth's house. Had on a hat too.

ZONIA: Yeah, that's my daddy.

REUBEN: You like Mr. Seth?

ZONIA: I ain't see him much.

REUBEN: My grandpap say he a great big old windbag. How come you living in Mr. Seth's house? Don't you have no house?

ZONIA: We going to find my mother.

REUBEN: Where she at?

ZONIA: I don't know. We got to find her. We just go all over.

REUBEN: Why you got to find her? What happened to her?

ZONIA: She ran away.

REUBEN: Why she run away?

ZONIA: I don't know. My daddy say some man named Joe Turner did something bad to him once and that made her run away.

REUBEN: Maybe she coming back and you don't have to go looking for her.

ZONIA: We ain't there no more.

REUBEN: She could have come back when you wasn't there.

ZONIA: My daddy said she ran off and left us so we going looking for her.

REUBEN: What he gonna do when he find her?

ZONIA: He didn't say. He just say he got to find her.

REUBEN: Your daddy say how long you staying in Mr. Seth's house?

ZONIA: He don't say much. But we never stay too long nowhere. He say we got to keep moving till we find her.

REUBEN: Ain't no kids hardly live around here. I had me a friend but he died. He was the best friend I ever had. Me and Eugene used to keep secrets. I still got his pigeons. He told me to let them go when he died. He say, "Reuben, promise me when I die you'll let my pigeons go." But I keep them to remember him by. I ain't never gonna let them go. Even when I get to be grown up. I'm just always gonna have Eugene's pigeons.
(*Pause.*)
Mr. Bynum a conjure man. My grandpap scared of him. He don't like me to come over here too much. I'm scared of him too. My grandpap told me not to let him get close enough to where he can reach out his hand and touch me.

ZONIA: He don't seem scary to me.

REUBEN: He buys pigeons from me . . . and if you get up early in the morning you can see him out in the yard doing something with them pigeons. My grandpap say he kill them. I sold him one yesterday. I don't know what he do with it. I just hope he don't spook me up.

229

ZONIA: Why you sell him pigeons if he's gonna spook you up?

REUBEN: I just do like Eugene do. He used to sell Mr. Bynum pigeons. That's how he got to collecting them to sell to Mr. Bynum. Sometime he give me a nickel and sometime he give me a whole dime.
(LOOMIS *enters from the house.*)

LOOMIS: Zonia!

ZONIA: Sir?

LOOMIS: What you doing?

ZONIA: Nothing.

LOOMIS: You stay around this house, you hear? I don't want you wandering off nowhere.

ZONIA: I ain't wandering off nowhere.

LOOMIS: Miss Bertha set that hot tub and you getting a good scrubbing. Get scrubbed up good. You ain't been scrubbing.

ZONIA: I been scrubbing.

LOOMIS: Look at you. You growing too fast. Your bones getting bigger everyday. I don't want you getting grown on me. Don't you get grown on me too soon. We gonna find your mamma. She around here somewhere. I can smell her. You stay on around this house now. Don't you go nowhere.

ZONIA: Yes, sir.
(LOOMIS *exits into the house.*)

REUBEN: Wow, your daddy's scary!

ZONIA: He is not! I don't know what you talking about.

REUBEN: He got them mean-looking eyes!

ZONIA: My daddy ain't got no mean-looking eyes!

REUBEN: Aw, girl, I was just messing with you. You wanna go see
Eugene's pigeons? Got a great big coop out the back of my house.
Come on, I'll show you.
(REUBEN *and* ZONIA *exit as the lights go down.*)

ACT ONE: Scene Two

It is Saturday morning, one week later. The lights come up on the kitchen. BERTHA *is at the stove preparing breakfast while* SETH *sits at the table.*

SETH: Something ain't right about that fellow. I been watching him all week. Something ain't right, I'm telling you.

BERTHA: Seth Holly, why don't you hush up about that man this morning?

SETH: I don't like the way he stare at everybody. Don't look at you natural like. He just be staring at you. Like he trying to figure out something about you. Did you see him when he come back in here?

BERTHA: That man ain't thinking about you.

SETH: He don't work nowhere. Just go out and come back. Go out and come back.

BERTHA: As long as you get your boarding money it ain't your cause about what he do. He don't bother nobody.

SETH: Just go out and come back. Going around asking everybody about Martha. Like Henry Allen seen him down at the church last night.

BERTHA: The man's allowed to go to church if he want. He say he a deacon. Ain't nothing wrong about him going to church.

SETH: I ain't talking about him going to church. I'm talking about him hanging around *outside* the church.

BERTHA: Henry Allen say that?

SETH: Say he be standing around outside the church. Like he be watching it.

BERTHA: What on earth he wanna be watching the church for, I wonder?

SETH: That's what I'm trying to figure out. Looks like he fixing to rob it.

BERTHA: Seth, now do he look like the kind that would rob the church?

SETH: I ain't saying that. I ain't saying how he look. It's how he do. Anybody liable to do anything as far as I'm concerned. I ain't never thought about how no church robbers look . . . but now that you mention it, I don't see where they look no different than how he look.

BERTHA: Herald Loomis ain't the kind of man who would rob no church.

SETH: I ain't even so sure that's his name.

BERTHA: Why the man got to lie about his name?

SETH: Anybody can tell anybody anything about what their name is. That's what you call him . . . Herald Loomis. His name is liable to be anything.

BERTHA: Well, until he tell me different that's what I'm gonna call him. You just getting yourself all worked up about the man for nothing.

SETH: Talking about Loomis—Martha's name wasn't no Loomis nothing. Martha's name is Pentecost.

BERTHA: How you so sure that's her right name? Maybe she changed it.

SETH: Martha's a good Christian woman. This fellow here look like he owe the devil a day's work and he's trying to figure out how he gonna pay him. Martha ain't had a speck of distrust about her the whole time she was living here. They moved the church out there to Rankin and I was sorry to see her go.

BERTHA: That's why he be hanging around the church. He looking for her.

SETH: If he looking for her, why don't he go inside and ask? What he doing hanging around outside the church acting sneaky like? (BYNUM *enters from the yard.*)

BYNUM: Morning, Seth. Morning, Sister Bertha. (BYNUM *continues through the kitchen and exits up the stairs.*)

BERTHA: That's who you should be asking the questions. He been out there in that yard all morning. He was out there before the sun come up. He didn't even come in for breakfast. I don't know what he's doing. He had three of them pigeons lined up out there. He dance around till he get tired. He sit down awhile then get up and dance some more. He come through here a little while ago looking like he was mad at the world.

SETH: I don't pay Bynum no mind. He don't spook me up with all that stuff.

BERTHA: That's how Martha come to be living here. She come to see Bynum. She come to see him when she first left from down South.

SETH: Martha was living here before Bynum. She ain't come on here when she first left from down there. She come on here after she went back to get her little girl. That's when she come on here.

BERTHA: Well, where was Bynum? He was here when she came.

SETH: Bynum ain't come till after her. That boy Hiram was staying up there in Bynum's room.

BERTHA: Well, how long Bynum been here?

234

SETH: Bynum ain't been here no longer than three years. That's what I'm trying to tell you. Martha was staying up there and sewing and cleaning for Doc Goldblum when Bynum came. This the longest he ever been in one place.

BERTHA: How you know how long the man been in one place?

SETH: I know Bynum. Bynum ain't no mystery to me. I done seen a hundred niggers like him. He's one of them fellows never could stay in one place. He was wandering all around the country till he got old and settled here. The only thing different about Bynum is he bring all this heebie-jeebie stuff with him.

BERTHA: I still say he was staying here when she came. That's why she came . . . to see him.

SETH: You can say what you want. I know the facts of it. She come on here four years ago all heartbroken cause she couldn't find her little girl. And Bynum wasn't nowhere around. She got mixed up in that old heebie-jeebie nonsense with him after he came.

BERTHA: Well, if she came on before Bynum I don't know where she stayed. Cause she stayed up there in Hiram's room. Hiram couldn't get along with Bynum and left out of here owing you two dollars. Now, I know you ain't forgot about that!

SETH: Sure did! You know Hiram ain't paid me that two dollars yet. So that's why he be ducking and hiding when he see me down on Logan Street. You right. Martha did come on after Bynum. I forgot that's why Hiram left.

BERTHA: Him and Bynum never could see eye to eye. They always rubbed each other the wrong way. Hiram got to thinking that Bynum was trying to put a fix on him and he moved out. Martha came to see Bynum and ended up taking Hiram's room. Now, I know what I'm talking about. She stayed on here three years till they moved the church.

SETH: She out there in Rankin now. I know where she at. I know where they moved the church to. She right out there in Rankin in that place used to be a shoe store. Used to be Wolf's shoe

235

store. They moved to a bigger place and they put that church in there. I know where she at. I know just where she at.

BERTHA: Why don't you tell the man? You see he looking for her.

SETH: I ain't gonna tell that man where that woman is! What I wanna do that for? I don't know nothing about that man. I don't know why he looking for her. He might wanna do her a harm. I ain't gonna carry that on my hands. He looking for her, he gonna have to find her for himself. I ain't gonna help him. Now, if he had come and presented himself as a gentleman—the way Martha Pentecost's husband would have done—then I would have told him. But I ain't gonna tell this old wild-eyed mean-looking nigger nothing!

BERTHA: Well, why don't you get a ride with Selig and go up there and tell her where he is? See if she wanna see him. If that's her little girl . . . you say Martha was looking for her.

SETH: You know me, Bertha. I don't get mixed up in nobody's business.

(BYNUM *enters from the stairs.*)

BYNUM: Morning, Seth. Morning, Bertha. Can I still get some breakfast? Mr. Loomis been down here this morning?

SETH: He done gone out and come back. He up there now. Left out of here early this morning wearing that coat. Hot as it is, the man wanna walk around wearing a big old heavy coat. He come back in here, paid me for another week, sat down there waiting on Selig. Got tired of waiting and went on back upstairs.

BYNUM: Where's the little girl?

SETH: She out there in the front. Had to chase her and that Reuben off the front porch. She out there somewhere.

BYNUM: Look like if Martha was around here he would have found her by now. My guess is she ain't in the city.

SETH: She ain't! I know where she at. I know just where she at. But I ain't gonna tell him. Not the way he look.

BERTHA: Here go your coffee, Bynum.

BYNUM: He says he gonna get Selig to find her for him.

SETH: Selig can't find her. He talk all that . . . but unless he get lucky and knock on her door he can't find her. That's the only way he find anybody. He got to get lucky. But I know just where she at.

BERTHA: Here go some biscuits, Bynum.

BYNUM: What else you got over there, Sister Bertha? You got some grits and gravy over there? I could go for some of that this morning.

BERTHA: (*Sets a bowl on the table.*) Seth, come on and help me turn this mattress over. Come on.

SETH: Something ain't right with that fellow, Bynum. I don't like the way he stare at everybody.

BYNUM: Mr. Loomis alright, Seth. He just a man got something on his mind. He just got a straightforward mind, that's all.

SETH: What's that fellow that they had around here? Moses, that's Moses Houser. Man went crazy and jumped off the Brady Street Bridge. I told you when I seen him something wasn't right about him. And I'm telling you about this fellow now.
(*There is a knock on the door.* SETH *goes to answer it. Enter* RUTHERFORD SELIG.)
Ho! Come on in, Selig.

BYNUM: If it ain't the People Finder himself.

SELIG: Bynum, before you start . . . I ain't seen no shiny man now.

BYNUM: Who said anything about that? I ain't said nothing about that. I just called you a first-class People Finder.

SELIG: How many dustpans you get out of that sheet metal, Seth?

SETH: You walked by them on your way in. They sitting out there on the porch. Got twenty-eight. Got four out of each sheet and

237

made Bertha a coffeepot out the other one. They a little small but they got nice handles.

SELIG: That was twenty cents apiece, right? That's what we agreed on.

SETH: That's five dollars and sixty cents. Twenty on top of twenty-eight. How many sheets you bring me?

SELIG: I got eight out there. That's a dollar twenty makes me owe you . . .

SETH: Four dollars and forty cents.

SELIG: (*Paying him.*) Go on and make me some dustpans. I can use all you can make.
(LOOMIS *enters from the stairs.*)

LOOMIS: I been watching for you. He say you find people.

BYNUM: Mr. Loomis here wants you to find his wife.

LOOMIS: He say you find people. Find her for me.

SELIG: Well, let's see here . . . find somebody, is it?
(SELIG *rummages through his pockets. He has several notebooks and he is searching for the right one.*)
Alright now . . . what's the name?

LOOMIS: Martha Loomis. She my wife. Got married legal with the paper and all.

SELIG: (*Writing.*) Martha . . . Loomis. How tall is she?

LOOMIS: She five feet from the ground.

SELIG: Five feet . . . tall. Young or old?

LOOMIS: She a young woman. Got long pretty hair.

SELIG: Young . . . long . . . pretty . . . hair. Where did you last see her?

LOOMIS: Tennessee. Nearby Memphis.

SELIG: When was that?

LOOMIS: Nineteen hundred and one.

SELIG: Nineteen . . . hundred and one. I'll tell you, mister . . . you better off without them. Now you take me . . . old Rutherford Selig could tell you a thing or two about these women. I ain't met one yet I could understand. Now, you take Sally out there. That's all a man needs is a good horse. I say giddup and she go. Say whoa and she stop. I feed her some oats and she carry me wherever I want to go. Ain't had a speck of trouble out of her since I had her. Now, I been married. A long time ago down in Kentucky. I got up one morning and I saw this look on my wife's face. Like way down deep inside her she was wishing I was dead. I walked around that morning and every time I looked at her she had that look on her face. It seem like she knew I could see it on her. Every time I looked at her I got smaller and smaller. Well, I wasn't gonna stay around there and just shrink away. I walked out on the porch and closed the door behind me. When I closed the door she locked it. I went out and bought me a horse. And I ain't been without one since! Martha Loomis, huh? Well, now I'll do the best I can do. That's one dollar.

LOOMIS: (Holding out the dollar suspiciously.) How you find her?

SELIG: Well now, it ain't no easy job like you think. You can't just go out there and find them like that. There's a lot of little tricks to it. It's not an easy job keeping up with you Nigras the way you move about so. Now you take this woman you looking for . . . this Martha Loomis. She could be anywhere. Time I find her, if you don't keep your eye on her, she'll be gone off someplace else. You'll be thinking she over here and she'll be over there. But like I say there's a lot of little tricks to it.

LOOMIS: You say you find her.

SELIG: I can't promise anything but we been finders in my family for a long time. Bringers and finders. My great-granddaddy used to bring Nigras across the ocean on ships. That wasn't no easy job either. Sometimes the winds would blow so hard you'd think the hand of God was set against the sails. But it set him well in pay and he settled in this new land and found him a wife of good Christian charity with a mind for kids and the like and well . . . here I am, Rutherford Selig. You're in good hands, mister. Me and my daddy have found plenty Nigras. My daddy, rest his soul, used to find runaway slaves for the plantation bosses. He was the best there was at it. Jonas B. Selig. Had him a reputation stretched clean across the country. After Abraham Lincoln give you all Nigras your freedom papers and with you all looking all over for each other . . . we started finding Nigras for Nigras. Of course, it don't pay as much. But the People Finding business ain't so bad.

LOOMIS: (*Hands him the dollar.*) Find her. Martha Loomis. Find her for me.

SELIG: Like I say, I can't promise you anything. I'm going back upriver, and if she's around in them parts I'll find her for you. But I can't promise you anything.

LOOMIS: When you coming back?

SELIG: I'll be back on Saturday. I come and see Seth to pick up my order on Saturday.

BYNUM: You going upriver, huh? You going up around my way. I used to go all up through there. Blawnox . . . Clairton. Used to go up to Rankin and take that first right-hand road. I wore many a pair of shoes out walking around that way. You'd have thought I was a missionary spreading the gospel the way I wandered all around them parts.

SELIG: Okay, Bynum. See you on Saturday.

SETH: Here, let me walk out with you. Help you with them dustpans. (SETH *and* SELIG *exit out the back.* BERTHA *enters from the stairs carrying a bundle of sheets.*)

BYNUM: Herald Loomis got the People Finder looking for Martha.

BERTHA: You can call him a People Finder if you want to. I know

240

Rutherford Selig carries people away too. He done carried a whole bunch of them away from here. Folks plan on leaving plan by Selig's timing. They wait till he get ready to go, then they hitch a ride on his wagon. Then he charge folks a dollar to tell them where he took them. Now, that's the truth of Rutherford Selig. This old People Finding business is for the birds. He ain't never found nobody he ain't took away. Herald Loomis, you just wasted your dollar.
(BERTHA *exits into the bedroom.*)

LOOMIS: He say he find her. He say he find her by Saturday. I'm gonna wait till Saturday.
(*The lights fade to black.*)

ACT ONE: Scene Three

It is Sunday morning, the next day. The lights come up on the kitchen.
SETH *sits talking to* BYNUM. *The breakfast dishes have been cleared away.*

SETH: They can't see that. Neither one of them can see that. Now, how much sense it take to see that? All you got to do is be able to count. One man making ten pots is five men making fifty pots. But they can't see that. Asked where I'm gonna get my five men. Hell, I can teach anybody how to make a pot. I can teach you. I can take you out there and get you started right now. Inside of two weeks you'd know how to make a pot. All you got to do is want to do it. I can get five men. I ain't worried about getting no five men.

BERTHA: (*Calls from the bedroom.*) Seth. Come on and get ready now. Reverend Gates ain't gonna be holding up his sermon cause you sitting out there talking.

SETH: Now, you take the boy, Jeremy. What he gonna do after he put in that road? He can't do nothing but go put in another one somewhere. Now, if he let me show him how to make some pots and pans . . . then he'd have something can't nobody take away from him. After a while he could get his own tools and go off somewhere and make his own pots and pans. Find him somebody to sell them to. Now, Selig can't make no pots and pans. He can sell them but he can't make them. I get me five men with some tools and we'd make him so many pots and pans he'd have to

242

open up a store somewhere. But they can't see that. Neither Mr. Cohen nor Sam Green.

BERTHA: (*Calls from the bedroom.*) Seth . . . time be wasting. Best be getting on.

SETH: I'm coming, woman! (*To* BYNUM.) Want me to sign over the house to borrow five hundred dollars. I ain't that big a fool. That's all I got. Sign it over to them and then I won't have nothing.
(JEREMY *enters waving a dollar and carrying his guitar.*)

JEREMY: Look here, Mr. Bynum . . . won me another dollar last night down at Seefus! Me and that Mattie Campbell went down there again and I played contest. Ain't no guitar players down there. Wasn't even no contest. Say, Mr. Seth, I asked Mattie Campbell if she wanna come by and have Sunday dinner with us. Get some fried chicken.

SETH: It's gonna cost you twenty-five cents.

JEREMY: That's alright. I got a whole dollar here. Say Mr. Seth . . . me and Mattie Campbell talked it over last night and she gonna move in with me. If that's alright with you.

SETH: Your business is your business . . . but it's gonna cost her a dollar a week for her board. I can't be feeding nobody for free.

JEREMY: Oh, she know that, Mr. Seth. That's what I told her, say she'd have to pay for her meals.

SETH: You say you got a whole dollar there . . . turn loose that twenty-five cents.

JEREMY: Suppose she move in today, then that make seventy-five cents more, so I'll give you the whole dollar for her now till she gets here.
(SETH *pockets the money and exits into the bedroom.*)

BYNUM: So you and that Mattie Campbell gonna take up together?

JEREMY: I told her she don't need to be by her lonesome, Mr.

Bynum. Don't make no sense for both of us to be by our lonesome. So she gonna move in with me.

BYNUM: Sometimes you got to be where you supposed to be. Sometimes you can get all mixed up in life and come to the wrong place.

JEREMY: That's just what I told her, Mr. Bynum. It don't make no sense for her to be all mixed up and lonesome. May as well come here and be with me. She a fine woman too. Got them long legs. Knows how to treat a fellow too. Treat you like you wanna be treated.

BYNUM: You just can't look at it like that. You got to look at the whole thing. Now, you take a fellow go out there, grab hold to a woman and think he got something cause she sweet and soft to the touch. Alright. Touching's part of life. It's in the world like everything else. Touching's nice. It feels good. But you can lay your hand upside a horse or a cat, and that feels good too. What's the difference? When you grab hold to a woman, you got something there. You got a whole world there. You got a way of life kicking up under your hand. That woman can take and make you feel like something. I ain't just talking about in the way of jumping off into bed together and rolling around with each other. Anybody can do that. When you grab hold to that woman and look at the whole thing and see what you got . . . why, she can take and make something out of you. Your mother was a woman. That's enough right there to show you what a woman is. Enough to show you what she can do. She made something out of you. Taught you converse, and all about how to take care of yourself, how to see where you at and where you going tomorrow, how to look out to see what's coming in the way of eating, and what to do with yourself when you get lonesome. That's a mighty thing she did. But you just can't look at a woman to jump off into bed with her. That's a foolish thing to ignore a woman like that.

JEREMY: Oh, I ain't ignoring her, Mr. Bynum. It's hard to ignore a woman got legs like she got.

244

BYNUM: Alright. Let's try it this way. Now, you take a ship. Be out there on the water traveling about. You out there on that ship sailing to and from. And then you see some land. Just like you see a woman walking down the street. You see that land and it don't look like nothing but a line out there on the horizon. That's all it is when you first see it. A line that cross your path out there on the horizon. Now, a smart man know when he see that land, it ain't just a line setting out there. He know that if you get off the water to go take a good look . . . why, there's a whole world right there. A whole world with everything imagin-able under the sun. Anything you can think of you can find on that land. Same with a woman. A woman is everything a man need. To a smart man she water and berries. And that's all a man need. That's all he need to live on. You give me some water and berries and if there ain't nothing else I can live a hundred years. See, you just like a man looking at the horizon from a ship. You just seeing a part of it. But it's a blessing when you learn to look at a woman and see in maybe just a few strands of her hair, the way her cheek curves . . . to see in that everything there is out of life to be gotten. It's a blessing to see that. You know you done right and proud by your mother to see that. But you got to learn it. My telling you ain't gonna mean nothing. You got to learn how to come to your own time and place with a woman.

JEREMY: What about your woman, Mr. Bynum? I know you done had some woman.

BYNUM: Oh, I got them in memory time. That lasts longer than any of them ever stayed with me.

JEREMY: I had me an old gal one time . . .
(*There is a knock on the door.* JEREMY *goes to answer it. Enter* MOLLY CUNNINGHAM. *She is about twenty-six, the kind of woman that "could break in on a dollar anywhere she goes." She carries a small cardboard suitcase, and wears a colorful dress of the fashion of the day.* JEREMY's *heart jumps out of his chest when he sees her.*)

MOLLY: You got any rooms here? I'm looking for a room.

245

JEREMY: Yeah . . . Mr. Seth got rooms. Sure . . . wait till I get Mr. Seth. (*Calls.*) Mr. Seth! Somebody here to see you! (*To* MOLLY.) Yeah, Mr. Seth got some rooms. Got one right next to me. This a nice place to stay, too. My name's Jeremy. What's yours?

(SETH *enters dressed in his Sunday clothes.*)

SETH: Ho!

JEREMY: This here woman looking for a place to stay. She say you got any rooms.

MOLLY: Mister, you got any rooms? I seen your sign say you got rooms.

SETH: How long you plan on staying?

MOLLY: I ain't gonna be here long. I ain't looking for no home or nothing. I'd be in Cincinnati if I hadn't missed my train.

SETH: Rooms cost two dollars a week.

MOLLY: Two dollars!

SETH: That includes meals. We serve two meals a day. That's breakfast and dinner.

MOLLY: I hope it ain't on the third floor.

SETH: That's the only one I got. Third floor to the left. That's pay up in advance week to week.

MOLLY: (*Going into her bosom.*) I'm gonna pay you for one week. My name's Molly. Molly Cunningham.

SETH: I'm Seth Holly. My wife's name is Bertha. She do the cooking and taking care of around here. She got sheets on the bed. Towels twenty-five cents a week extra if you ain't got none. You get breakfast and dinner. We got fried chicken on Sundays.

MOLLY: That sounds good. Here's two dollars and twenty-five cents. Look here, Mister . . . ?

SETH: Holly. Seth Holly.

MOLLY: Look here, Mr. Holly. I forgot to tell you. I likes me some company from time to time. I don't like being by myself.

SETH: Your business is your business. I don't meddle in nobody's business. But this is a respectable house. I don't have no riffraff around here. And I don't have no women hauling no men up to their rooms to be making their living. As long as we understand each other then we'll be alright with each other.

MOLLY: Where's the outhouse?

SETH: Straight through the door over yonder.

MOLLY: I get my own key to the front door?

SETH: Everybody get their own key. If you come in late just don't be making no whole lot of noise and carrying on. Don't allow no fussing and fighting around here.

MOLLY: You ain't got to worry about that, mister. Which way you say that outhouse was again?

SETH: Straight through that door over yonder.
(MOLLY *exits out the back door.* JEREMY *crosses to watch her.*)

JEREMY: Mr. Bynum, you know what? I think I know what you was talking about now.
(*The lights go down on the scene.*)

ACT ONE: Scene Four

The lights come up on the kitchen. It is later the same evening. MATTIE *and all the residents of the house, except* LOOMIS, *sit around the table. They have finished eating and most of the dishes have been cleared.*

MOLLY: That sure was some good chicken.

JEREMY: That's what I'm talking about. Miss Bertha, you sure can fry some chicken. I thought my mama could fry some chicken. But she can't do half as good as you.

SETH: I know it. That's why I married her. She don't know that, though. She think I married her for something else.

BERTHA: I ain't studying you, Seth. Did you get your things moved in alright, Mattie?

MATTIE: I ain't had that much. Jeremy helped me with what I did have.

BERTHA: You'll get to know your way around here. If you have any questions about anything just ask me. You and Molly both. I get along with everybody. You'll find I ain't no trouble to get along with.

MATTIE: You need some help with the dishes?

BERTHA: I got me a helper. Ain't I, Zonia? Got me a good helper.

ZONIA: Yes, ma'am.

SETH: Look at Bynum sitting over there with his belly all poked out. Ain't saying nothing. Sitting over there half-asleep. Ho, Bynum!

BERTHA: If Bynum ain't saying nothing what you wanna start him up for?

SETH: Ho, Bynum!

BYNUM: What you hollering at me for? I ain't doing nothing.

SETH: Come on, we gonna Juba.

BYNUM: You know me, I'm always ready to Juba.

SETH: Well, come on, then.
(SETH *pulls out a harmonica and blows a few notes.*)
Come on there, Jeremy. Where's your guitar? Go get your guitar. Bynum say he's ready to Juba.

JEREMY: Don't need no guitar to Juba. Ain't you never Juba without a guitar?
(JEREMY *begins to drum on the table.*)

SETH: It ain't that. I ain't never Juba with one! Figured to try it and see how it worked.

BYNUM: (*Drumming on the table.*) You don't need no guitar. Look at Molly sitting over there. She don't know we Juba on Sunday. We gonna show you something tonight. You and Mattie Campbell both. Ain't that right, Seth?

SETH: You said it! Come on, Bertha, leave them dishes be for a while. We gonna Juba.

BYNUM: Alright. Let's Juba down!
(*The Juba is reminiscent of the ring shouts of the African slaves. It is a call and response dance.* BYNUM *sits at the table and drums. He calls the dance as others clap hands, shuffle, and stomp around the table. It should be as African as possible, with the performers working themselves up into a near frenzy. The words can be improvised, but should include some mention of the Holy Ghost. In the middle of the dance* HERALD LOOMIS *enters.*)

249

LOOMIS: (*In a rage.*) Stop it! Stop!
(*They stop and turn to look at him.*)
You all sitting up here singing about the Holy Ghost. What's so holy about the Holy Ghost? You singing and singing. You think the Holy Ghost coming? You singing for the Holy Ghost to come? What he gonna do, huh? He gonna come with tongues of fire to burn up your woolly heads? You gonna tie onto the Holy Ghost and get burned up? What you got then? Why God got to be so big? Why he got to be bigger than me? How much big is there? How much big do you want?
(LOOMIS *starts to unzip his pants.*)

SETH: Nigger, you crazy!

LOOMIS: How much big you want?

SETH: You done plumb lost your mind!
(LOOMIS *begins to speak in tongues and dance around the kitchen.* SETH *starts after him.*)

BERTHA: Leave him alone, Seth. He ain't in his right mind.

LOOMIS: (*Stops suddenly.*) You all don't know nothing about me. You don't know what I done seen. Herald Loomis done seen some things he ain't got words to tell you.
(LOOMIS *starts to walk out the front door and is thrown back and collapses, terror-stricken by his vision.* BYNUM *crawls to him.*)

BYNUM: What you done seen, Herald Loomis?

LOOMIS: I done seen bones rise up out the water. Rise up and walk across the water. Bones walking on top of the water.

BYNUM: Tell me about them bones, Herald Loomis. Tell me what you seen.

LOOMIS: I come to this place . . . to this water that was bigger than the whole world. And I looked out . . . and I seen these bones rise up out the water. Rise up and begin to walk on top of it.

BYNUM: Wasn't nothing but bones and they walking on top of the water.

250

LOOMIS: Walking without sinking down. Walking on top of the water.

BYNUM: Just marching in a line.

LOOMIS: A whole heap of them. They come up out the water and started marching.

BYNUM: Wasn't nothing but bones and they walking on top of the water.

LOOMIS: One after the other. They just come up out the water and start to walking.

BYNUM: They walking on the water without sinking down. They just walking and walking. And then . . . what happened, Herald Loomis?

LOOMIS: They just walking across the water.

BYNUM: What happened, Herald Loomis? What happened to the bones?

LOOMIS: They just walking across the water . . . and then . . . they sunk down.

BYNUM: The bones sunk into the water. They all sunk down.

LOOMIS: All at one time! They just all fell in the water at one time.

BYNUM: Sunk down like anybody else.

LOOMIS: When they sink down they made a big splash and this here wave come up . . .

BYNUM: A big wave, Herald Loomis. A big wave washed over the land.

LOOMIS: It washed them out of the water and up on the land. Only . . . only . . .

BYNUM: Only they ain't bones no more.

LOOMIS: They got flesh on them! Just like you and me!

251

BYNUM: Everywhere you look the waves is washing them up on the land right on top of one another.

LOOMIS: They black. Just like you and me. Ain't no difference.

BYNUM: Then what happened, Herald Loomis?

LOOMIS: They ain't moved or nothing. They just laying there.

BYNUM: You just laying there. What you waiting on, Herald Loomis?

LOOMIS: I'm laying there . . . waiting.

BYNUM: What you waiting on, Herald Loomis?

LOOMIS: I'm waiting on the breath to get into my body.

BYNUM: The breath coming into you, Herald Loomis. What you gonna do now?

LOOMIS: The wind's blowing the breath into my body. I can feel it. I'm starting to breathe again.

BYNUM: What you gonna do, Herald Loomis?

LOOMIS: I'm gonna stand up. I got to stand up. I can't lay here no more. All the breath coming into my body and I got to stand up.

BYNUM: Everybody's standing up at the same time.

LOOMIS: The ground's starting to shake. There's a great shaking. The world's busting half in two. The sky's splitting open. I got to stand up.
(LOOMIS *attempts to stand up.*)
My legs . . . my legs won't stand up!

BYNUM: Everybody's standing and walking toward the road. What you gonna do, Herald Loomis?

LOOMIS: My legs won't stand up.

BYNUM: They shaking hands and saying good-bye to each other and walking every whichaway down the road.

LOOMIS: I got to stand up!

252

BYNUM: They walking around here now. Mens. Just like you and me. Come right up out the water.

LOOMIS: Got to stand up.

BYNUM: They walking, Herald Loomis. They walking around here now.

LOOMIS: I got to stand up. Get up on the road.

BYNUM: Come on, Herald Loomis.
(LOOMIS *tries to stand up.*)

LOOMIS: My legs won't stand up! My legs won't stand up!
(LOOMIS *collapses on the floor as the lights go down to black.*)

ACT TWO: Scene One

The lights come up on the kitchen. BERTHA *busies herself with breakfast preparations.* SETH *sits at the table.*

SETH: I don't care what his problem is! He's leaving here!

BERTHA: You can't put the man out and he got that little girl. Where they gonna go then?

SETH: I don't care where he go. Let him go back where he was before he come here. I ain't asked him to come here. I knew when I first looked at him something wasn't right with him. Dragging that little girl around with him. Looking like he be sleeping in the woods somewhere. I knew all along he wasn't right.

BERTHA: A fellow get a little drunk he's liable to say or do anything. He ain't done no big harm.

SETH: I just don't have all that carrying on in my house. When he come down here I'm gonna tell him. He got to leave here. My daddy wouldn't stand for it and I ain't gonna stand for it either.

BERTHA: Well, if you put him out you have to put Bynum out too. Bynum right there with him.

SETH: If it wasn't for Bynum ain't no telling what would have happened. Bynum talked to that fellow just as nice and calmed him down. If he wasn't here ain't no telling what would have happened. Bynum ain't done nothing but talk to him and kept

255

him calm. Man acting all crazy with that foolishness. Naw, he's leaving here.

BERTHA: What you gonna tell him? How you gonna tell him to leave?

SETH: I'm gonna tell him straight out. Keep it nice and simple. Mister, you got to leave here!
(MOLLY *enters from the stairs.*)

MOLLY: Morning.

BERTHA: Did you sleep alright in that bed?

MOLLY: Tired as I was I could have slept anywhere. It's a real nice room, though. This is a nice place.

SETH: I'm sorry you had to put up with all that carrying on last night.

MOLLY: It don't bother me none. I done seen that kind of stuff before.

SETH: You won't have to see it around here no more.
(BYNUM *is heard singing offstage.*)
I don't put up with all that stuff. When that fellow come down here I'm gonna tell him.

BYNUM: (*Singing.*)
Soon my work will all be done
Soon my work will all be done
Soon my work will all be done

I'm going to see the king.

BYNUM: (*Enters.*) Morning, Seth. Morning, Sister Bertha. I see we got Molly Cunningham down here at breakfast.

SETH: Bynum, I wanna thank you for talking to that fellow last night and calming him down. If you hadn't been here ain't no telling what might have happened.

BYNUM: Mr. Loomis alright, Seth. He just got a little excited.

256

SETH: Well, he can get excited somewhere else cause he leaving here.
(MATTIE *enters from the stairs.*)

BYNUM: Well, there's Mattie Campbell.

MATTIE: Good morning.

BERTHA: Sit on down there, Mattie. I got some biscuits be ready in a minute. The coffee's hot.

MATTIE: Jeremy gone already?

BYNUM: Yeah, he leave out of here early. He got to be there when the sun come up. Most working men got to be there when the sun come up. Everybody but Seth. Seth work at night. Mr. Olowski so busy in his shop he got fellows working at night.
(LOOMIS *enters from the stairs.*)

SETH: Mr. Loomis, now . . . I don't want no trouble. I keeps me a respectable house here. I don't have no carrying on like what went on last night. This has been a respectable house for a long time. I'm gonna have to ask you to leave.

LOOMIS: You got my two dollars. That two dollars say we stay till Saturday.
(LOOMIS *and* SETH *glare at each other.*)

SETH: Alright. Fair enough. You stay till Saturday. But come Saturday you got to leave here.

LOOMIS: (*Continues to glare at* SETH. *He goes to the door and calls.*) Zonia. You stay around this house, you hear? Don't you go anywhere.
(LOOMIS *exits out the front door.*)

SETH: I knew it when I first seen him. I knew something wasn't right with him.

BERTHA: Seth, leave the people alone to eat their breakfast. They don't want to hear that. Go on out there and make some pots and pans. That's the only time you satisfied is when you out

257

there. Go on out there and make some pots and pans and leave them people alone.

SETH: I ain't bothering anybody. I'm just stating the facts. I told you, Bynum.
(BERTHA *shoos* SETH *out the back door and exits into the bedroom.*)

MOLLY: (*To* BYNUM.) You one of them voodoo people?

BYNUM: I got a power to bind folks if that what you talking about.

MOLLY: I thought so. The way you talked to that man when he started all that spooky stuff. What you say you had the power to do to people? You ain't the cause of him acting like that, is you?

BYNUM: I binds them together. Sometimes I help them find each other.

MOLLY: How do you do that?

BYNUM: With a song. My daddy taught me how to do it.

MOLLY: That's what they say. Most folks be what they daddy is. I wouldn't want to be like my daddy. Nothing ever set right with him. He tried to make the world over. Carry it around with him everywhere he go. I don't want to be like that. I just take life as it come. I don't be trying to make it over.
(*Pause.*)
Your daddy used to do that too, huh? Make people stay together?

BYNUM: My daddy used to heal people. He had the Healing Song. I got the Binding Song.

MOLLY: My mama used to believe in all that stuff. If she got sick she would have gone and saw your daddy. As long as he didn't make her drink nothing. She wouldn't drink nothing nobody give her. She was always afraid somebody was gonna poison her. How your daddy heal people?

BYNUM: With a song. He healed people by singing over them. I seen him do it. He sung over this little white girl when she was sick. They made a big to-do about it. They carried the girl's bed

258

out in the yard and had all her kinfolk standing around. The little girl laying up there in the bed. Doctors standing around can't do nothing to help her. And they had my daddy come up and sing his song. It didn't sound no different than any other song. It was just somebody singing. But the song was its own thing and it come out and took upon this little girl with its power and it healed her.

MOLLY: That's sure something else. I don't understand that kind of thing. I guess if the doctor couldn't make me well I'd try it. But otherwise I don't wanna be bothered with that kind of thing. It's too spooky.

BYNUM: Well, let me get on out here and get to work.
(BYNUM *gets up and heads out the back door.*)

MOLLY: I ain't meant to offend you or nothing. What's your name . . . Bynum? I ain't meant to say nothing to make you feel bad now.
(BYNUM *exits out the back door.*)
(*To* MATTIE.) I hope he don't feel bad. He's a nice man. I don't wanna hurt nobody's feelings or nothing.

MATTIE: I got to go on up to Doc Goldblum's and finish this ironing.

MOLLY: Now, that's something I don't never wanna do. Iron no clothes. Especially somebody else's. That's what I believe killed my mama. Always ironing and working, doing somebody else's work. Not Molly Cunningham.

MATTIE: It's the only job I got. I got to make it someway to fend for myself.

MOLLY: I thought Jeremy was your man. Ain't he working?

MATTIE: We just be keeping company till maybe Jack come back.

MOLLY: I don't trust none of these men. Jack or nobody else. These men liable to do anything. They wait just until they get one woman tied and locked up with them . . . then they look around to see if they can get another one. Molly don't pay them no mind. One's just as good as the other if you ask me. I ain't never met one that meant nobody no good. You got any babies?

MATTIE: I had two for my man, Jack Carper. But they both died.

MOLLY: That be the best. These men make all these babies, then run off and leave you to take care of them. Talking about they wanna see what's on the other side of the hill. I make sure I don't get no babies. My mama taught me how to do that.

MATTIE: Don't make me no mind. That be nice to be a mother.

MOLLY: Yeah? Well, you go on, then. Molly Cunningham ain't gonna be tied down with no babies. Had me a man one time who I thought had some love in him. Come home one day and he was packing his trunk. Told me the time come when even the best of friends must part. Say he was gonna send me a special delivery some old day. I watched him out the window when he carried that trunk out and down to the train station. Said if he was gonna send me a special delivery I wasn't gonna be there to get it. I done found out the harder you try to hold onto them, the easier it is for some gal to pull them away. Molly done learned that. That's why I don't trust nobody but the good Lord above, and I don't love nobody but my mama.

MATTIE: I got to get on. Doc Goldblum gonna be waiting.
(MATTIE *exits out the front door.* SETH *enters from his workshop with his apron, gloves, goggles, etc. He carries a bucket and crosses to the sink for water.*)

SETH: Everybody gone but you, huh?

MOLLY: That little shack out there by the outhouse . . . that's where you make them pots and pans and stuff?

SETH: Yeah, that's my work shed. I go out there . . . take these hands and make something out of nothing. Take that metal and bend and twist it whatever way I want. My daddy taught me that. He used to make pots and pans. That's how I learned it.

MOLLY: I never knew nobody made no pots and pans. My uncle used to shoe horses.

(JEREMY *enters at the front door.*)

SETH: I thought you was working? Ain't you working today?

JEREMY: Naw, they fired me. White fellow come by told me to give him fifty cents if I wanted to keep working. Going around to all the colored making them give him fifty cents to keep hold to their jobs. Them other fellows, they was giving it to him. I kept hold to mine and they fired me.

SETH: Boy, what kind of sense that make? What kind of sense it make to get fired from a job where you making eight dollars a week and all it cost you is fifty cents. That's seven dollars and fifty cents profit! This way you ain't got nothing.

JEREMY: It didn't make no sense to me. I don't make but eight dollars. Why I got to give him fifty cents of it? He go around to all the colored and he got ten dollars extra. That's more than I make for a whole week.

SETH: I see you gonna learn the hard way. You just looking at the facts of it. See, right now, without the job, you ain't got nothing. What you gonna do when you can't keep a roof over your head? Right now, come Saturday, unless you come up with another two dollars, you gonna be out there in the streets. Down up under one of them bridges trying to put some food in your belly and wishing you had given that fellow that fifty cents.

JEREMY: Don't make me no difference. There's a big road out there. I can get my guitar and always find me another place to stay. I ain't planning on staying in one place for too long noway.

SETH: We gonna see if you feel like that come Saturday!

(SETH *exits out the back.* JEREMY *sees* MOLLY.)

JEREMY: Molly Cunningham. How you doing today, sugar?

MOLLY: You can go on back down there tomorrow and go back to work if you want. They won't even know who you is. Won't even

261

know it's you. I had me a fellow did that one time. They just went ahead and signed him up like they never seen him before.

JEREMY: I'm tired of working anyway. I'm glad they fired me. You sure look pretty today.

MOLLY: Don't come telling me all that pretty stuff. Beauty wanna come in and sit down at your table asking to be fed. I ain't hardly got enough for me.

JEREMY: You know you pretty. Ain't no sense in you saying nothing about that. Why don't you come on and go away with me?

MOLLY: You tied up with that Mattie Campbell. Now you talking about running away with me.

JEREMY: I was just keeping her company cause she lonely. You ain't the lonely kind. You the kind that know what she want and how to get it. I need a woman like you to travel around with. Don't you wanna travel around and look at some places with Jeremy? With a woman like you beside him, a man can make it nice in the world.

MOLLY: Molly can make it nice by herself too. Molly don't need nobody leave her cold in hand. The world rough enough as it is.

JEREMY: We can make it better together. I got my guitar and I can play. Won me another dollar last night playing guitar. We can go around and I can play at the dances and we can just enjoy life. You can make it by yourself alright, I agrees with that. A woman like you can make it anywhere she go. But you can make it better if you got a man to protect you.

MOLLY: What places you wanna go around and look at?

JEREMY: All of them! I don't want to miss nothing. I wanna go everywhere and do everything there is to be got out of life. With a woman like you it's like having water and berries. A man got everything he need.

MOLLY: You got to be doing more than playing that guitar. A dollar a day ain't hardly what Molly got in mind.

JEREMY: I gambles real good. I got a hand for it.

MOLLY: Molly don't work. And Molly ain't up for sale.

JEREMY: Sure, baby. You ain't got to work with Jeremy.

MOLLY: There's one more thing.

JEREMY: What's that, sugar?

MOLLY: Molly ain't going South.
  (*The lights go down on the scene.*)

ACT TWO: Scene Two

The lights come up on the parlor. SETH *and* BYNUM *sit playing a game of dominoes.* BYNUM *sings to himself.*

BYNUM: (*Singing.*)
  They tell me Joe Turner's come and gone
  Ohhh Lordy
  They tell me Joe Turner's come and gone
  Ohhh Lordy
  Got my man and gone

  Come with forty links of chain
  Ohhh Lordy
  Come with forty links of chain
  Ohhh Lordy
  Got my man and gone

SETH: Come on and play if you gonna play.

BYNUM: I'm gonna play. Soon as I figure out what to do.

SETH: You can't figure out if you wanna play or you wanna sing.

BYNUM: Well sir, I'm gonna do a little bit of both.
  (*Playing.*)
  There. What you gonna do now?
  (*Singing.*)
  They tell me Joe Turner's come and gone
  Ohhh Lordy

They tell me Joe Turner's come and gone
Ohhh Lordy

SETH: Why don't you hush up that noise.

BYNUM: That's a song the women sing down around Memphis. The women down there made up that song. I picked it up down there about fifteen years ago.
(LOOMIS *enters from the front door.*)

BYNUM: Evening, Mr. Loomis.

SETH: Today's Monday, Mr. Loomis. Come Saturday your time is up. We done ate already. My wife roasted up some yams. She got your plate sitting in there on the table. (*To* BYNUM.) Whose play is it?

BYNUM: Ain't you keeping up with the game? I thought you was a domino player. I just played so it got to be your turn.
(LOOMIS *goes into the kitchen, where a plate of yams is covered and set on the table. He sits down and begins to eat with his hands.*)

SETH: (*Plays.*) Twenty! Give me twenty! You didn't know I had that ace five. You was trying to play around that. You didn't know I had that lying there for you.

BYNUM: You ain't done nothing. I let you have that to get mine.

SETH: Come on and play. You ain't doing nothing but talking. I got a hundred and forty points to your eighty. You ain't doing nothing but talking. Come on and play.

BYNUM: (*Singing.*)
They tell me Joe Turner's come and gone
Ohhh Lordy
They tell me Joe Turner's come and gone
Ohhh Lordy
Got my man and gone
He come with forty links of chain
Ohhh Lordy

265

LOOMIS: Why you singing that song? Why you singing about Joe Turner?

BYNUM: I'm just singing to entertain myself.

SETH: You trying to distract me. That's what you trying to do.

BYNUM: (*Singing.*)
Come with forty links of chain
Ohhh Lordy
Come with forty links of chain
Ohhh Lordy

LOOMIS: I don't like you singing that song, mister!

SETH: Now, I ain't gonna have no more disturbance around here, Herald Loomis. You start any more disturbance and you leavin here, Saturday or no Saturday.

BYNUM: The man ain't causing no disturbance, Seth. He just say he don't like the song.

SETH: Well, we all friendly folk. All neighborly like. Don't have no squabbling around here. Don't have no disturbance. You gonna have to take that someplace else.

BYNUM: He just say he don't like the song. I done sung a whole lot of songs people don't like. I respect everybody. He here in the house too. If he don't like the song, I'll sing something else. I know lots of songs. You got "I Belong to the Band," "Don't You Leave Me Here." You got "Praying on the Old Campground," "Keep your Lamp Trimmed and Burning" . . . I know lots of songs.
(*Sings.*)
Boys, I'll be so glad when payday come
Captain, Captain, when payday comes
Gonna catch that Illinois Central
Going to Kankakee

SETH: Why don't you hush up that hollering and come on and play dominoes.

266

BYNUM: You ever been to Johnstown, Herald Loomis? You look like a fellow I seen around there.

LOOMIS: I don't know no place with that name.

BYNUM: That's around where I seen my shiny man. See, you looking for this woman. I'm looking for a shiny man. Seem like everybody looking for something.

SETH: I'm looking for you to come and play these dominoes. That's what I'm looking for.

BYNUM: You a farming man, Herald Loomis? You look like you done some farming.

LOOMIS: Same as everybody. I done farmed some, yeah.

BYNUM: I used to work at farming . . . picking cotton. I reckon everybody done picked some cotton.

SETH: I ain't! I ain't never picked no cotton. I was born up here in the North. My daddy was a freed man. I ain't never even seen no cotton!

BYNUM: Mr. Loomis done picked some cotton. Ain't you, Herald Loomis? You done picked a bunch of cotton.

LOOMIS: How you know so much about me? How you know what I done? How much cotton I picked?

BYNUM: I can tell from looking at you. My daddy taught me how to do that. Say when you look at a fellow, if you taught yourself to look for it, you can see his song written on him. Tell you what kind of man he is in the world. Now, I can look at you, Mr. Loomis, and see you a man who done forgot his song. Forgot how to sing it. A fellow forget that and he forget who he is. Forget how he's supposed to mark down life. Now, I used to travel all up and down this road and that . . . looking here and there. Searching. Just like you, Mr. Loomis. I didn't know what I was searching for. The only thing I knew was something was keeping me dissatisfied. Something wasn't making my heart smooth and easy. Then one day my daddy gave me a song. That song had a weight to it

267

that was hard to handle. That song was hard to carry. I fought against it. Didn't want to accept that song. I tried to find my daddy to give him back the song. But I found out it wasn't his song. It was my song. It had come from way deep inside me. I looked long back in memory and gathered up pieces and snatches of things to make that song. I was making it up out of myself. And that song helped me on the road. Made it smooth to where my footsteps didn't bite back at me. All the time that song getting bigger and bigger. That song growing with each step of the road. It got so I used all of myself up in the making of that song. Then I was the song in search of itself. That song rattling in my throat and I'm looking for it. See, Mr. Loomis, when a man forgets his song he goes off in search of it . . . till he find out he's got it with him all the time. That's why I can tell you one of Joe Turner's niggers. Cause you forgot how to sing your song.

LOOMIS: You lie! How you see that? I got a mark on me? Joe Turner done marked me to where you can see it? You telling me I'm a marked man. What kind of mark you got on you?
(BYNUM *begins singing.*)

BYNUM:
They tell me Joe Turner's come and gone
Ohhh Lordy
They tell me Joe Turner's come and gone
Ohhh Lordy
Got my man and gone

LOOMIS: Had a whole mess of men he catched. Just go out hunting regular like you go out hunting possum. He catch you and go home to his wife and family. Ain't thought about you going home to yours. Joe Turner catched me when my little girl was just born. Wasn't nothing but a little baby sucking on her mama's titty when he catched me. Joe Turner catched me in nineteen hundred and one. Kept me seven years until nineteen hundred and eight. Kept everybody seven years. He'd go out hunting and bring back forty men at a time. And keep them seven years.

268

I was walking down this road in this little town outside of Memphis. Come up on these fellows gambling. I was a deacon in the Abundant Life Church. I stopped to preach to these fellows to see if maybe I could turn some of them from their sinning when Joe Turner, brother of the governor of the great sovereign state of Tennessee, swooped down on us and grabbed everybody there. Kept us all seven years.

My wife Martha gone from me after Joe Turner catched me. Got out from under Joe Turner on his birthday. Me and forty other men put in our seven years and he let us go on his birthday. I made it back to Henry Thompson's place where me and Martha was sharecropping and Martha's gone. She taken my little girl and left her with her mama and took off north. We been looking for her ever since. That's been going on four years now we been looking. That's the only thing I know to do. I just wanna see her face so I can get me a starting place in the world. The world got to start somewhere. That's what I been looking for. I been wandering a long time in somebody else's world. When I find my wife that be the making of my own.

BYNUM: Joe Turner tell why he caught you? You ever asked him that?

LOOMIS: I ain't never seen Joe Turner. Seen him to where I could touch him. I asked one of them fellows one time why he catch niggers. Asked him what I got he want? Why don't he keep on to himself? Why he got to catch me going down the road by my lonesome? He told me I was worthless. Worthless is something you throw away. Something you don't bother with. I ain't seen him throw me away. Wouldn't even let me stay away when I was by my lonesome. I ain't tried to catch him when he going down the road. So I must got something he want. What I got?

SETH: He just want you to do his work for him. That's all.

LOOMIS: I can look at him and see where he big and strong enough to do his own work. So it can't be that. He must want something he ain't got.

269

BYNUM: That ain't hard to figure out. What he wanted was your song. He wanted to have that song to be his. He thought by catching you he could learn that song. Every nigger he catch he's looking for the one he can learn that song from. Now he's got you bound up to where you can't sing your own song. Couldn't sing it them seven years cause you was afraid he would snatch it from under you. But you still got it. You just forgot how to sing it.

LOOMIS: (*To* BYNUM.) I know who you are. You one of them bones people.
(*The lights go down to black.*)

ACT TWO: Scene Three

The lights come up on the kitchen. It is the following morning. MATTIE *and* BYNUM *sit at the table.* BERTHA *busies herself at the stove.*

BYNUM: Good luck don't know no special time to come. You sleep with that up under your pillow and good luck can't help but come to you. Sometimes it come and go and you don't even know it's been there.

BERTHA: Bynum, why don't you leave that gal alone? She don't wanna be hearing all that. Why don't you go on and get out the way and leave her alone?

BYNUM: (*Getting up.*) Alright, alright. But you mark what I'm saying. It'll draw it to you just like a magnet.
(BYNUM *exits up the stairs as* LOOMIS *enters.*)

BERTHA: I got some grits here, Mr. Loomis.
(BERTHA *sets a bowl on the table.*)
If I was you, Mattie, I wouldn't go getting all tied up with Bynum in that stuff. That kind of stuff, even if it do work for a while, it don't last. That just get people more mixed up than they is already. And I wouldn't waste my time fretting over Jeremy either. I seen it coming. I seen it when she first come here. She that kind of woman run off with the first man got a dollar to spend on her. Jeremy just young. He don't know what he getting into. That gal don't mean him no good. She's just using him to keep from being by herself. That's the worst use of a man you can

271

have. You ought to be glad to wash him out of your hair. I done seen all kind of men. I done seen them come and go through here. Jeremy ain't had enough to him for you. You need a man who's got some understanding and who willing to work with that understanding to come to the best he can. You got your time coming. You just tries too hard and can't understand why it don't work for you. Trying to figure it out don't do nothing but give you a troubled mind. Don't no man want a woman with a troubled mind.

You get all that trouble off your mind and just when it look like you ain't never gonna find what you want . . . you look up and it's standing right there. That's how I met my Seth. You gonna look up one day and find everything you want standing right in front of you. Been twenty-seven years now since that happened to me. But life ain't no happy-go-lucky time where everything be just like you want it. You got your time coming. You watch what Bertha's saying.
(SETH *enters.*)

SETH: Ho!

BERTHA: What you doing come in here so late?

SETH: I was standing down there on Logan Street talking with the fellows. Henry Allen tried to sell me that old piece of horse he got.
(*He sees* LOOMIS.)
Today's Tuesday, Mr. Loomis.

BERTHA: (*Pulling him toward the bedroom.*) Come on in here and leave that man alone to eat his breakfast.

SETH: I ain't bothering nobody. I'm just reminding him what day it is.
(SETH *and* BERTHA *exit into the bedroom.*)

LOOMIS: That dress got a color to it.

MATTIE: Did you really see them things like you said? Them people come up out the ocean?

272

LOOMIS: It happened just like that, yeah.

MATTIE: I hope you find your wife. It be good for your little girl for you to find her.

LOOMIS: Got to find her for myself. Find my starting place in the world. Find me a world I can fit in.

MATTIE: I ain't never found no place for me to fit. Seem like all I do is start over. It ain't nothing to find no starting place in the world. You just start from where you find yourself.

LOOMIS: Got to find my wife. That be my starting place.

MATTIE: What if you don't find her? What you gonna do then if you don't find her?

LOOMIS: She out there somewhere. Ain't no such thing as not finding her.

MATTIE: How she got lost from you? Jack just walked away from me.

LOOMIS: Joe Turner split us up. Joe Turner turned the world upside-down. He bound me on to him for seven years.

MATTIE: I hope you find her. It be good for you to find her.

LOOMIS: I been watching you. I been watching you watch me.

MATTIE: I was just trying to figure out if you seen things like you said.

LOOMIS: (Getting up.) Come here and let me touch you. I been watching you. You a full woman. A man needs a full woman. Come on and be with me.

MATTIE: I ain't got enough for you. You'd use me up too fast.

LOOMIS: Herald Loomis got a mind seem like you a part of it since I first seen you. It's been a long time since I seen a full woman. I can smell you from here. I know you got Herald Loomis on your mind, can't keep him apart from it. Come on and be with Herald Loomis.

273

(LOOMIS *has crossed to* MATTIE. *He touches her awkwardly, gently, tenderly. Inside he howls like a lost wolf pup whose hunger is deep. He goes to touch her but finds he cannot.*)
I done forgot how to touch.
(*The lights fade to black.*)

ACT TWO: Scene Four

It is early the next morning. The lights come up on ZONIA *and* REUBEN *in the yard.*

REUBEN: Something spooky going on around here. Last night Mr. Bynum was out in the yard singing and talking to the wind . . . and the wind it just be talking back to him. Did you hear it?

ZONIA: I heard it. I was scared to get up and look. I thought it was a storm.

REUBEN: That wasn't no storm. That was Mr. Bynum. First he say something . . . and the wind it say back to him.

ZONIA: I heard it. Was you scared? I was scared.

REUBEN: And then this morning . . . I seen Miss Mabel!

ZONIA: Who Miss Mabel?

REUBEN: Mr. Seth's mother. He got her picture hanging up in the house. She been dead.

ZONIA: How you seen her if she been dead?

REUBEN: Zonia . . . if I tell you something you promise you won't tell anybody?

ZONIA: I promise.

REUBEN: It was early this morning . . . I went out to the coop to

275

feed the pigeons. I was down on the ground like this to open up the door to the coop . . . when all of a sudden I seen some feets in front of me. I looked up . . . and there was Miss Mabel standing there.

ZONIA: Reuben, you better stop telling that! You ain't seen nobody!

REUBEN: Naw, it's the truth. I swear! I seen her just like I see you. Look . . . you can see where she hit me with her cane.

ZONIA: Hit you? What she hit you for?

REUBEN: She says, "Didn't you promise Eugene something?" Then she hit me with her cane. She say, "Let them pigeons go." Then she hit me again. That's what made them marks.

ZONIA: Jeez man . . . get away from me. You done seen a haunt!

REUBEN: Shhhh. You promised, Zonia!

ZONIA: You sure it wasn't Miss Bertha come over there and hit you with her hoe?

REUBEN: It wasn't no Miss Bertha. I told you it was Miss Mabel. She was standing right there by the coop. She had this light coming out of her and then she just melted away.

ZONIA: What she had on?

REUBEN: A white dress. Ain't even had no shoes or nothing. Just had on that white dress and them big hands . . . and that cane she hit me with.

ZONIA: How you reckon she knew about the pigeons? You reckon Eugene told her?

REUBEN: I don't know. I sure ain't asked her none. She say Eugene was waiting on them pigeons. Say he couldn't go back home till I let them go. I couldn't get the door to the coop open fast enough.

ZONIA: Maybe she an angel? From the way you say she look with that white dress. Maybe she an angel.

REUBEN: Mean as she was . . . how she gonna be an angel? She used to chase us out her yard and frown up and look evil all the time.

ZONIA: That don't mean she can't be no angel cause of how she looked and cause she wouldn't let no kids play in her yard. It go by if you got any spots on your heart and if you pray and go to church.

REUBEN: What about she hit me with her cane? An angel wouldn't hit me with her cane.

ZONIA: I don't know. She might. I still say she was an angel.

REUBEN: You reckon Eugene the one who sent old Miss Mabel?

ZONIA: Why he send her? Why he don't come himself?

REUBEN: Figured if he send her maybe that'll make me listen. Cause she old.

ZONIA: What you think it feel like?

REUBEN: What?

ZONIA: Being dead.

REUBEN: Like being sleep only you don't know nothing and can't move no more.

ZONIA: If Miss Mabel can come back . . . then maybe Eugene can come back too.

REUBEN: We can go down to the hideout like we used to! He could come back everyday! It be just like he ain't dead.

ZONIA: Maybe that ain't right for him to come back. Feel kinda funny to be playing games with a haunt.

REUBEN: Yeah . . . what if everybody came back? What if Miss Mabel came back just like she ain't dead? Where you and your daddy gonna sleep then?

ZONIA: Maybe they go back at night and don't need no place to sleep.

277

REUBEN: It still don't seem right. I'm sure gonna miss Eugene. He's the bestest friend anybody ever had.

ZONIA: My daddy say if you miss somebody too much it can kill you. Say he missed me till it liked to killed him.

REUBEN: What if your mama's already dead and all the time you looking for her?

ZONIA: Naw, she ain't dead. My daddy say he can smell her.

REUBEN: You can't smell nobody that ain't here. Maybe he smelling old Miss Bertha. Maybe Miss Bertha your mama?

ZONIA: Naw, she ain't. My mamma got long pretty hair and she five feet from the ground!

REUBEN: Your daddy say when you leaving?
(ZONIA *doesn't respond.*)
Maybe you gonna stay in Mr. Seth's house and don't go looking for your mama no more.

ZONIA: He say we got to leave on Saturday.

REUBEN: Dag! You just only been here for a little while. Don't seem like nothing ever stay the same.

ZONIA: He say he got to find her. Find him a place in the world.

REUBEN: He could find him a place in Mr. Seth's house.

ZONIA: It don't look like we never gonna find her.

REUBEN: Maybe he find her by Saturday then you don't have to go.

ZONIA: I don't know.

REUBEN: You look like a spider!

ZONIA: I ain't no spider!

REUBEN: Got them long skinny arms and legs. You look like one of them black widows.

ZONIA: I ain't no black window nothing! My name is Zonia!

REUBEN: That's what I'm gonna call you . . . Spider.

ZONIA: You can call me that, but I don't have to answer.

REUBEN: You know what? I think maybe I be your husband when I grow up.

ZONIA: How you know?

REUBEN: I ask my grandpap how you know and he say when the moon falls into a girl's eyes that how you know.

ZONIA: Did it fall into my eyes?

REUBEN: Not that I can tell. Maybe I ain't old enough. Maybe you ain't old enough.

ZONIA: So there! I don't know why you telling me that lie!

REUBEN: That don't mean nothing cause I can't see it. I know it's there. Just the way you look at me sometimes look like the moon might have been in your eyes.

ZONIA: That don't mean nothing if you can't see it. You supposed to see it.

REUBEN: Shucks, I see it good enough for me. You ever let anybody kiss you?

ZONIA: Just my daddy. He kiss me on the cheek.

REUBEN: It's better on the lips. Can I kiss you on the lips?

ZONIA: I don't know. You ever kiss anybody before?

REUBEN: I had a cousin let me kiss her on the lips one time. Can I kiss you?

ZONIA: Okay.
(REUBEN *kisses her and lays his head against her chest.*)
What you doing?

REUBEN: Listening. Your heart singing!

ZONIA: It is not.

279

REUBEN: Just beating like a drum. Let's kiss again.
(*They kiss again.*)
Now you mine, Spider. You my girl, okay?

ZONIA: Okay.

REUBEN: When I get grown, I come looking for you.

ZONIA: Okay.
(*The lights fade to black.*)

ACT TWO: Scene Five

The lights come up on the kitchen. It is Saturday. BYNUM, LOOMIS, *and* ZONIA *sit at the table.* BERTHA *prepares breakfast.* ZONIA *has on a white dress.*

BYNUM: With all this rain we been having he might have ran into some washed-out roads. If that wagon got stuck in the mud he's liable to be still upriver somewhere. If he's upriver then he ain't coming until tomorrow.

LOOMIS: Today's Saturday. He say he be here on Saturday.

BERTHA: Zonia, you gonna eat your breakfast this morning.

ZONIA: Yes, ma'am.

BERTHA: I don't know how you expect to get any bigger if you don't eat. I ain't never seen a child that didn't eat. You about as skinny as a bean pole.
(*Pause.*)
Mr. Loomis, there's a place down on Wylie. Zeke Mayweather got a house down there. You ought to see if he got any rooms.
(LOOMIS *doesn't respond.*)
Well, you're welcome to some breakfast before you move on.
(MATTIE *enters from the stairs.*)

MATTIE: Good morning.

BERTHA: Morning, Mattie. Sit on down there and get you some breakfast.

281

BYNUM: Well, Mattie Campbell, you been sleeping with that up under your pillow like I told you?

BERTHA: Bynum, I done told you to leave that gal alone with all that stuff. You around here meddling in other people's lives. She don't want to hear all that. You ain't doing nothing but confusing her with that stuff.

MATTIE: (*To* LOOMIS.) You all fixing to move on?

LOOMIS: Today's Saturday. I'm paid up till Saturday.

MATTIE: Where you going to?

LOOMIS: Gonna find my wife.

MATTIE: You going off to another city?

LOOMIS: We gonna see where the road take us. Ain't no telling where we wind up.

MATTIE: Eleven years is a long time. Your wife . . . she might have taken up with someone else. People do that when they get lost from each other.

LOOMIS: Zonia. Come on, we gonna find your mama.
(LOOMIS *and* ZONIA *cross to the door.*)

MATTIE: (*To* ZONIA.) Zonia, Mattie got a ribbon here match your dress. Want Mattie to fix your hair with her ribbon?
(ZONIA *nods.* MATTIE *ties the ribbon in her hair.*)
There . . . it got a color just like your dress.
(*To* LOOMIS.)
I hope you find her. I hope you be happy.

LOOMIS: A man looking for a woman be lucky to find you. You a good woman, Mattie. Keep a good heart.
(LOOMIS *and* ZONIA *exit.*)

BERTHA: I been watching that man for two weeks . . . and that's the closest I come to seeing him act civilized. I don't know what's between you all, Mattie . . . but the only thing that man needs is somebody to make him laugh. That's all you need in the world is love and laughter. That's all anybody needs. To have love in one hand and laughter in the other.

(BERTHA *moves about the kitchen as though blessing it and chasing away the huge sadness that seems to envelop it. It is a dance and demonstration of her own magic, her own remedy that is centuries old and to which she is connected by the muscles of her heart and the blood's memory.*)

You hear me, Mattie? I'm talking about laughing. The kind of laugh that comes from way deep inside. To just stand and laugh and let life flow right through you. Just laugh to let yourself know you're alive.

(*She begins to laugh. It is a near-hysterical laughter that is a celebration of life, both its pain and its blessing.* MATTIE *and* BYNUM *join in the laughter.* SETH *enters from the front door.*)

SETH: Well, I see you all having fun.

(SETH *begins to laugh with them.*)

That Loomis fellow standing up there on the corner watching the house. He standing right up there on Manila Street.

BERTHA: Don't you get started on him. The man done left out of here and that's the last I wanna hear of it. You about to drive me crazy with that man.

SETH: I just say he standing up there on the corner. Acting sneaky like he always do. He can stand up there all he want. As long as he don't come back in here.

(*There is a knock on the door.* SETH *goes to answer it. Enter* MARTHA LOOMIS [PENTECOST]. *She is a young woman about twenty-eight. She is dressed as befitting a member of an Evangelist church.* RUTHERFORD SELIG *follows.*)

SETH: Look here, Bertha. It's Martha Pentecost. Come on in, Martha. Who that with you? Oh . . . that's Selig. Come on in, Selig.

BERTHA: Come on in, Martha. It's sure good to see you.

BYNUM: Rutherford Selig, you a sure enough first-class People Finder!

SELIG: She was right out there in Rankin. You take that first right-hand road . . . right there at that church on Wooster Street. I started to go right past and something told me to stop at the church and see if they needed any dustpans.

SETH: Don't she look good, Bertha.

BERTHA: Look all nice and healthy.

MARTHA: Mr. Bynum . . . Selig told me my little girl was here.

SETH: There's some fellow around here say he your husband. Say his name is Loomis. Say you his wife.

MARTHA: Is my little girl with him?

SETH: Yeah, he got a little girl with him. I wasn't gonna tell him where you was. Not the way this fellow look. So he got Selig to find you.

MARTHA: Where they at? They upstairs?

SETH: He was standing right up there on Manila Street. I had to ask him to leave cause of how he was carrying on. He come in here one night—
(The door opens and LOOMIS and ZONIA enter. MARTHA and LOOMIS stare at each other.)

LOOMIS: Hello, Martha.

MARTHA: Herald . . . Zonia?

LOOMIS: You ain't waited for me, Martha. I got out the place looking to see your face. Seven years I waited to see your face.

MARTHA: Herald, I been looking for you. I wasn't but two months behind you when you went to my mama's and got Zonia. I been looking for you ever since.

LOOMIS: Joe Turner let me loose and I felt all turned around inside. I just wanted to see your face to know that the world was still there. Make sure everything still in its place so I could reconnect myself together. I got there and you was gone, Martha.

MARTHA: Herald . . .

LOOMIS: Left my little girl motherless in the world.

MARTHA: I didn't leave her motherless, Herald. Reverend Tolliver
wanted to move the church up North cause of all the trouble the
colored folks was having down there. Nobody knew what was
gonna happen traveling them roads. We didn't even know if we
was gonna make it up here or not. I left her with my mama so she
be safe. That was better than dragging her out on the road having
to duck and hide from people. Wasn't no telling what was gonna
happen to us. I didn't leave her motherless in the world. I been
looking for you.

LOOMIS: I come up on Henry Thompson's place after seven years of
living in hell, and all I'm looking to do is see your face.

MARTHA: Herald, I didn't know if you was ever coming back. They
told me Joe Turner had you and my whole world split half in two.
My whole life shattered. It was like I had poured it in a cracked
jar and it all leaked out the bottom. When it go like that there
ain't nothing you can do to put it back together. You talking
about Henry Thompson's place like I'm still gonna be working
the land by myself. How I'm gonna do that? You wasn't gone but
two months and Henry Thompson kicked me off his land and I
ain't had no place to go but to my mama's. I stayed and waited
there for five years before I woke up one morning and decided
that you was dead. Even if you weren't, you was dead to me. I
wasn't gonna carry you with me no more. So I killed you in my
heart. I buried you. I mourned you. And then I picked up what
was left and went on to make life without you. I was a young
woman with life at my beckon. I couldn't drag you behind me
like a sack of cotton.

LOOMIS: I just been waiting to look on your face to say my good-
bye. That good-bye got so big at times, seem like it was gonna
swallow me up. Like Jonah in the whale's belly I sat up in that
good-bye for three years. That good-bye kept me out on the road
searching. Not looking on women in their houses. It kept me

bound up to the road. All the time that good-bye swelling up in my chest till I'm about to bust. Now that I see your face I can say my good-bye and make my own world.
(LOOMIS *takes* ZONIA's *hand and presents her to* MARTHA.)
Martha . . . here go your daughter. I tried to take care of her. See that she had something to eat. See that she was out of the elements. Whatever I know I tried to teach her. Now she need to learn from her mother whatever you got to teach her. That way she won't be no one-sided person.
(LOOMIS *stoops to* ZONIA.)
Zonia, you go live with your mama. She a good woman. You go on with her and listen to her good. You my daughter and I love you like a daughter. I hope to see you again in the world somewhere. I'll never forget you.

ZONIA: (*Throws her arms around* LOOMIS *in a panic.*) I won't get no bigger! My bones won't get no bigger! They won't! I promise! Take me with you till we keep searching and never finding. I won't get no bigger! I promise!

LOOMIS: Go on and do what I told you now.

MARTHA: (*Goes to* ZONIA *and comforts her.*) It's alright, baby. Mama's here. Mama's here. Don't worry. Don't cry.
(MARTHA *turns to* BYNUM.)
Mr. Bynum, I don't know how to thank you. God bless you.

LOOMIS: It was you! All the time it was you that bind me up! You bound me to the road!

BYNUM: I ain't bind you, Herald Loomis. You can't bind what don't cling.

LOOMIS: Everywhere I go people wanna bind me up. Joe Turner wanna bind me up! Reverend Tolliver wanna bind me up. You wanna bind me up. Everybody wanna bind me up. Well, Joe Turner's come and gone and Herald Loomis ain't for no binding. I ain't gonna let nobody bind me up!
(LOOMIS *pulls out a knife.*)

BYNUM: It wasn't you, Herald Loomis. I ain't bound you. I bound the little girl to her mother. That's who I bound. You binding yourself. You bound onto your song. All you got to do is stand up and sing it, Herald Loomis. It's right there kicking at your throat. All you got to do is sing it. Then you be free.

MARTHA: Herald . . . look at yourself! Standing there with a knife in your hand. You done gone over to the devil. Come on . . . put down the knife. You got to look to Jesus. Even if you done fell away from the church you can be saved again. The Bible say, "The Lord is my shepherd I shall not want. He maketh me to lie down in green pastures. He leads me beside the still water. He restoreth my soul. He leads me in the path of righteousness for His name's sake. Even though I walk through the shadow of death—"

LOOMIS: That's just where I be walking!

MARTHA: "I shall fear no evil. For thou art with me. Thy rod and thy staff, they comfort me."

LOOMIS: You can't tell me nothing about no valleys. I done been all across the valleys and the hills and the mountains and the oceans.

MARTHA: "Thou preparest a table for me in the presence of my enemies."

LOOMIS: And all I seen was a bunch of niggers dazed out of their woolly heads. And Mr. Jesus Christ standing there in the middle of them, grinning.

MARTHA: "Thou annointest my head with oil, my cup runneth over."

LOOMIS: He grin that big old grin . . . and niggers wallowing at his feet.

MARTHA: "Surely goodness and mercy shall follow me all the days of my life, and I shall dwell in the house of the Lord forever."

LOOMIS: Great big old white man . . . your Mr. Jesus Christ.

Standing there with a whip in one hand and tote board in another, and them niggers swimming in a sea of cotton. And he counting. He tallying up the cotton. "Well, Jeremiah . . . what's the matter, you ain't picked but two hundred pounds of cotton today? Got to put you on half rations." And Jeremiah go back and lay up there on his half rations and talk about what a nice man Mr. Jesus Christ is cause he give him salvation after he die. Something wrong here. Something don't fit right!

MARTHA: You got to open up your heart and have faith, Herald. This world is just a trial for the next. Jesus offers you salvation.

LOOMIS: I been wading in the water. I been walking all over the River Jordan. But what it get me, huh? I done been baptized with blood of the lamb and the fire of the Holy Ghost. But what I got, huh? I got salvation? My enemies all around me picking the flesh from my bones. I'm choking on my own blood and all you got to give me is salvation?

MARTHA: You got to be clean, Herald. You got to be washed with the blood of the lamb.

LOOMIS: Blood make you clean? You clean with blood?

MARTHA: Jesus bled for you. He's the Lamb of God who takest away the sins of the world.

LOOMIS: I don't need nobody to bleed for me! I can bleed for myself.

MARTHA: You got to be something, Herald. You just can't be alive. Life don't mean nothing unless it got a meaning.

LOOMIS: What kind of meaning you got? What kind of clean you got, woman? You want blood? Blood make you clean? You clean with blood?
(LOOMIS *slashes himself across the chest. He rubs the blood over his face and comes to a realization.*)
I'm standing! I'm standing! My legs stood up! I'm standing now!
(*Having found his song, the song of self-sufficiency, fully resurrected, cleansed and given breath, free from any encumbrance other than the*

workings of his own heart and the bonds of the flesh, having accepted the responsibility for his own presence in the world, he is free to soar above the environs that weighed and pushed his spirit into terrifying contractions.)

Good-bye, Martha.

(LOOMIS turns and exits, the knife still in his hands. MATTIE looks about the room and rushes out after him.)

BYNUM: Herald Loomis, you shining! You shining like new money!

The lights go down to black.

AUGUST WILSON'S
BLUES POETICS

> *This world is not my home*
> *This world is not my home*
> *This world is a howling wilderness*
> *This world is not my home*
> —traditional slave lament/song

Early in 1990, an august body of military governors, scholars, artists, village chiefs and elders assembled for the Eagle on Iroko
Symposium at the University of Nigeria—its locus being the ancestral hearth for many Africans of the New World diaspora—to
celebrate the sixtieth birthday of the distinguished native-born author, Chinua Achebe. Rising to the occasion in the appropriate
role of extended family member, the Jamaican author, Michael
Thelwell, christened the proceedings with an inaugural address that
attributed Achebe's achievement to an ability to retrieve from the
impact of a colonial cultural hegemony, a Nigerian particularity in
his prose, and cites James Baldwin as the American author whose
work best reflects such an achievement.

> Baldwin, whose uncompromisingly clear vision and
> magnificent prose was firmly anchored in the rich cultural
> traditions and bitter historical experience of Black
> America . . . in texture . . . a prose voice informed by, and
> fashioned out of, the blues' rough-edged poetry; the gospel's
> soaring rhythms; the prophetic fires of the Old Testament; the
> mournful affirmation of the sorrow songs; the preacher's shout;

291

the field-hand's holler; the blues man's growl and the disciplined freedom of jazz improvisation. On the smithy of his art, all these elements were forged and transmuted into an imperishable prose instrument of black—which is to say universal—struggle and moral affirmation.[1]

Similarly, the expressive ethos of August Wilson's twentieth-century cycle—each play regarding a decade in the African-American experience—is hewn from the same bedrock of racial memory and particularity of experience. Memory enshrines experience, unless otherwise burdened with an uneasy reconciliation with the middle passage that leads to spiritual vitiation in the process of Anglo-American assimilation. Wilson, as chronicler of the African-American experience, has responded to the durable ethos of the African continuum, which is the cultural mooring of black expression throughout the diaspora. Unlike Topsy—the picca-ninny house servant of *Uncle Tom's Cabin* whose rude separation from Africa had so throughly arrested her memory of any continuity with an ancestral homeland that she would submit to the on-tological conclusion that she "jes growed"—Wilson's memory has fashioned a vernacular voice that resonates, with archetypical sonority, the rhythms of West African "talking drums" and the riffs of Delta blues guitars. As an expression of the African-American oral tradition, the "signifyin'" voice of the blues bears witness to a particularity of experience that is universally illuminating.

Uumh, standing at the crossroad, I tried to flag a ride,
Standing at the crossroad, I tried to flag a ride,
Didn't nobody seem to know me, everybody passed me by.
                              —Robert Johnson, "Crossroad Blues"

Irrespective of African adaptation to the Eurocentric priorities of dominant culture, marginalization prompted African-Americans to probe the recesses of ancestral memory for recognizable Afri-can values, linguistic techniques, and aesthetic constructions that could be cultivated as a source of ethnic reaffirmation. The African-American moral personality, then, is shaped and validated by a value system gleaned from the folkloric repository of experience that stores the culturally specific sanctions and embargos that perpetuate a common world view. The recursive reappearance of Afrocentric values in social rituals and common beliefs has served to solidify both secular and sacred mythologies of group affiliation, as described by Ralph Ellison in "The Art of Fiction."

> The clue to this can be found in folklore, which offers the first drawings of any group's character. It preserves mainly those situations which have repeated themselves again and again in the history of any given group. It describes those rites, manners, customs and so forth, which insure the good life, or destroy it; and it describes those boundaries of feeling, thought and action which that particular group has found to be the limitation of the human condition. It projects this wisdom in symbols which express the group's will to survive; it embodies those values by which the group lives and dies.[2]

Certainly, it can be argued that the African-American experience is not monolithic nor otherwise without its diversity; however, the psychic response to the dislocations shared in American history binds the collective consciousness into an ethos that strives for material and spiritual cohesion. The stories and gestures that codify collective experience are framed ideologically by myths which serve to preserve the essential metaphors of the cultural worldview. In respect to myths and ideologies, Richard Stokin notes that myths "are stories, drawn from history, that have acquired through usage over many generations a symbolizing function central to the culture of the society that produces them . . . [and] suggests that by understanding and imaginatively reenacting conflict resolutions of the past, we can interpret and control the unresolved conflicts of the present."[3] Whereas history is the logos of time, mythos is the aggrandizement of collective experience that invariably looms larger in our consciousness than the conceits and deceits contrived by descriptive reality.

Thus, embedded in the mythological store of black experience are the many symbolic gestures that correspond to the changing ideals that lead to moral and ethical perfection. The source of

revelation might be located in the Bible, or Duke Ellington's orchestration book, or the orally transmitted boasts recalling the
ribald adventures of the Signifyin' Monkey. Those who claim creative access to the experience—the poet/musician/artist—must
consciously tune into the mythologies of folk experience for the recurring ancestral residue of symbolic gestures that lift material life
from the ground level of profane acquisition to a cosmic scale
which frames reality with the appropriate paradigms required for
adaptation to the many social transformations anticipated in a
dynamically changing world. The expressive tradition of the folk
vernacular has had many adherents—including W.E.B. Du Bois,
Jean Toomer, Langston Hughes, Zora Neale Hurston, Ralph
Ellison, and Leadbelly—in the first half of the twentieth century
and sustained in the second half of the century by the poststructural
inventions of Amiri Baraka, Ishmael Reed, Alice Walker,
Adrienne Kennedy, Toni Morrison, and Thelonious Monk, to
mention but a few of the luminaries August Wilson has joined in
the expressive continuum.

The vernacular products forged from ancestral memory, including the improvisational configuration of the blues, work songs,
church and field hollers, and verbal dexterity coupled with the
mythic significations of folktales, boasts, toasts, and the dozens—
the entire panoply of expressive strategies that serves as a unifying
principle for black identity—had once been disdained by Richard
Wright as "Forms of Things Unknown" that were "wrung from
a bleak and barren environment, an environment that stung,
crushed, all but killed" and had merely exotic appeal while inhibit-
ing the practice of more conventional standards that would launch
black art into the mainstream.[4] Wright had joined many other
post-Harlem-renaissance men of letters in retreating from the cultural dialectics of the scholar/activist W.E.B. Du Bois who, in the
mid-twenties, called for a folk play movement that was ethno-
centrically informed by the unadorned expressive modes of the
"true blood" experience of the rural south, what Houston A. Baker,
Jr., has described as the "blues matrix," where the hoots and hollers
of a "world of transcience, instability, hard luck, brutalizing work,

294

lost love, minimal security, and enduring human wit and resource-fulness in the face of disaster" was most evident.[5]

When grounded by sociological explication, the recondite aura of "Forms of Things Unknown" becomes naturalized, the magic of folk expression arrested, its products' potential to reveal ontologically significant images vitiated. Lost, for example, is the aesthetic ap-preciation of discontinuity—rather than linear continuity—as a rhythmic device in the expressive modes of African socialization, including the polymorphic orchestration of off-beats, counterbeats, and breaks in music and storytelling, and the visual tension of asymmetrical patterns woven in West African Kente cloth and the African-American quilts of the rural south, as well as the testimonial vitality expressed in discordant primary colors that energizes the street attire of black folks in a rhythmic spectacle of potency.

The vitality of "Forms of Things Unknown," however, was not lost on Langston Hughes, whose boyhood response to the arrival of a new schoolmate up from the South inspired the poem "When Sue Wears Red," rhapsodized with the appropriate repetition and call 'n' response pattern peculiar to the blues:

> When Susanna Jones wears red
> Her face is like an ancient cameo
> Turned brown by the ages.
>
> Come with a blast of trumpets,
> Jesus!
>
> When Susanna Jones wears red
> A queen from some time-dead Egyptian night
> Walks once again.
>
> Blow trumpets, Jesus!
>
> And the beauty of Susanna Jones in red
> Wakes in my heart a love-fire sharp like pain.
>
> Sweet silver trumpets,
> Jesus!

Rather than crude corruptions of accepted standards, the narrator of the *Invisible Man* viewed "Forms of Things Unknown" as the retrieval of ancient residue from a netherworld when he encounters three boys wearing zoot suits, the spectacle of their discordant colors and billowing trousers giving them the "secret" countenance of "men outside of historical time," their rhythmical swagger having the potency of ancestral spirits in the act of deliverance.

> It was as though I'd never seen their likes before: Walking slowly, their shoulders swaying, their legs swinging from their hips in trousers that ballooned upward from cuffs fitting snug about their ankles; their coats long and hip-tight with shoulders far too broad to be those of natural western men. . . . But who knew (and now I began to tremble so violently I had to lean against a refuse can)—who knew but they were the saviors, the true leaders, the bearers of something uncomfortable, burdensome, which they hated because, living outside of history, there was no one to applaud their value and they themselves failed to understand it.[6]

Those well-intentioned men of the post-Harlem-Renaissance literati withheld their "applause" for a linguistic style "fashioned out of the blues' rough-edged poetry" which, however persuasive its adherence to authentic experience, seemed subversive and threatened to deconstruct the canon of their inspirations. They had concerned themselves with the formal language of *belle lettres* and were resistant to the familiar maxim of the uptown-fast-life crowd that claimed "style is eva'thang, chile!," an observation quite consonant with the postmodern reconstruction theorist Roland Barthes who notes that style, "the decorative voice of hidden, secret flesh" goes beyond language because "imagery, delivery, vocabulary spring from the body and the past of the writer and gradually become the very reflexes of his art."[7] The cultural specificity of style, then, is the depth sounding of the author's experience, the resonance of his or her personal and collective mythology which urges the phenomenology of language to illuminate, for better or worse, the important themes of existence. Our collective sensibilities are aroused to the iconographic significance of the narrator when the poet massages our consciousness with a language infused

296

with Afrocentric codes that transform the ordinary (with subtle nuance) into multilayers of transcendental meaning.

> Poems are bullshit, unless they are
> teeth or trees or lemons piled
> on a step. Or black ladies dying
> of men leaving nickle hearts
> beating them down. Fuck poems
> and they are useful, they shoot
> come at you, love what you are,
> breathe like wrestlers, or shudder
> strangely after pissing. We want live
> words of the hip world live fresh &
> coursing blood.
> —from "Black Art," Amiri Baraka

The upheavals of the sixties encouraged a new aesthetic orthodoxy which was framed by black nationalism and led by poet/dramatist Amiri Baraka (LeRoi Jones), whose pursuit of ideological focus inspired artists to search among the folk for the expressive techniques necessary to create an Afrocentric cultural identity. The initial thrust of the black theater movement in the sixties was political, catalyzed by icons like Malcolm, at times Martin, and often featured adversarial confrontations between characters shaped by the necessary stereotypes for agitation/propaganda productions. The black artist community, deciding that the dominant culture could not conduct business as usual, set about to the task of constructing emotionally charged theatrical exercises that owned language and images consistent with the urgency of black folks to overcome the many social inequities experienced in America. A predictable amount of rhetorical parochialism emerged in the form of images that depicted black as beautiful and white as ugly. Polarization, or at least a heightening of the social contradictions, was necessary to deconstruct the value system that had held black people hostage to promises of a better life in the great by-and-by.

While the firebrand writers were often overzealous, inflaming hearts and minds if not otherwise producing raging fires in the streets, they were never culturally ambivalent or indifferent. Few

297

plays during the period reached the level of the poetic expositions into the black experience such as were revealed in Adrienne Kennedy's existential ritual, *Funnyhouse of a Negro*, Amiri Baraka's epic-ritual, *Slaveship*, Ed Bullin's absurd realism in *Goin' a Buffalo*, and Douglas Turner Ward's scathing social satire, *Day of Absence*. However, the less fully realized works served as a convenient forum for focusing on the oppressive landscape of America—an exercise which raised the eye and the ire of the nation—with texts and images configured like a tortured, passionate song that was sometimes crudely performed with inflated rhetoric and elaboration of African ascendancy.

This preoccupation with African symbology, however, was not simply a matter of atavistic nostalgia or cosmetics. It was, rather, a reaffirmation of ethnic kinship which invited spiritual renewal. The revival of a collective African memory had a chastening effect on contemporary black artists, urging them away from a posture of cultural ambivalence to achieve a vigorous, uncompromised expression of ethnic ethos in the creative process. The excavation of art from the social products of ordinary black life became the source of a new aesthetic which was articulated by Larry Neal in his now famous 1968 manifesto, "The Black Arts Movement": "The Black Arts Movement is radically opposed to any concept of the artist that alienates him from his community. Black Art is the aesthetic and spiritual sister of the Black Power concept. As such, it envisions an art that speaks directly to the needs and aspirations of Black America. In order to perform this task, the Black Arts Movement proposes a radical reordering of the western cultural aesthetic. It proposes a separate symbolism, mythology, critique, and iconology."[8]

It has been more than twenty-five years since the black theater surfaced as a subterranean movement of the American theater. Earlier definitions proposed by W.E.B. Du Bois during the twenties and later demanded in the sixties argued that the sole criteria for black theater were plays about the black experience authored by black writers and performed by black actors. The missing ingredient was style, some form of particularized presentation—more textual in its orientation than the highly esoteric kinetic rituals of Barbara

Ann Teer's National Black Theatre—resourceful enough to reveal mythic layers of folk culture without becoming burdened with the familiar sociological formulations on the black experience that had constrained the *blues voice* of Lorraine Hansberry *Raisin in the Sun*, subordinating her dramaturgy to the structural limitations of social realism popularized in the traditional American theater.

Wilson's work, on the other hand, faithfully corresponds with Neal's demand for black self-authentication. Rhetorically, however, Wilson is concerned with the significations of ontology rather than the objective documentation of casually related responses to oppression formulated in direct protest. In the process of placing a face on the Invisible Man while refiguring the turbulent angst of Bigger Thomas into gestures of liberation, Wilson charts the social disruptions of the "blues matrix" that lock his characters into a constant state of psychic and spiritual liminality as they struggle for existential definition. Stylistically, Wilson's plays are compatible with Neal's call for the self-determination of artistic purpose that is located in an oral tradition codified by the aesthetics of black church oratory and folk blues performances.

> *I'm goin' away to a world unknown,*
> *I'm goin' away to a world unknown,*
> *I'm worried now, but I won't be worried long.*
> —Charley Patton, "Down the Dirt Road Blues"

The cosmic, or the sacred experience, is also a vital inspirational index for black aesthetics. In "Black Culture and Black Consciousness," Lawrence Levine notes that religiosity in traditional African societies "is a means of extending the world spatially upward so that communication with the other world becomes ritually possible, and extending it temporally backward so that the paradigmatic acts of god and mythical ancestors can be continually re-enacted and indefinitely recoverable."[9] In order to access the lessons of myth secured in the inner world of experience, what Wole Soyinka refers to as the "psychic substructure and the temporal subsidence, the cumulative history and empirical observations of the community,"[10] Wilson has

299

lyrically tuned his voice to the expressive modes of black church and black music to reveal the archetypes in *Joe Turner's Come and Gone* (turn of the century), *Ma Rainey's Black Bottom* (the twenties), and *Fences* (mid-fifties). The plays' aspirations to achieve "paradigmatic acts of god and mythical ancestors" become legitimate testaments of struggle within the "blues matrix." While the black church is the repository of a very formal, culturally specific call-and-response ritual that leads to spiritual illumination, the blues is the secular resonator of collective oppression in America. As Ellison observes, the blues is "an impulse to keep the painful details and episodes of a brutal experience alive in one's aching consciousness, to finger its jagged grain, and to transcend it, not by consolation of philosophy but by squeezing from it a near-tragic, near comic lyricism. As a form, the blues is an autobiographical chronicle of personal catastrophe expressed lyrically,"[11] a survival tactic which is echoed in *Ma Rainey's Black Bottom:*

> MA RAINEY: White folks don't understand about the blues. They hear it come out but they don't know how it got there. They don't understand that's life's way of talking. You don't sing to feel better. You sing cause that's a way of understanding life. . . . The blues help you get out of bed in the morning. You get up knowing you ain't alone. There's something else in the world. Something's been added by that song. This be an empty world without the blues. I take that emptiness and try to fill it up with something. (Act II)

On stage, life is an illusion, a masquerade where impersonation, dialogue, plot, and conflict are amalgamated into a secular ritual. The process is designed to achieve a symbolic universe that might provide the observer/participant with an enlightened view of an otherwise static apprehension of experience. Poetic language, voiced by the archetypically conceived character, transforms the familiar into mythic revelations that are universally cogent, as opposed to rhetorically bogus. In *Fences*, a litany of social ruptures are signified in a blues narrative that gives the illusion of action when in fact it is the mind/heart that is galvanized. Here, the brooding passages of the text seem to create their own momentum, disregarding logical constructions of time. The accumulation of unrelenting anecdotes summons the emotionally invocative, incantatory power of traditional blues/church oratory before subsiding without catharsis, and the resolution is suspended in a space of heightened tension that is carried out of the theater. The mythic voice of the character archetype is qualitative, rather than quantitative, and thus is unsubjugated to the limits of temporal closure—*mockin'* time rather than marking time—telling stories that enlarge the time and space of reality by weaving a circuitous course of parenthetical anecdotes, asides, and utterances into a coherent pattern that encourages unanticipated tensions which amplify the coded significations inherent in the story. Thus, the mythic characters are annointed with the symbolic freedom reflected in Baraka's poem, "Scenario VI":

> and I came out of it
> with this marvelous yellow cane
> in my hand, yellow cashmere jacket
> green felt pants & green boater . . . & green &
> black clack shoes, polished & fast, jiggling
> in the wings . . . till Vincente says "rolllem"
> & I jiggle out on the stage, hands in my pockets,
> the cane balanced delicately under my arm, spinning
> & clack clack clacking across the bare sunday clothesline
> tilting the hat to avoid the sun & gingerly missing
> the dried branch I had put there yesterday.[12]

Deep inside the rhythm of *clack clack & clack* is the familiar resonance of a common black experience, the beginnings of a tale we all recognize, a mythic image reclaimed. We may not know the narrator by common name—could be Cool Breeze, Shine, or just plain ol' Slick—but we do recognize the style of his balancing act, the existential dilemma of liminality, suspended between being and nonbeing. He is the mythic hero as underdog, the trickster legacy of Yoruba mythology, Eshu—reinvented throughout the diaspora as Exu in Brazil, Elegua in Cuba, Papa Legba in Haiti, and the Signifyin' Monkey in urban black America—who mediates the obstacles that threaten survival and harmony with wit, cunning, guile, and a

301

godly sense of self-empowerment which accords him extravagant transgressions. Alogical and nontraditional—at least more adept at improvisation—he is unimpressed with social constraints established for mortals of average size. An awkward rhythm accompanies both his physical gait and mental convolutions as a result of having "one leg among humans and the other among the gods" and it forces him to exist in a state of liminality, suspended between the social and cosmic universe of Nature/Man/God, which he views as inextricable parts of his personal worldview. Divined with the potent, unfettered rhythms of Nature, the trickster is a source of fecund vitality, which is given phallocentric expression through his procreative issue. Levee (*Ma Rainey*), Troy (*Fences*), and Loomis (*Joe Turner*) each owe their pedigree to the trickster.

Wilson brings to the American theater, then, the oracular voice of the poet as a communal griot and has reaffirmed a kinship with the tradition of blues narratives, advancing the aesthetic strategies of polyrhythm and repetition, choric call 'n' response, double entendre and improvisation, signifyin' text that resists closure, and the re-enactment of experience by the narrator/trickster figure whose self-parodic tactics allow him to suspend the painful consequences of reality.

> *Well trouble, oh trouble*
> *Trouble on my worried mind,*
> *When you see me laughin',*
> *I'm laughin' to keep from cryin'.*
> —Bertha "Chippie" Hill, "Trouble in Mind"

Irony, as opposed to self-indulgent pathos, is how the blues voice negotiates the dilemma. The narrator/trickster must step gingerly through an emotional minefield of pathologies presumed to be irrevocably related to the naturalistic documentation of the "blues matrix." This "blues matrix" threatens to unmask and reduce an otherwise self-inspired strategy for redemption to a posture of self-pity. Wilson carefully avoids freezing the social landscape into tidy frames of social realism by invoking authentic mythic insinuations

302

which amplify the African experience in America with cosmic resonance.

The dry spell blues are falling, drove me from door to door,
Dry spell blues are falling, drove me from door to door,
The dry spell blues have put everybody on the killing floor.
—Son House, "Dry Spell Blues"

In *Fences*, the patriarchal potency of Troy Maxson cannot be gauged through socio-metric calculations on how the "haves" and "have-nots" respond to material reality. Unlike Willie Loman in *Death of a Salesman*, whose shrinking world causes him to experience a sense of marginalization, Troy has no respect for the limitations imposed on him by a hostile world and thus avoids engaging in cynical devaluations of self-esteem that might reduce him to a victim. Neither does he repress the immutable hostilities of the world. Instead, in the spirit of the Yoruba trickster, Eshu—who in addition to being the guardian of the crossroads, master of style and stylus, and phallic god of procreativity, is also the master of mystical barriers—Troy will erect a fence to set the boundaries of his universe, a barrier that serves the dual function of keeping the profane at bay and containing divine order within his immediate province where, on the heels of hard labor, he engages in weekly payday drinking rituals to signify his sexual prowess and testify to his personal heroics while straddling the brink of despair. Even Death is no match for this old trickster who, when stricken with a pneumonia fever, naturalizes Death with a signifying riff:

TROY: Death standing there staring at me . . . carrying that sickle in his hand. Finally he say, "You want bound over for another year? See, just like that . . . "You want bound over for another year?" I told him, "Bound over hell! Let's settle this now!

It seem like he kinda fell back when I said that, and all the cold went out of me. I reached down and grabbed that sickle and threw it just as far as I could throw it . . . and me and him commenced to wrestling.

303

We wrestled for three days and three nights. I can't say where I found the strength from. Every time it seemed like he was gonna get the best of me, I'd reach way down deep inside myself and find the strength to do him one better. (I, i)

But then, Troy is a survivor, enjoying the extravagant transgressions of a trickster, reinventing himself as the occasion requires. When he walks through the house, as his wife Rose laments, he "fill[s] it up," absorbing all the spaces, nullifying the independent thoughts and actions of his son Cory, who tries to access the outer world beyond Troy's sanctified province. Cory's confrontation with Troy is a rite of passage which is often misconstrued as a struggle between father and son for dominance when, in fact, there are no rights shared by sons with their fathers in traditional African-American households. Rather than embodying the achievement of an egalitarian spirit in the natural order, Troy archetypically represents the entitlements of cosmic prerogative which are implied in the indisputable declarations of patriarchal authority that continue to resonate in the hearts and minds of most black folks today: "I brought you into the world . . . I'll take you out of the world!" The posture of cosmic prerogative that allows Troy to reign without injunction is designed to transform a life of aborted expectations into a reasonable reality without appeals to sentimental judgment. Cory, whose feelings are scaled to mortal size, asks whether or not his father likes him, invoking the unanticipated irony of Troy's cosmic paternal sensibility:

TROY: Like you? I go out of here every morning . . . bust my butt . . . putting up with them crackers everyday . . . cause I like you? You about the biggest fool I ever saw. (*Pause.*) It's my responsibility! You understand that? A man got to take care of his family. You live in my house . . . sleep you behind on my bedclothes . . . fill you belly up with my food . . . cause you my son. You my flesh and blood. Not cause I like you! Cause it's my duty to take care of you. I owe a responsibility to you!

Let's get this straight right here . . . before it go along any further . . . I ain't got to like you. (I, iii)

304

Troy—in response to a phallocentric legacy from Eshu—engages in sexual excesses with impunity. The birth of a daughter out of wedlock, and his resolve to care for her, is a testament to his procreative force, a fecund issue that demonstrates his cosmic role as progenitor in the recurring cycle of personal immortality. When Death catches up with Troy, it is less a tragic defeat for him than a reinvention of his vitality, more like the transcendental passing of a redeemer. His ascension, heralded through the gates of heaven by the muted immanence of a trumpet played by his brain-damaged brother, Gabriel, is a soundless ritual gesture which is at once grotesque and triumphant in its revelry of Troy's transformation into the spirit which promises a new day. The heraldic moment, however, is apostrophized by Gabriel at the end of the "performance" with a sense of renewal: "That's the way that go!" The subtle humility of Gabriel's confrontation with reality, though phonically unspectacular, does manage to restore order and a sense of cosmic harmony that suppress the need for cynical self-estimations about the best or worst of times in a life profaned by intolerable social limitations that might cause one to view reality as nothing more than an illusory speck in the collective time of humanity.

Gabriel's muted, yet potent, performance summons to mind Albert Murray's appraisal of Ellison's *Invisible Man* as a work that held "new dimensions of rhetorical resonance (based on lying and signifying). It employed a startling effective fusion of narrating realism and surrealism, and it achieved a unique but compelling combination of the naturalistic, the ridiculous, and the down right hallucinatory."[13] Wilson, as blues raconteur, orchestrates his tale with a recursive language that allows words, mood, and potential resolutions to shift and reappear almost improvisationally, at least, creating an unanticipated suspension of closure in the event. "In blues and jazz," observes Shelly Wong, "improvising becomes a way of keeping the world open to its own potentiality. Jazz articulates meaning through attention to the particulars of the moment, to the work under hand, rather than through any strict adherence to received and preconceived notions of the bar or the line."[14] A Thelonious Monk tune that abandons the fixed patterns associated with the linear expectations of musical exposition and closure is an appropriate model for the transformative power of language. The spaces created by Monk suspend the listener's response to the familiar, repeating the sound, then placing it into unfamiliar territory, which revitalizes the tune. Repetition is a common expressive technique in the language of Africans throughout the diaspora, perhaps indicative of what Peter Brook views as "returns to origin and returns of the repressed,"[15] but most clearly witnessed in the riffs of African music where, as observed by John Miller Chernoff, "there is a dominant point of repetition developed from a dominant conversation with a clearly defined alternation, a swinging back and forth from solo to chorus or from solo to an emphatic instrumental reply,"[16] which is also apparent in the contrapuntal strategy generated by the recursive texts of Toni Morrison, who noted in a discussion that her writing invited the reader to "Come on in!"

As an expressive strategy in blues and jazz improvisations, the modal distribution of related and nonrelated ideas often revivifies the familiar story/image with new illumination. We encounter in *Joe Turner's Come and Gone* the bizzare juxtaposition of an unanticipated symbiosis between Seth, the crafter of pots from sheet metal—perhaps the incarnation of the Yoruba diety, Ogun, the master of iron and creativity?—who owns the boardinghouse way station for itinerant travelers, and Selig, a traveling salesman who sells the pots and claims to be the People Finder whose great granddaddy was a slaveship seaman, and whose father had a reputation for locating and returning runaway slaves to plantations. Their relationship is made possible by the noncontradictory "soundscape" of human experience envisioned in Wilson's blues poetics which, like Toni Morrison's texts, "are a constant exchange between an implicit mythic voice, one that struggles against the wall of history to assert itself and an explicit narrator, one that is inextricably bound to its spoken counterpart," and invite the audience to *come on in.*[17]

Typically we discover in *Ma Rainey's Black Bottom* intinerant blues musicians in a rehearsal room engaged in the male ritual aggression of "lyin' and signifyin'" while exchanging survival tales about coming and going in a hostile world, taunting each other with a contrapuntal—call 'n' response—choral configuration which presses them to the edge of physical confrontation. This is followed by a cathartic subsidence, then personal illumination.

> CUTLER: I'm gonna tell you something. Reverend Gates . . . you know Reverend Gates? Slow Drag know who I'm talking about. Reverend Gates . . . now I'm gonna show you how this go where the white man don't care a thing about who you is. Reverend Gates was coming from Tallahassee to Atlanta, going to see his sister, who was sick at that time with the consumption. The train come up through Thomasville, then past Moultrie, and stopped in this little town called Sigsbee . . .

> LEVEE: You can stop telling that right there! That train don't stop in Sigsbee. I know what train you talking about. That train got four stops before it reach Macon to go on to Atlanta. One in Thomasville, one in Moultrie, and one in Cordele . . . and it stop in Centerville.

> CUTLER: Nigger, I know what I'm talking about. You gonna tell me where the train stop?

> LEVEE: Hell, yeah, if you talking about it stop in Sigsbee. I'm gonna tell you the truth.

> CUTLER: I'm talking about *this* train! I don't know what train you been riding. I'm talking about *this* train!

> LEVEE: Ain't but one train. Ain't but one train come out of Tallahassee heading north to Atlanta, and it don't stop at Sigsbee. Tell him, Toledo . . . that train don't stop at Sigsbee. The only train that stops at Sigsbee is the Yazoo Delta, and you have to transfer at Moultrie to get it!

> CUTLER: Well, hell, maybe that what he done! I don't know. I'm just telling you the man got off the train at Sigsbee . . .

> LEVEE: Alright . . . you telling it. Tell it your way. Just make up anything. (Act II)

Levee symbolizes the urban blues archetype—his very name signifying a possible kinship with the new music soundings of jazz being created along the Mississippi levees of New Orleans during the period—attempting to use the music to carve out the necessary *sacred* time and space required for himself and his gods to impose order on the chaos of his specific universe. It is a universe of endless itinerancy, self-indulgence, and the vague fulfillment of instant gratification in bucket of blood joints, testifies Slow Drag to Cutler:

> SLOW DRAG: We been doing this together for twenty-two
> years. All up and down the back roads, the side roads, the
> front roads . . . We done played the juke-joints, the whore-
> houses, the barn dances, and city sit-downs . . . I done lied
> for you and lied with you . . . We done laughed together,
> fought together, slept in the same bed together, done sucked
> the same titty . . . and now don't wanna give me no
> reefer. (Act I)

White paternalism and control is included in the uncharitable universe and must also be negotiated. Toledo, who serves the play as a singular choral figure, an unofficial griot or chronicler of the collective history, identifies the deities responsible for the altered universe of black experience and offers contingencies connected to past "paradigmatic acts of gods."

> TOLEDO (*pedantically*): See, now . . . I'll tell you something.
> As long as the colored man look to white folks to put the
> crown on what he say . . . as long as he looks to white folks
> for approval . . . then he ain't never gonna find out who he
> is and what he's about. He just gonna be about what white
> folks want him to be about. That's one sure thing. (Act I)

Levee, the unperturbable trickster, ignores Toledo's sage instruction and, like a pesty boll weevil with an indiscriminating appetite, sets his sights on a feast in the midst of moral and spiritual famine. Reveling in a sense of indestructibility, he will pursue his claim to the music by any means necessary, even through the appearance of obsequiousness. He adorns a mask that allows him to play *his* "song," in a manner gleaned from a childhood episode when his father smiled in the face of the white men that had assaulted his mother, sold the family land to one of the men, left town, and stealthily returned to vindicate the assault, a strategy for survival quite redolent of the sentient warning offered by the dying father to his son in Ellison's *Invisible Man:* "Live with your head in the mouth of the lion's mouth. I want you to overcome 'em with yeses, undermine 'em with grins, agree 'em to death and destruction, let 'em swoller you till they vomit or bust wide open."

Ma Rainey, "unruly and let loose"—to borrow Toni Morrison's description of her personal liberation of the female imagination—flaunts her "black bottom" around with the parodic gesture of male empowerment. Her actions revive the haunting specter of Clay's apocalyptic speech in Baraka's *Dutchman,* which conjectured that it would not have been necessary for Bessie Smith to sing if she could have vindicated her oppression with a white man's blood, her song amounting to an invitation to "kiss my black unruly ass." The boss lady throws her weight around as she demands to sing *her* song her way: "I don't care what you say, Irvin. Levee ain't messing up my song. If he got what the people want, let him take it somewhere else. I'm singing Ma Rainey's song. I ain't singing Levee's song. Now that's all there is to it" (Act I).

Omnipresent in the plays of Wilson is the character's objective to *sing one's own song,* which seems to signify that all-important quest for self-authentication in black life. Everybody has their personal song. Even Rose credits Troy's expansiveness for her song. In *Joe Turner's Come and Gone,* Wilson introduces young Jeremy with the stage note that *he is a proficient guitar player, though his spirit has yet to be molded into a song.* Bynum, the conjure man in *Joe Turner* who boasts a direct descendancy to a father whose Healing Song cured the infirm, claims possession of a Binding Song used to bind together dislocated lives of displaced families. Bynum is quick to conclude that Loomis's peripatetic roving is the sign of a man who has lost his personal song: "Now, I can look at you, Mr. Loomis, and see you a man who done forgot his song. Forgot how to sing it. A fellow forget that and he forget who he is. Forget how he's supposed to mark down life" (Act II, scene ii).

Bynum's folk wisdom brings to mind the Larry Neal essay, "Uncle Rufus Raps on the Squared Circle," where the narrator is figured as an elderly Harlem dandy/trickster—perhaps a slick, urbane cousin of Uncle Remus—who "peacocks" as he "bops" into a bar wearing "a pearl gray homburg" and "blue cashmere" coat, sporting "a golden-headed serpent cane," and shoes with gray spats from "French, Shriner, and Urner," his entrance alone revealing an unmistakably personal song. Uncle Rufus then begins to proffer the metaphysics of negotiating the squared circle—the boxing ring—and explains why Muhammad Ali lost the fight to Joe Frazier:

> All fighters must understand the principles of rhythmic modality . . . it also refers to the artistic or technical manipulation of the space encompassed by the square which these fools erroneously call the "ring." . . . Now, Ali understands these principles of rhythm and music. . . . You see, he believes in riffing. He's got the body, the legs, and the mouth for it. But Frazier is somewhere else in the musical universe. Frazier is stomp-down blues, bacon, grits, and Sunday church. . . . Ali is body bebop, while Frazier is slow brooding blues with a gospel bearing . . . most likely, Frazier wants to shout in church. However, Ali, as a Muslim intellectual, has been forced to suppress his gospel impulse. But he can't suppress it totally. You can still hear it in his voice when he speaks, or when he tries to sing. But blues and gospel ain't his thing. Frazier can't sing, but he sings better than Ali. And that's why Frazier won the fight.[18]

Levee's song is apocalyptic. It challenges the metaphysical potency of gods erected by men of average size, which he disregards as an inappropriate match for his self-empowered will to survive. Levee's song leaves no space for reappraisal or calculated negotiation of the squared circle. It is a battle cry with malevolent intent.

> LEVEE: Cutler's God! Come on and save this nigger! Come on and save him like you did my mama! Save him like you did my mama! I heard her when she called you! I heard her when she said, "Lord, have mercy! Jesus help me! Please, God, have mercy on me, Lord Jesus, help me!" And did

you turn your back? Did you turn your back, motherfucker?
Did you turn your back? (*Stabs at the air above his head
frantically.*) Come on! Come on and turn your back on me!
Turn your back on me! Come on! Where is you? Come on
and turn your back on me! Come on! Turn your back on
me, motherfucker. I'll cut your heart out! Come on, turn
your back on me! Come on! What's the matter? Where is
you? Come on and turn your back on me! Come on, what
you scared of? Turn your back on me! Come on, coward,
motherfucker! (LEVEE *folds his knife and stands triumphantly.*)
Your God ain't shit, Cutler. (Act II)

There is no joy inside the song of the trickster's "sardonic grin,"
an ominous gesture that amplifies a stridently pitched imputation
against the world which can be inspired in a moment's notice by the
slightest provocation. The listener might very well anticipate that
the magnitude of the venom spewed in the song would necessarily be
earmarked for the person who initiated so much rage. But then, the
spirit of his song is random, as unanticipated as the shift of notes in a
Monk tune. Dispirited by the white studio owner's appropriation of
his music, Levee releases his final wrath on Toledo, who had acci-
dentally stepped on his shoes. In the annals of black rage, it is not
uncommon for the oppressed to ventilate their hostility toward those
in power on their equally oppressed kith and kin. However, with the
slaying of Toledo, the tributary of collective consciousness, Levee
has not only desecrated a natural life, but also cut himself off from
ontological continuity, a sort of cosmic suicide, which is more
apocalyptic in its crushing, psychic devastation than mortal guilt.

> *They tell me Joe Turner been here and gone,*
> *Lord, they tell me Joe Turner been here and gone,*
> *They tell me Joe Turner been here and gone.*
> —Big Bill Broonzy, "Joe Turner Blues"

Metaphysical challenges are frequent among the tricksters of Wilson's plays. Herald Loomis, vigilantly stalking the crossroads, is
drawn into the boardinghouse by a frenzied, improvised, contra-

311

puntal ritual call of the Holy Ghost, which was generated in the remnants of a ring shout retrieved from African memory and now configured as the Juba dance. Loomis, the redeemer trickster who seeks salvation without submission to powers larger than his own, challenges the authority of the Holy Ghost:

> LOOMIS: Stop it! Stop! . . . You all sitting up here singing about the Holy Ghost. What's so holy about the Holy Ghost? You singing and singing. You think the Holy Ghost coming? You singing for the Holy Ghost to come? What he gonna do, huh? He gonna come with tongues of fire to burn up your woolly heads? You gonna tie onto the Holy Ghost and get burned up? What you got then? Why God got to be so big? Why he got to be bigger than me? How much big is there? How much big do you want? (LOOMIS starts to unzip his pants.) (Act I, scene iv)

By all appearances, Herald Loomis arrives at the boarding house a spiritually crippled—if not mad—man, whose true identity even is questionable. A Yoruba proverb says, "There is nothing that there is not; whatever we have a name for, that is." Seth is not certain of what to call Loomis, whose symbolic freedom is located in the cosmic significations of his name, Herald. The act of naming, and, in some cases, unnaming, is a linguistic ritual of self-possession and communal aggrandizement. "Don't call me out my name" is a common injunction by most black children in response to the magic involved in whatever significant ceremony created the name. Ralph Ellison, in "Hidden Names and Complex Fate," reports, "We must learn to wear our names within all the noise and confusion in which we find ourselves. They must become our masks and our shields and the containers of all those values and traditions which we learn and/or imagine being the meaning of our familial past."[19] Herald Loomis, the trickster as redeemer, arrives formless at the way station of itinerant travelers, his identity shrouded in a liminal zone between bondage and liberation. He is a freed man consumed with the memory of hellhounds on his heels. His countenance reveals the trauma of domestic and spiritual rupture resulting from several

312

years of the illegal servitude and hard labor forced upon him by the fabled Tennessee bounty hunter, Joe Turner.

I got to keep moving, I got to keep moving,
Blues falling down like hail, blues falling down like hail,
Ummm, blues falling down like hail, blues falling down like hail,
And the days keep on reminding me there's a hellhound on my trail,
Hellhound on my trail, hellhound on my trail.

—Robert Johnson, "Hellhound on My Trail"

While stalking the crossroads for signs of his wife, Martha Pentecost, he becomes witness to a vision of ancestral bones that walk on water until they are swept under by a great wave that washes them ashore, their bodies now covered with flesh. Loomis envisions himself among these ancestors and unites himself ontologically to the past—an act of spiritual transformation that portends his mission of personal and collective deliverance. However, Loomis has lost his song and is unable to stand up on his own legs and is thus unable to effectuate his spiritual commission. Bynum, the conjure man, who is unwavering in his faith in song as a healing force, has foreseen the arrival of the redeemer in the specter of a shiny man. He reunites Zonia with Martha Pentecost so that Loomis is able to reclaim his song by letting his own blood in a cleansing ritual, the redemptive gesture empowering him to walk erect in the world once more "shining like new money!"

A closer inspection of Loomis's ritual gesture of self-inflicted bloodletting reveals Wilson's acknowledgment of the ancient Egyptian mythos attributed to the dark god Osiris—the hidden one who is key to light—who offers humanity the opportunity to become one with God, which is to become God, through the spiritual cleansing associated with death and rebirth. The Osirian mythos, which invites the death of the body in order to allow for the resurrection of the spirit/body, is the foundation of Judeo-Christian messianic sacrifice, salvation, transfiguration, and self-redemption. Loomis seeks such redemption, which is revealed to him in the specter of the slave ancestors. Despite the trauma of slavery and the consequent degradation of the body, the ancestors achieve spiritual ascendancy as they "walk on water" and arrive in the New World with flesh on their bones. Inside the spiritual dynamism of the ancestors—perceived and made useful in the present as opposed to being arrested in the past—is the true song of redemption and liberation. While the condition of slavery and forced labor in the New World has caused psychic and physical rupture, it resisted the cosmic vitiation of the true song, and spiritual resilience encouraged reclamation for the sake of liberation and freedom. The ancestors had experienced forced deaths. Loomis's self-infliction symbolizes insightful "death." Once he bears witness to the true song in the vision of the ancestors, he seeks to become part of this spirituality for his own self-redemption. If renewal of spirit is to be made possible, the body must become transfigured. The ritual sacrifice of Loomis's body becomes the seeding of the new soul, the body gilded with the precious life-force—blood—until it shines like the armor of pure song/spirit. Thus, Wilson seems to infer that the discernment of the ancestral experience is a cosmic rather than a psycho-physical drama that offers the oppressed an opportunity to disregard flesh and spirit as opposing forces and to view their suffering in the context of a spiritual continuum that reassures physical liberation.

Joe Turner's Come and Gone is a metaphysically engaging excursion into the tributaries of the African diaspora. It extends backward into the past where ancestors reside for "paradigmatic acts of gods," revealing both the natural and supernatural in a single universe of experience. The play operates outside the logic of naturalism which can only serve to restrain the ritualistic passage of time and burden the potential enlargement of events with fixed expectations of cause and effect. For example, the repetitive serving of hot biscuits in the kitchen is not a prosaic expression of domesticity, but rather a rhythmic gesture of the play's ritual mode, the recursive issuance of biscuits reaffirming the nurturing atmosphere of the boardinghouse way station. Also amplifying the ritual, though easily lost amid the scale of driving forces that move the principle characters, is the densely packed symbolic signification released by the choric testimonies of the children.

In all three plays, the choric element is subtly placed. In *Fences*, Bono is the singular choric figure whose testimony textualizes the social and moral landscape of black life, codifying the transient nature of the folk as the "walking blues": "Back in those days what you talking about . . . they walk out their front door and just take on down one road or another and keep on walking" (Act I, scene iv). And in *Ma Rainey* the choral figure is Toledo, who offers a culinary parable that signifies the fragility of the "blues matrix" in the stew pot called America:

> TOLEDO: Now you take and eat the stew. You take and make your history with that stew. Alright. Now it's over. Your history's over and you done ate the stew. But you look around and you see some carrots over here, some potatoes over there. That stew's still there. You done made your history and it's still there. You can't eat it all. So what you got? You got some leftovers. That's what it is. You got leftovers and you can't do nothing with it. You already making you another history . . . cooking you another meal, and you don't need them leftovers no more. What to do?
> See, we's the leftovers. The colored man is the leftovers. Now what's the colored man gonna do with himself? That's what we waiting to find out. But first we gotta know we the leftovers. (Act I)

In *Joe Turner* we discover that the backyard of the rooming house where the children play is hallowed ground, fecund with roots and self-sustaining edibles and consecrated with daily animal sacrifices. Embraced by the immanent nature of these grounds and away from the tide of tensions gripping the adult universe, Reuben and Zonia offer a choric testimony that mediates between the natural and spiritual worlds. Almost immediately, Reuben inducts Zonia into the psychic underworld of children's secrets: the pigeons used for the sacrificial rituals belonged to Reuben's boyhood friend who died and left behind explicit instructions to release the pigeons upon his death. Reuben intends to keep the birds, despite the materialization of dead Miss Mabel, who admonishes him. The children conjecture that if Miss Mabel can materialize, perhaps Reuben's boyhood friend could as well. They conspire to wait for the boy's spirit at the secret hideout. On these hallowed grounds, Reuben parodies the ritual of renaming Zonia to "Spider," a subtle gesture of personal claim that divests her father of possession. The liminal rite of passage is sealed with a kiss and Reuben promises to locate her in the world one day for marriage, portending another generation of transient black souls in search of domestic and spiritual harmony.

Wilson's plays arguably represent the culmination of political, social, and aesthetic objectives presaged by the Harlem Renaissance in the twenties and the Black Arts Movement of the sixties. His plays reflect a sovereignty of personal and collective ethnocentric aspiration and are indicative of a dramaturgy of classical proportion that is aesthetically based in the African-American cultural vernacular. We discover in his work an authentic reclamation of the blues voice—dredged up from the oral and musical traditions of black life—as the vehicle for folk narratives. These narratives are profoundly rooted in the mythic sediments of reality in a way that eschews "folksiness" as a convenient index to folk life. The ironic significations of the blues, like the testimonial strategies of folk language, allow an encounter with good and evil, negotiated as part of a noncontradictory social universe. Wilson's appreciation of the blues' transcendental significance is facilitated by personal intimacy with the rhythms and repetitions that characterize ordinary black speech, which invests the narrative with a heightened quality of poetry and song. Safely ensconced within the oral tradition, Wilson has been able to explore the icons and cosmic sensibilities of folk culture to reveal the interrelationship between physical and metaphysical reality, demonstrating the impact of the spirit world upon the concrete aspects of black life without trivializing the experience or reducing such revelations to superstitious encounters with the supernatural. Most importantly, Wilson has reaffirmed the potency of the African continuum as a psychic and spiritual repository of values and survival strategies that authenticates experience and fuels the imagination for a creative achievement capable of promoting personal renewal and collective healing. The very authenticity of Wilson's blues voice shares much in common with Michael Thelwell's observation that the prose of Chinua Achebe is "gracefully masking in its deceptive simplicity undercurrents of the utmost profundity and originality of craft and purpose," and is a welcome model for future African-American dramaturgy.

PAUL CARTER HARRISON
Columbia College, Chicago

NOTES

1. Michael Thelwell, opening address, *Chinua Achebe's Birthday Symposium,* Eagle on Iroko, University of Nigeria, Nusukka, 12 February 1990.

2. Ralph Ellison, "The Act of Fiction," *Shadow and Act* (New York: Signet, 1966), p. 172.

3. Richard Stotkin, "Myth and the Production of History," in *Ideology and Classic American Literature,* ed. Sacvan Berkovitch and Myra Jehlen (New York: Cambridge University Press, 1986), pp. 70–90.

4. Richard Wright, "The Literature of the Negro in the U.S.," *White Man, Listen* (Garden City, N.Y.: Anchor Books, 1964), pp. 69–105.

5. Houston A. Baker, Jr., *Blues, Ideology, and Afro-American Literature* (Chicago: University of Chicago Press, 1984), p. 2.

6. Ralph Ellison, *Invisible Man* (New York: Signet Books, 1952).

7. Roland Barthes, *Writing Degree Zero and Elements of Semiology,* trans. Annette Lavers and Colin Smith (Boston: Beacon Press, 1970), p. 10.

8. Larry Neal, "The Black Arts Movement," *Visions of a Liberated Future* (New York: Thunder Mouth Press, 1989), p. 62.

9. Lawrence Levine, *Black Culture and Black Consciousness* (Oxford: Oxford University Press, 1977), pp. 30–55.

10. Wole Soyinka, *Myth, Literature, and the African World* (Cambridge: Cambridge University Press, 1976).

11. Ralph Ellison, "Richard Wright's Blues," *Shadow and Act,* pp. 78–79.

12. LeRoi Jones (Amiri Baraka), "Scenario VI," *Preface to a Twenty Volume Suicide Note* (New York: Totem/Corinth, 1961), p. 22.

13. Albert Murray, *The Omni-Americans: Black Experience and American Culture* (New York: Avon Books, 1977), p. 167.

14. Shelly Wong, "Transgression as Poesis in *The Bluest Eye,*" *Callaloo* 13 (1990), pp. 471–81.

15. Peter Brook, *Reading for the Plot* (New York: Vintage, 1985), p. 125.

16. John Miller Chernoff, *African Rhythm and African Sensibility: Aesthetics and*

Social Action in African Musical Idioms (Chicago: University of Chicago Press, 1979), p. 55.

17. Karla F. C. Holloway, *"Beloved: A Spiritual,"* *Callaloo* 13 (1990), pp. 516–25.

18. Larry Neal, "Uncle Rufus Raps on the Squared Circle," *Visions of a Liberated Future* (New York: Thunder Mouth Press, 1989), pp. 97–106.

19. Ralph Ellison, "Hidden Names and Complex Fate," *Shadow and Act* (New York: New American Library, 1966), p. 151.